OUTSPOKEN: The Olly Neal Story

OUTSPOKEN
The Olly Neal Story

by Olly Neal Jr., as told to Jan Wrede

The CALS Butler Center for Arkansas Studies
Bobby L. Roberts Library of Arkansas History & Art

Central Arkansas Library System
100 Rock Street
Little Rock, Arkansas 72201
robertslibrary.org

May 2020

ISBN 978-1-945624-25-4 (paperback)
Cover and book design: Mike Keckhaver
Copyeditor: Ali Welky
Cover photograph: Courtesy ©Eugene Richards, 2010

Library of Congress Cataloging-in-Publication Data

Names: Neal, Olly, Jr., 1941- author. | Wrede, Jan, 1943- author. | Butler Center
for Arkansas Studies, publisher.
Title: Outspoken : the Olly Neal story / Olly Neal Jr. as told to Jan Wrede.
Description: Little Rock : Butler Center Books, Central Arkansas Library System,
2020. | Includes index. |
Identifiers: LCCN 2020005764 | ISBN 9781945624254 (paperback)
Subjects: LCSH: Neal, Olly, Jr., 1941- | African American judges--
Arkansas--Biography.
Classification: LCC KF373.N43 A3 2020 | DDC 347.737/03334 [B]--dc23
LC record available at https://lccn.loc.gov/2020005764

Printed in the United States of America

This book is printed on archival-quality paper that meets requirements of the
American National Standard for Information Sciences, Permanence of Paper,
Printed Library Materials, ANSI Z39.48-1984.

Butler Center Books, the publishing division of the CALS Butler Center for
Arkansas Studies, was made possible by the generosity of Dora Johnson
Ragsdale and John G. Ragsdale Jr.

We dedicate OUTSPOKEN *to those whose lives and conduct may court disaster and to those who offer a helping hand and show safe passage to a better future.*

—O. N. and J. W.

Well, son, I'll tell you:
Life for me ain't been no crystal stair.
It's had tacks in it,
And splinters,
And boards torn up,
And places with no carpet on the floor—
Bare
But all the time
I'se been a-climbin' on,
And reachin' landin's,
And turnin' corners,
And sometimes goin' in the dark
Where there ain't been no light.
So boy, don't you turn back.
Don't you set down on the steps
'Cause you finds it's kinder hard.
Don't you fall now—
For I'se still goin', honey,
I'se still climbin',
And life for me ain't been no crystal stair.

—poem by Langston Hughes

"The brave are not those who feel no fear, and the generous are not those who never feel selfish. Extraordinary people are not extraordinary because they are invulnerable to unconscious biases. They are extraordinary because they choose to do something about it."

—Shankar Vedantam

Table of Contents:

Part Four: Family

Part Five: Legacy

Preface, by Olly Neal and Jan Wrede

Olly: When I got to be seventy, I knew that I wanted to write down something about my life, but I wasn't sure what to write. I only knew that I wanted to tell what came out of my life and time in Marianna and Lee County, Arkansas. That was all. It took me awhile to realize that I had to look closely at myself. I had to examine both my strengths and weaknesses, successes and failures, so I could reach a better understanding of my life. Then maybe I could pass on some of what I have learned.

Jan: Olly and I worked together for a relatively short period in 1970. I moved away from Arkansas, and we had been in touch only a couple of times. When I retired, I started looking back at my life and decided to write about our experiences starting the Lee County Cooperative Clinic (LCCC). It was an intense time when many social and political changes happened quickly. I thought that we needed to write about it, so events could be put down as they happened. Time was taking the lives and memories of those who were there, and if we didn't do this now it would be too late.

I met with Olly in April 2016 and proposed we join forces. Olly was interested, but his health was troublesome and he was not sure that he could uphold his side of the deal. So we made a tentative plan to talk for an hour once a week on Tuesday mornings. Olly kept talking and I kept listening every week for four years. After only a month of our process, I realized the bigger story was the life of this complicated, locally popular yet little known civil rights activist. So my focus shifted to writing about the full arc of Olly's life, with the Clinic being as major a pivotal point for him personally as it was for race relations in the Arkansas Delta.

Olly: As Jan asked questions and I told my stories, I wanted to let it all hang out. I didn't know what I would discover, and I can tell you this has been a powerful exploration for me. Some of the time, I had to laugh at myself. My approach was not academic. I was amused because often I couldn't tell Jan that I had thought things through so I could figure out what I should do. The work of my life caused economic, political, and social discomfort, but I don't apologize. I didn't get it all right, that's for sure, but most of the time that's what the real world is like. You get some things right, and some things don't go quite as well.

Jan: I chose to be faithful to Olly's words without including any comments from me. I recorded, transcribed, and used our weekly interviews. Through the years, I researched what he told me for accuracy and interviewed others who could contribute to Olly's stories. I organized his words into a cohesive narrative of his life and his time and place in the history of Arkansas.

No historian or storyteller is neutral. Here, Olly Neal speaks with the personal knowledge of how events affected him and the black community. History is not an exact science. Facts can be interpreted in different ways. And historians insert suggestions by the way they present what happened. For example, concerning the 1970s Marianna boycotts, a white historian might say, "There were younger whites who would accept some form of political power for blacks, but it would take time." That statement could have been true, but Olly would never say that. Never. That statement suggests that blacks were not being sufficiently patient, and Olly knew from personal experience that black folks had been patient for too long. No more waiting. NOW was the time for change.

Olly: Some readers might question the wisdom of a black civil rights leader telling his story to a middle-class white woman. In fact, my first choice had been my brother Prentiss, but he was not available, so Jan became a solid second choice. She has had some influence on my story through the questions she asked me and the arrangement of my words and thoughts. Jan's questions sometimes made me uncomfortable. To answer them I had to look at actions that do not make me proud, and I'd think, "Hell, I don't want to answer that!" Then I'd remember I had told myself I was going to let it all hang out and I had to talk about that shit. It was part of my life. I think those probing questions helped me be honest.

I also can say I trusted Jan because she had already proved that in spite of being white, she could see and understand the perspectives of a black person. My trust started fifty years ago when Jan left Marianna. She was part of setting up the Clinic's community-controlled structure and she worked on fundraising and other parts of the administration. When she was getting ready to leave her work at the Clinic, Jan told me that she was putting everything she had done in my hands and the rest was up to me. Then she disappeared. Completely. By leaving, she gave up all control. She recognized me as legitimate, a complete human being, who could think and work without any influence from a white person. None at all.

Jan: In the early 1970s, we were thinking far beyond our actual age. We were young and ignorant of how to run a community health center. But for us that didn't matter because, as with many others in the 1960s and 1970s, we were charged with an unreasonable courage to create change. Now, we want to pass that passionate courage on to a new generation of activists. We want to inform and inspire our readers to be unreasonably strong in their commitment to the change they want to see.

Part One: Background, Family, Schooling, and Out on My Own

David Maclin, his wife Rose, and my Momma Willie B. when she was two years old in front of their house in the New Hope community.

Chapter 1
My Family and the New Hope Community

Before I tell you about my time as an activist and clinic administrator and judge, I have to tell you about my life growing up and going to school in Lee County, Arkansas, during a different time—the 1940s and 1950s.

My earliest years were in the New Hope community of Lee County, about ten miles west of Marianna. One of my first memories is going out to the hen house on a hot day when I was two or three years old. I reached up and got this egg out of an empty nest. I had heard somebody say that it was hot enough to fry eggs out there, so I broke the egg and left it on the ground to fry. I didn't tell anybody, but I had to do it. Another time I reached up under a chicken sitting on her nest to pull out an egg like I had seen my Momma do. The hen pecked me, and I still have a little round scar on my forehead.

My Granddad Mose Neal

I am the grandson of a man who was born a slave. His name was Mose Neal and he was born in 1859 in Kemper County, Mississippi. I saw a document one time that showed Mose as somebody's property. Mose was my Daddy's father. Mose became a preacher. He was married to Georgianna and died in Mississippi.

My Daddy Ollie Neal

My Daddy's name is Ollie Neal. He only told me a few little things about his teenage years, like the time he was driving a wagon from Yazoo City to Jackson, Mississippi. The load was so heavy that he had to stop the wagon and block the wheels to let the mules rest now and then. Each time the same mule would get down on his knees. I never knew a mule that liked to get down on his knees to rest.

Daddy was born in 1896 and was drafted into the U.S. Army in 1917 during World War I. When the war ended, he was in France. Back then it was rare for blacks to be in combat. I think he just did the cleanup work of a janitor. After he came back from the military, Daddy married his first wife, Willie Lee, around 1920. His mother-in-law Betty was an independent and well-known woman who was born without any arms. She could do all kinds of things with her feet like thread a needle and sew. She made pretty good money going around putting on shows. Folks didn't pay to come in. They just gave her money after they saw the show. By 1928, she had kind of played out the Bentonia area where they lived in Mississippi and she wasn't making enough money anymore.

Daddy heard that you could buy land in Arkansas, so they moved to Lee County, and during the winter of 1929, they settled in the New Hope community where he bought forty acres. They sent their furniture in a railway car and his farming equipment, wagon, and mules in a second rail car to Aubrey, Arkansas. They must have had some money to do that. Daddy drove the three of them, Miss Betty, himself, and his wife Willie Lee plus their two children Betty and Georgia in his Momma-in-law's 1927 Ford car. Willie Lee was or soon after was pregnant with my twin brothers Willie and Billie.

After they came to Arkansas, Daddy was not "spending enough time at home," so Willie Lee left him. The car belonged to Miss Betty, so when Willie Lee left it went with them. I don't believe Miss Betty, Willie Lee, or her children ever went back to Mississippi though.

Daddy had come to Arkansas with two suits and in 1933 or 1934 he had a house fire that burned up both of those suits. So, between 1933 and 1950, Daddy didn't go back to Mississippi either. He was embarrassed to go back less well off than when he left. He and I used to laugh about this story.

Daddy and my Momma Willie B. had six children—five boys and one girl—and we started out on Daddy's farm in the New Hope community. I was named for my Daddy even though I was Momma and Daddy's third son. Daddy told me that Momma wouldn't name a son after him until they were married. They were married in 1940 and I was born in July 1941. Daddy's name is spelled O-l-l-i-e and mine is O-l-l-y because Momma thought O-l-l-y was the better spelling for a man. I get my mouth, or you could say my outspoken personality and the way I react to circumstances, from my Momma.

My Great-Granddaddy David Maclin

Momma was raised by her grandfather David Maclin. He died when I was two and a half years old, and my only memory of him is a mental picture of a man on a big gray horse. The story about him was passed down in my family. I heard it from my Momma, and I think that she heard it from David Maclin himself. He was born around 1855 in either Fayette or Henderson County, Tennessee, somewhere near the county line. He remembered hearing big guns going off during the Civil War. My brother Rowan checked the history of that area and found out that there was an 1864 or 1865 Civil War battle near where David Maclin lived, so he could have heard those guns.

I don't have much information about David Maclin's folk. But in 1867, about two years after the Civil War ended, he was twelve years old. Another family story goes that he was walking down a country road and met some white boys who threatened him. He picked up a rock as they were coming at him and threw it. He hit one of them, who fell down. He didn't know what happened to the white boy who fell down, because he ran away and got himself to Memphis as fast as he could. He crossed the Mississippi River and kept going down into the country. I don't know how long it took him, but I believe that is how my great-granddaddy David Maclin got to Arkansas.

David Maclin settled in Thomasville, which was in the New Hope community, just west of Aubrey in Lee County. Thomasville was named in the 1870s or 1880s for a black man who owned the land around there and donated a piece of it for the town and school.

David Maclin ran the little Thomasville store, and he was the Thomasville postmaster until he got into some trouble for loaning someone ten cents of the U.S. post office money. He was accused of theft and he might have gone to jail, but he got out after a short time. He could have been pardoned. I'm not sure. Anyway, it all worked out okay, and he remained a big man in the community.

David Maclin was also a preacher and a teacher who taught at the New Hope School. At some point he attended Arkansas Baptist College, a school in Little Rock started in 1884 to educate black ministers. Back in those days they were taking people for all levels of academic training, and I don't know for sure if he actually got a college or high school degree because those records were lost in a fire. But he was always called Professor Maclin.

Between 1945 and 1960, Thomasville declined and lost its population. The closing of my grandfather's store was part of that decline. When I was a child, the building was still there, but it was never used and eventually fell down.

David Maclin was married to three women throughout his life: Joanna, Narciss, and Rose. He and Joanna had three children: James, Frank, and Thomas (who died in his teenage years). He and Narciss had one child, Mary, who was my Momma's mother. When Narciss died, David married

Rose, who helped raise Momma. So, we called her Momma Rose.

My Momma Willie B. Maclin Neal

Momma was born November 12, 1912, and named Willie B. Maclin. She knew who her father was, but since she was raised by David Maclin, people called her by his name. At the time Momma was born, her Momma Mary was only seventeen and unmarried, so David Maclin and Momma Rose were raising both Mary and Momma. Mary stayed with them until 1917 when she married Pleas McCowan. I understand that he was a good-looking, light-skinned man who took their daughter Azell, born in 1917, with them but would not take Momma, who was five years old.

Mary and Pleas had seven children, and we had a good relationship with all of them. They lived nearby and Mary was a mouthy woman. Daddy would wave at Mary when we went by and she was outside and he would say, "Hey, Mary." And Mary would wave back and say, "Go to hell." I remember one day Daddy called out, "How you feelin', Sister Mary." And Mary said, "What the hell you want to know for? You ain't no damn doctor." She was a terrible little woman. So, we could talk trash with her too. I knew her well and called her Grand Momma. She died in 1958 when I was seventeen.

My Momma was real smart, and she started doing some teaching at the New Hope School when she was fourteen. That would have been 1926 or 1927. When her grandfather David Maclin needed help, she would go and assist him like a substitute or assistant teacher. Later she taught there full time, and before we moved to Marianna she was my teacher in the first and second grade. New Hope School closed in May 1948 when they combined the three little two-room schools in Springfield, Freedonia, and New Hope into Carver Elementary out on Highway 79.

The House Where I Was Born

Our New Hope house was on a dirt road with some gravel spots. It was on the east side of the road and faced the west. It had two rooms. The one on the north side was big and had some cracks in the walls and the floor. The one on the south side was newer with no cracks. It might have been tongue and groove. Its floor was six inches higher than the other part. I guess when Daddy built it he couldn't get the floors to match. The big room was the front room and the kitchen and where all the kids slept. We used kerosene lamps and had a well where we hand-pumped our water.

I was born in that house, and I grew up with six brothers—DL, Thaddeus, Donnie, Granville, Rowan, and Prentiss—and one sister, Gloria. We were born between 1931 and 1948. I also had five older brothers and sisters—Betty, Georgia, Willie, Billie, and Bertha—who were my Daddy's children with his first wife, Willie Lee, but they didn't live with us.

We had plenty of tasks that we could do, based on our size. We all helped sweep the yard. We kept our yard nice and clean. That was how we liked it—with nothing in it. As a little kid, my job was to bring in stove wood and put it in the heater and the cook stove. I helped with dishes and other clean-up stuff, and I fed the chickens and slopped the hogs. There was always something to do.

My sister Gloria was two years and three months under me, and I took care of her. I took responsibility for her and kept an eye out for her. One time when I was about four, I was holding her hand on the way to talk to Momma in the field. We saw a snake crossing the road and I had to go kill it to make sure Gloria didn't get bit. That was a big deal. Thinking back, it could have been a blue racer, which is not poisonous, but all snakes were awful to us. We didn't trust any of them.

Moro

The closest town center was Moro, with a population of about 150. Moro was six or seven miles away, and it had a cotton gin. This wasn't common, but sometimes Daddy let us ride on top of the cotton when he drove his wagon to the gin. There were two stores where we could go in and buy soda water. These were white-owned establishments. Moro had a justice of the peace but no town hall. I never had any contact with police authorities all the time we lived out there. Only one or two black families actually lived in Moro. And when I came back home in 1969, the black families had been forced out. Moro had become a "sundown town." That means that no blacks were allowed in town after sunset.

Church

There were only a few pickup trucks in New Hope. I think that Old Man Nelson Scott Sr. and his son Willie "Bob" Scott had pickups. There were some old flatbed trucks in New Hope that we called "stake bottom" because they had wooden stakes on the sides to hold the side boards together. The stakes were usually cut from a good, straight, four- to five-inch hickory limb. Stake bottoms were not pretty. They were used primarily for big loads of farm equipment, wood, peas or cotton. A big stake bottom might hold 4,000 pounds. The smaller ones had shorter stakes and lower sides so they couldn't be overloaded. A guy named Deuce Bonner had one with real tight sides that he tried to use to haul ice. One time I saw a white man haul five or six cows in his.

The name New Hope was for both the school and the church. They were not on the same property. I don't know where the name came from. The New Hope Church was Missionary Baptist, as were most of the churches in that general area. There also was a Missionary Baptist Church in Springfield about five miles away, one in Freedonia about three miles away, and two in Aubrey about four miles away. Peter's Rock Methodist Church was down the road about six miles toward Marianna.

I remember that when we went to church, there were lots of mules and wagons in the churchyard. The big boys in my family liked to be cool and did not ride in our old wagon, so as soon as Momma would let me, I walked with the big boys. They left for church a little earlier.

In subsequent years, the pastors could read, but when I was a little kid, the preacher usually was somebody who did not read very well at all. He would learn scriptures by memory, and his sermon always started off with a teaching lesson. As he moved into the sermon, he changed into a high-pitched, rhythmic voice that we called a "squall." Toward the end, he would talk about when Jesus died on the cross. Everybody felt bad about the crucifixion, so that started the people shouting and crying. We used to say, "That preacher tore down the church." It meant that he caused the congregation to shout, scream, and jump. That sort of thing.

Daddy liked to read the scriptures. Maybe it was because his father Mose had been a preacher. Momma and Daddy were not ones to jump and scream in church. Momma believed church was necessary to give guideposts for her children, and she wanted to be a model for us. Singing in the church choir was the big part for her. We didn't have a church piano. We had "shaped note" music books with the notes on the music staff and shaped a certain way, so folks didn't have to learn what each line meant. The songs were the sound-and-call style, with the choir singing the words and then the congregation repeating: "I'd like to be here. I'd like to be here. And living that day. And living that day. When Jesus come down. When Jesus come down. To take us away. To take us away." Like that. And there was a lot of harmonizing too. My Momma and her Momma sang alto. They would try to out-sing each other. Like who could sing the loudest.

Usually church attendance would be twenty-five to thirty folk, and that would be a good crowd. New Hope Church had a service two Sundays per month—on the second and fourth Sundays. We had Sunday School every Sunday, so on the first and third Sundays you could go to Sunday School and then go home or go to another church for a service if you wanted. Since Daddy was a strong church person, we went to a church service every Sunday.

Church was fun. In the rural areas, most of our entertainment related to something around church or baseball. Sometimes we had Wednesday prayer meeting where folks would get together—usually not many. From time to time, we had church socials or church suppers. We had regular baseball games in the warm season, and each community had a team. I didn't play baseball. I never could catch that ball. I had no sports ability. I did play a little football in high school, but for me it was more mouth than physical skill.

There were very few dances. In school, we had the 4-H Club, and little kids could go somewhere once or twice a year to show their skills on whatever they were doing. Older women had what they called their Home Demonstration Club, with contests on who could make the prettiest preserves and that kind of thing. They called it canning but it was in Mason jars.

Animals, Work, and Chores

Momma couldn't keep up with me, and I always liked to be out with the big boys. We had two wagon horses and another young one called Corinne; she was born after I was. My older brothers would tame everything and one day they were trying to catch Corinne, who was about two years old and not very big. I was out in the pasture with them, and I dropped down to hide in some bushes when I heard her running. As she came through the bushes she hit me hard with her shoulder or the upper part of her leg. I don't know how she didn't hurt me. She bumped me hard. I did learn to ride horses, but I never rode the bucking horses like my older brother Donnie did.

Another time, when I was five or six, Daddy's milk cow had a big bull calf. So my brother Donnie was out there trying to ride the calf, and it threw him up on some bricks and hurt his face. He just caught the calf, beat on him, and rode him again.

I never did learn to shoot a gun very well either. Daddy didn't have a lot of guns, but he had a shotgun. He only kept three or four shells. He wasn't a good shot himself, and he often went hunting and came back without killing anything. We generally wanted to shoot so we could kill an animal to eat. My older brother Thaddeus was a very good shot, but the rest of us were not, except for my brother Willie who was not raised with us. He was a perfect shot. In later years he could shoot a rattlesnake with his pistol and hit it in the eye so as not to mess up the skin.

When I was five, I started going in the fields to help pick cotton. When I was seven, I could help chop the cotton. (You know chopping cotton really means chopping the weeds.) That was in the summer. When we were working in the field, the four of us—Thad, Donnie, Granville, and me—together could catch a rabbit. If we scared up a rabbit, we'd circle around it, move in, and catch it with our hands. Of course we ate the rabbit. We weren't just killing it. The family ate it.

The first time I worked by the day chopping cotton was for a farmer who paid me $2.50 for ten hours. I went with my brothers, and neither my Momma nor Daddy was there. My brother Thad was kind of my guide. I was seven and he was fifteen.

We always had wood stoves. I think that I was out of high school before Momma got natural gas to heat the house in Marianna. Cutting and hauling wood always was a significant job. When I was ten or twelve, I helped chop wood, and about this time Daddy bought a place back in the Warrior Bottoms in the far southwest corner of Lee County. We had big axes with a wide blade on them. And to make money my brothers and I would make eight-foot-long crossties out of oak or sweetgum wood. Nowadays, they are made with automated saws, but we cut them the right length and hewed them into a rectangle shape. There were three different sizes, and we sold them to the railroad for between $2 and $3 each, depending on the size and kind of wood. Oak was the best.

After we moved to Marianna in 1949, on weekends we went to work on the farm. When I was about twelve, I was in the woods with the wagon and mules cutting wood to take back to our house in town. My brother Rowan, who must have been about eight, was with me. We ran over a beehive, or maybe it was those wasps that live in the ground, and they came all over me. I jumped down off the wagon to get them away from the mules and told Rowan, "Git in the wagon. You got to git the mules out of here fast." I told him that because if the bees started stinging the mules, they would run and catch the wagon on a tree and tear it up. I knew Daddy didn't have money for a new wagon. After Rowan drove the mules out of there, I ran away in the other direction. I had on a shirt and pants, but I got stung all over my face, arms, and hands.

I was proud of my decision to keep the mules from running, but my face was swollen big and my breathing was messed up. I was wheezing so bad that Momma and Daddy thought I wasn't going to make it. They had to take me to the doctor. We drove all the way to Marianna, which was an hour's drive even though it was only about thirty miles. We had to drive twenty miles of dirt and gravel roads and ten miles of paved. Those bee stings made my asthma act up, and I was sick for a week after that. Dr. Grey, like most of the doctors in Marianna, had "colored" and "white" waiting rooms to keep his black patients separate from the white patients. I think that he gave me a shot, but I don't know what it was. I went to school the next day, but I was feeling real bad.

Another time when we were ten and eight, my mother let me and my sister Gloria ride the train to Memphis to visit our Great-Uncle James Maclin. I held on to Gloria's hand when we got on the train and until we found our seats. When we got to Memphis, I had to catch a taxi to take us to the house. It was a lot of responsibility and I felt proud.

Food and Agriculture

Growing up on the farm in New Hope, we always had plenty of food and did fine, and I never really thought we were poor. Daddy raised some hogs and when he slaughtered a hog, it was salted down and the meat would keep for a year. Cattle were more expensive, so we didn't eat very much beef, but I remember one time we had a steer, and we had plenty of meat that year. We were like the others around us. We were all black families out there except for two white families, and they weren't doing as well as the rest of us.

Even back then, the New Hope area seemed to be declining, but the black community did get together to do some good things. We had scrub hogs of poor genetic quality, the kind that ate a lot and didn't gain much weight. With advice from the agricultural extension service man, in around 1945, some of the black farmers in New Hope formed a co-op and went together to buy a registered Poland China (we called it "polen china") boar to breed to all their sows and improve the hog stock. This was really something, in my opinion.

Unfortunately, that polen china boar got out and one of the other black farmers, Mr. King, shot it. He was not part of the co-op and he was mad at the others who were co-op members. He said that the hog came onto his place and was rooting up his field, so he shot it. The co-op farmers got the dead polen china, ground up the meat, and divided it among the members.

Later on, the co-op bought a combine to harvest peas and soybeans. That was good, but the biggest thing the black farmers did together was in 1948 or 1949 when they started the black-owned, co-op cotton gin. It was called the Peoples Co-op Cotton Gin. Mr. Andrew Howard (my friend Andrea Hope Howard's father) was the manager, and he really made it run. I was too young to have anything to do with these cooperative efforts, but I grew up seeing folks working together and helping each other. It was a good example for me.

Marianna House

We moved to Marianna in January 1949. Our house in town was a shot-gun. It had a door in the front, a door in the back, and a door in the middle, and if all the doors were open you could look straight through (or shoot a gun!) from front to back. The rooms were relatively small, probably 10′ x 10′ or 10′ x 12′. It was in town, but we had an open well, meaning we had to drop a bucket down to get water. Eventually, they put a water line close enough so we could get our water from the hydrant. But that house did not have running water until after my graduation from high school in 1958.

Even with Daddy out on the farm during the week, that little Marianna house was small. Momma and Gloria slept in a bed in the middle room. Thaddeus, Granville, and Rowan slept on the foldout couch in the front room. It was the kind where you pulled up the bottom and the back would lay down into a double bed. There was a chest of drawers and maybe a dresser in there too. My brother Donnie and I slept on a folding bed in the kitchen behind the stove. During the day, we kept our bed folded up behind the kitchen door. After we put it down, you couldn't come in the kitchen. When Daddy came home on the weekends, Gloria had to move someplace else. I can't remember exactly where. It was so small. One time a friend asked me how all of us fit in there. He just was curious.

Momma had kind of an expensive wood stove. It had a tank on the side that held water. So, there was hot water whenever we had a fire in the stove. I can't remember what they called that. The cheaper stoves just had the barrel where you put the wood and the warm surface up above. There was also a cab-inet in our kitchen with some shelves, a bin for flour, and a bin for cornmeal.

In 1956–57, my Great-Uncle James Maclin built us a bigger house that made my Momma real proud. I remember him cutting all the rafters out in the yard and then when he was putting them up on the roof he would say to us boys, "Oh, it fit! I guessed right!" But he knew what he was doing. He had measured. He was just playing with us.

I only lived there one year. That house faced south and had six rooms with a hallway. The hall was kind of a gathering space. I believe they added the bathroom in 1961 or 1962. When Uncle James built the house, he had put in a space for the bathroom with just enough room for a tub, a commode, and a sink. The living room was elongated and to the west of that was the dining room.

Before she died, Momma got a tea service that my sister Gloria has now. Momma always wanted a tea service. It was considered to be kind of upper crust. All this time when we lived in Marianna during the school week, we also had a place on Daddy's farm. That made us a dual household, so I guess you could call us pretty high level, with a weekday home and a weekend home. Both of them were pretty rough, but we had them.

Tenant Farming in Warrior Bottoms

On weekends, we went to work the farm. Daddy was intent on keeping his boys out of trouble, and he used the farm work to keep us busy. That certainly worked, for the most part. We were all damn fool teenagers, but we stayed out of the worst kind of trouble. And except for my oldest brother DL, we all made it through high school and did not go to jail.

After we moved to Marianna and Momma started teaching school at LaGrange, she needed a good car because LaGrange was quite a distance away. Daddy and Momma bought a new Chevrolet pickup truck. It was Daddy's truck, but Momma drove it to school most of the time. The next year his crops were not very good, and Daddy couldn't quite keep up with the truck payments. In early 1951, Daddy put together a deal to sell his place in New Hope for $3,500 to O. C. Broadway, a black man who owned the adjoining land. Then, he was able to pay off the truck, and for $1,500, buy eighty acres in Warrior Bottoms with twenty acres cleared for cultivation. It was a clean start.

The trouble with Warrior Bottoms was the gumbo. Gumbo is clay that sticks like glue when it gets wet. When it dries it turns to rock and has to be hammered off. That's what this place was—gumbo. And it was not on a road. It was back in the woods. You could not drive a pickup in there at all when it rained. But that year, we made a decent crop, so the next year Daddy was trying to do a little bit more. Plus, he had all us boys to keep busy and he thought that we needed a little more work to do.

He didn't have money to buy more land, so in 1952 Daddy started to tenant farm some land owned by a white man named Mr. MacDonald. His land was on a graded road, so it dried up pretty quick after the rain and was good most of the time. Being on that road was one of the big advantages. We moved into the house on MacDonald's place because it was better than ours. But it didn't have electricity, so our Ag teacher Mr. Burnett came out, and he and my older brother Donnie wired the house.

Tenant farming was better than sharecropping because in sharecropping all you have is your body and your children. The landowner supplies the land, equipment, and mules, and he advances money for all the other farming and family expenses. Then, when the crop is harvested and sold, the landowner gets his half plus all the money he advanced. That often left nothing for the sharecropper.

Tenant farming is when, as the tenant, you furnish all of the labor, equipment, and seed, and you pay the landowner either a third or fourth of what you make when you sell the crop. Cotton and corn were our primary crops. Cotton was labor intensive, so the tenant farmer got more for cotton than for corn. For a cotton crop, Daddy's contribution was one-fourth for mules and equipment and one-half for labor, and one-fourth went to MacDonald. For the corn, Daddy's contribution was one-third for mules and equipment and one-third for labor, and one-third went to MacDonald.

We never grew soybeans, but we did grow some summer wheat that mostly was fed to the mules, and we had five or six acres of purple-hull peas that we picked by hand and sold for cash. The peas were important because they were harvested in July and August, during the hard months when no other money was coming in. They supplied a little cash plus they helped keep us boys busy.

Then It All Fell Apart

Daddy was a tenant farmer for three years. The first year, we worked MacDonald's thirty acres and Daddy's twenty acres of cultivated land, which was less than a mile away. The second year, we added another sixty acres of MacDonald's land that was adjacent. So, we worked over 100 acres in total. That was the year that we made the big crop. Daddy worked hard. He stayed there working all week, and we came out to work with him on the weekends. When the school year started, we went to the farm on Friday afternoon and worked until dark and then worked all day Saturday. We didn't work on Sundays, though, because Daddy always went to church.

The tenant farming deal fell apart when Mr. MacDonald came out one weekday and all of Daddy's boys were in school. Rowan and Prentiss were still little, but I was in the ninth grade, Granville was in eleventh, Donnie was in twelfth, and we were big boys. Daddy didn't work any of us like the other folks worked their children. We all went to school. So, MacDonald got upset because we were not picking cotton. And he probably was right that we would have had a better yield if we worked more days getting our crops out on time.

We moved off the MacDonald place in 1955, because of the conflict with Mr. MacDonald. Both Momma and Daddy insisted that we go to school. I would say they went beyond the call of duty. Momma didn't care about anything but keeping us in school. Daddy could have insisted on taking us out of school because he had to harvest his crop, but he never did.

The Security of a Close Family

I always thought that both my mother and father were good people. My Momma was home more than Daddy, so I was closer to her in that way. I was much like her, outspoken and pushy, and we were in conflict every day. She established principles in me, but sometimes I just didn't want to do what was right. She whipped me, but I never did develop a dislike for her because I understood that she was doing what she had to do.

My Daddy was calm all the time. He didn't holler. He didn't scream. He didn't curse. He just said what he wanted and that was that. I never knew what to do against him, so I couldn't take him on. When he was in the mix I would calm down quickly, and things would go the way they were supposed to go.

I was not surrounded by a safe cocoon like the children growing up on land inherited from their ancestors. Where they lived was significant. It gave them a sense of security that was a fine thing for them. It gave them confidence. My impression was that they just expected things to go right. Children in my family were uncomfortable because we knew Daddy was having a hard time making a living. He didn't hide it from us. I knew he was a good, hard-working farmer because he only had forty acres and was still getting six to seven bales of cotton. He just didn't have enough land.

On the other hand, we were fairly close in my family. My brother Thad was seven and a half years older than me, and that is a lot of years when you are five, six, or seven years old. Momma started me to school when I was five, and my brother Granville and I got to walk to school with Thad and I. V. McKenzie. They were the big boys, and they would make comments to me like I belonged. I felt comfortable with them. That was a very warm time. And in school, I was well received by others around me too because of my older brothers. Even when we moved to Marianna, they were well received so I was well received.

Disrespect

When I was very young, there were two times I was bothered by white folks. Our school was two and a half miles away, and we did not have a motorized vehicle, so all of us walked back and forth each day. One time, a school bus with a white driver and carrying the white students came by. It swerved real close to spray rocks all over us. That made me mad. The other time was when I was six or seven. We were walking to church in the other direction and we passed in front of one of the white families' houses. My brothers and I were walking together and a white boy about my age ran out at me and pulled my tie, so I knocked him down. Nothing happened to me, but I remember that Momma was worried about it. She always told us to behave and get good grades, so we could go to college and be like our great-grandfather David Maclin.

As a young teenager, I was treated with disrespect several times at the five-and-dime store in Marianna. The incident I remember most clearly is the time I went to buy a white handkerchief with my initial on it. When I asked the little white girl who worked there, she answered kind of sharp, "We don't carry it." So I pointed at them and said, "There they are right there." She snatched one out and sort of snapped the handkerchief before carrying it to the checkout counter. Her blatant disdain sort of riled me up, but what could I do?

Taboos

When I was nine or ten and we were living in Marianna, my Daddy, my brother Thaddeus, and I were walking down the street and Thad spoke to this girl Georgia Carolyn Bush, who was so light skinned that she looked white. Daddy knocked Thad off the sidewalk because he thought that Thad was speaking to a white girl. That was taboo. Thad knew why Daddy hit him and kept explaining vigorously, "She's not white; she is my classmate."

I thought this thing was just unfair but had no thought about what could be done.

Then, in 1955, when Emmett Till was tortured and murdered by white men in a little town across the Mississippi River only sixty miles away, that shook me up. Emmett Till and I were the same age—fourteen—when he was killed. We heard somehow that he had whistled at a white woman. Another taboo. Momma and Daddy sat us down and told Granville and Rowan and me to be very careful. Momma usually was loud when she disciplined, but this time there was no screaming. They both were so solemn. And their seriousness made a big impression on me. I didn't accept it, but I knew I could get in bad trouble if I ever whistled at a white girl. So as children we came up knowing you got to be scared.

Always on the Bottom End

In my community, there weren't many who went to college. But I knew that Momma placed a high value on education. She always told us about my great-grandfather David Maclin, who had been to college. He ran a store and a post office. He was a preacher and taught school. I grew up admiring him because he was in charge, and I thought that was cool. I guess he was my childhood hero and remained a role model. My Momma built that into us: David Maclin was black and in charge because he was a college man.

What happened outside Lee County usually didn't mean much to me, and there was comfort and perhaps a false security in the isolated life we led. I didn't know many people. My interests were pretty much those of a child, and few adults beyond my family had any influence on me. There were some people I thought were cool or cute, as I would have said at that time. When I was eight or nine years old, there was Nelson Scott Sr., who always made some funny comment in church when everyone else was serious. I thought another man, E. C. Wilder, was really cool because he talked tenor and sang bass.

I rarely thought beyond our life in Lee County. I had no grasp of what the rest of the world was like, and I felt that wishes had to be reality-based, so I never had big dreams. My dreams were about the farm. In the early 1950s, when we had a pretty good year on the farm and were doing better, I thought everything would be great if we could just have some more land and a tractor. To me, 150 or 160 acres seemed like the perfect amount to farm. I was hoping Daddy would buy more land and a tractor and was real disappointed when he came home one day with a new team of mules.

"All is well" is what Daddy used to say. It meant that he was ready to meet his maker if he was called to go. It gets your mind right. It's a wonderful position. Whatever happens, you know there is a better place coming. But my concerns were in our world, and I thought Daddy should have been living as good as some of those well-to-do white people. That always was very frustrating to me. We were always on the bottom end. Daddy never had any money and couldn't do the things he wanted to do. He was always having difficulties paying for something.

Chapter 2
School Years

I started school in 1946 and grew up in a segregated school system all the way. We did not have kindergarten. In first and second grades, I went to the New Hope School and my Momma was my teacher. As far as I know, the New Hope School always had black teachers, mostly women and an occasional man. The male teachers were called Professor. Before I started at New Hope, the head teacher was Professor Stroud, and Professor Maclin had taught there in the 1920s and 1930s.

During the winter when I was four, I liked to walk around in some big boots. We called them knee boots, and they had a little red ring around the top. I used to love to walk in deep water up to just before the red line so the water wouldn't get in the boot, but water usually got in the boot anyway. I'd get my feet wet and run around with wet feet all day. I had a cold all that winter. Momma decided that the way to keep up with me and keep me from being sick all the time was to have me in school with her, so I started school the next fall when I was five. I think that my brother Granville, who is two years older than me, started school early too. We only started early because we were troublesome at home.

Most kids started school at six or seven, so I was always younger than my classmates. At the New Hope School, dropouts increased exponentially starting with the fourth grade. My Momma taught three grades—first, second, and third—in one room. Mrs. Maggie Shepherd taught five grades, fourth through eighth, in the other room. There were more students in Momma's room than in Mrs. Shepherd's.

Mrs. Shepherd was the head teacher. Students called her Miss Shepherd because she was from Marianna. Students called my Momma Miss Willie because she was part of the New Hope community. That is what she was called out there, so all the kids knew her that way. I called her Momma most of the time except when I was trying to get some lenient treatment. There was a boy in my class and when he didn't know a word, he said, "Miss Willie, I don't know that word." And she left him alone, so I tried calling her Miss Willie, but that didn't make any difference; she was still hard on me.

We had tables and benches. No desks. I didn't see school desks until third grade in Marianna. But they were doing a decent job with us in that little school. The big kids who were good students taught the little kids. It was whatever you call that kind of system of education. The teachers were in charge, but the students helped teach too. We didn't have a principal at the New Hope School. The head teacher reported to the white superintendent in Moro. The black schools had what they called "Tellers" or school advisors, who were responsible men in the community. They provided wood for the stove and replaced windows when they were broken out. Sometimes when it was cold outside and a window didn't get fixed right away, we had cardboard instead of a windowpane. My Daddy was a Teller.

I could learn things pretty fast, but generally I was disinterested. My problem was that I had a short attention span for the school stuff. I was most interested in who was doing what and that sort of thing. I wasn't a slow student at all and got credit for that, but I didn't give school much of my attention.

I was interested in the big boys coming on their horses. I always wanted to run with the boys who were six or eight years older than me, but they probably thought I was just a little kid. I had a friend named Nelson Scott Jr. who I used to fight with. He was a year or two older than me but in the same classroom. I hesitate to say that he was my best friend, because I really wanted to be with the big boys. I always wanted to be somebody big. That's how silly I was.

I have to say that from the time I was little, my Momma and I were in a battle. My brothers and sister Gloria still say they don't understand how I got away with all the stuff I got away with, but I can assure you she gave me plenty of whippins. The whippins just didn't do any good. There wasn't bitterness or hostility between me and Momma. We were in a war of the wills. And I think that was because we were alike.

Discipline was different in the 1940s and 1950s because corporal punishment was common, especially for the boys. A "whippin" was not a beating meant to harm the child. You could get over it pretty fast. For whippins, we had switches and straps, and I think Miss Shepherd had a paddle. These implements were used regularly, and I don't think that anyone was damaged except maybe psychologically, but we didn't know about that then. Whippins were just routine discipline. My Momma used a switch on me. I got two a day many times—one in the morning at school when I didn't know something and again in the evening because I was out playing in the mud, getting wet, or doing something else I wasn't supposed to do. After a whippin my butt would hurt. I cried real easy because that meant she was getting to me, and it would make her stop. But after I got the whippin, I would go to my brothers, who were laughing at me, and I'd say that it didn't hurt. I was acting tough.

Through her teaching career, Momma taught at New Hope, LaGrange, and Strong Elementary in Marianna. I think she was an effective teacher, because the folk I talk to tell me how much she taught them and that she was an excellent teacher and tough. I don't remember her teaching me all that much, but I know that when I came out of the second grade I could spell some big words like camouflage and blitzkrieg. That was pretty good for the second grade, but I have to look up how to spell them now. She taught reading, spelling, penmanship and cursive, and arithmetic. I don't remember anything about composition. Maybe it was integrated into other things. My impressions were always colored by the fact that my teacher was my Momma, and she was tougher on me than she was on the other students.

While she taught at New Hope, Momma took some extension classes for school teachers in Forrest City and Helena, and later she went to summer school at Agricultural, Mechanical, and Normal College (AM&N), which is now the University of Arkansas at Pine Bluff. She graduated from college in 1959, a year after I graduated from high school. She was smart and tough, and she had high expectations.

My Brothers and the Move to Town

What I remember about my brother DL is that he was always getting into trouble. He graduated from eighth grade at New Hope in 1946. Moro's school district didn't have a high school for black people, and he had to walk about three miles to catch the bus to go to Moton Training School in Marianna. But the problem was that Momma couldn't make DL go to school anymore. She had to whip him to get him out of bed. He would just go off somewhere and not go to school. She would whip him until he cried, but she could not make him go to school.

The boys who called themselves "slick" didn't want to go to school because school was for little kids. And DL was big. My brother Willie said that he would talk trash to everybody but never to DL because DL was too damn big. DL also had a resistance to authority and a resistance to the social order. When he left and went to Texas, DL ended up in jail. Then he went to Florida and ended up in jail again. He went to North Carolina and was in jail there too until he got out in 1979. The last I heard he was back in Florida, but I really don't know where he is anymore.

Thad graduated from eighth grade at New Hope two years after DL. He only had to walk and catch the bus for one semester because Momma and Daddy had decided to move to Marianna. Part of their decision was to make it easier for their younger children to go all the way through school. Another part of it was that Momma was mad at the Moro school district. When Carver Elementary opened after consolidation, they hired four teachers for each of the two-grade classrooms: first and second, third and fourth, fifth and sixth, seventh and eighth. But Momma was large pregnant with my brother Prentiss at the time and she was not assigned one of those jobs.

Prentiss was born September 8, and Daddy took care of him as a baby because after a few months Momma got a new teaching job at another Lee County school district in LaGrange. Back then, Arkansas had something like 300 school districts, one in each little community. She always taught elementary and only missed a little time when she was sick with the fatal colon cancer.

Daddy bought a small lot in Marianna. Now, I may be halving this or doubling it, but my best recollection is that he paid $200 for the lot and borrowed the money from Mr. Ramsey, a black man in Marianna who was kind of well to do. Mr. Ramsey didn't look it, but he had money. Daddy had the little shotgun house built on the lot, and we moved into the house in January when I was halfway through the third grade. This was where we lived until the year before I graduated from high school.

Moton and Mrs. Strong

We were told that Moton Training School was the best school for blacks in the state of Arkansas. It was named after Dr. Robert Russa Moton, who had been a student of Booker T. Washington and who became the second president of Tuskegee Institute, serving from 1915 to 1935. The Moton school had first through twelfth grades, and Mrs. Anna Strong was the principal—but she acted like the superintendent of black education. She really ran that school. One time, Mr. Whitten, the white superintendent of all the Marianna schools, came into our building and he didn't take his hat off. Mrs. Strong asked him to remove his hat and said, "How can I train these boys to be more respectful if you don't take off your hat?" So, he pulled his hat off and shut up. That was pretty tough because those white men didn't take off their hats to black folks.

When I was there, Mrs. Strong brought Dr. Moton to speak to the student body one time. I don't remember anything about him. He must have come when I was in the third or fourth grade and I was too young to remember. Dr. Mary McCloud Bethune came to our school twice. There is a historically black school in Florida named for her called Bethune-Cookman. Mrs. Strong brought fun things too: the Harlem Globetrotters came twice.

We had a little auditorium where all the students could sit. Mrs. Strong was known for not giving whippins to students, but she would have order. When I was in fourth grade and my sister Gloria was in second, Gloria coughed during a program and Mrs. Strong took her right out of the auditorium. She didn't want any noise whatsoever. She was that strict. When I was in the eighth grade, Mrs. Strong brought Dr. Kelly Miller Smith from Nashville. Later I learned that he was one of the black leaders who got Nashville on the road to desegregation in the 1950s. He and Jim Lawson, who I would meet during the Memphis sit-ins, were the ones to make change in Nashville a long time before we got any desegregation in Memphis. I don't remember exactly what Dr. Smith said to us at Moton, but it must have been something like, "Follow your dreams, do something positive, and make the world a better place."

Many Moton graduates have grateful memories of Mrs. Strong and the influence she had on them. My brother Rowan told me this when we were talking about her:

> Mrs. Strong gave off an air of superiority, and she taught us to take care of our own. She made me feel like I was not being the best I could be if I dropped paper in the school grounds or would even think of writing on the school walls. I never heard her give a speech about this, but I don't remember any graffiti ever being in the bathrooms. As an adult, I managed a distribution center that was a million and a half square feet, and I always stopped to pick up trash from the floor. I still can't walk over a piece of paper on the lawn. I have to lean over and pick it up.

Harry Durham was a student Mrs. Strong more or less adopted because she recognized his potential and willingness to take advantage of what she had to offer. Harry is well known in our community as someone who "made it" in spite of starting out with so much working against him. To start, it was 1936 when he was born into the poverty of the Brickeys area, one of the poorest parts of one of the poorest counties in a country soon to fall into the big depression. Harry's father died when he was only six months old, and Harry was raised by his elderly grandparents.

To really understand the importance of Mrs. Strong, take a look at how Harry remembers her:

I started attending Moton in fifth grade and we moved to Marianna in 1951. My grandfather worked as a cotton chopper and a cotton picker and was an independent contractor. He owned a 1946 truck, but he couldn't drive because he had come up in the horse and buggy era. I got my driver's license early because he needed me to drive, and I did all of his driving. We hauled laborers out to the fields for different farmers around the area. And then I would come back to Marianna in time to go to school. After school and football practice, I would go back and pick up the laborers from the fields. I did that all through high school.

Mrs. Strong started asking me to drive her places where she had her meetings like Memphis, Little Rock, and Nashville, plus to Cleveland and Kentucky to meet her son. She was president of the national black PTA and one time I drove her to their meeting at Bethune-Cookman College in Daytona, Florida. Mrs. Strong introduced me to a lot of people too. One time, she introduced me to the president of Fisk University. And she would talk to me when we were driving. That is how we got real close. It was inspirational to be with her.

Mrs. Strong was a wonderful lady. I heard that her husband was killed. This was before my time and I don't know exactly what happened. But I do know that Mrs. Strong didn't take a backseat to anyone. She would speak very politely, but she was forthright and always wanted the best for her children. Most black schools had what was called a split term. They closed during the growing and harvest seasons when black children worked the fields. Moton didn't do that until after Mrs. Strong retired. Also, our white superintendent was supposed to hire all the teachers, but Mrs. Strong recruited and hired her own teachers.

It was tough back in those times. When I was growing up, black menfolk could not be outspoken like Mrs. Strong. It was common for the girls to step up and boys to stay in the background, but Mrs. Strong didn't think it ought to be that way. Mrs. Strong wanted boys to grow up to be men and leaders in their community. She preached that all the time. She taught me a tremendous amount through her actions and her words.

I am the youngest of ten children. Two or three of my sisters finished high school, but I was the only one who went to college. I was not a great athlete, but I was good enough to win a college football scholarship. When I graduated from college in 1960, I wanted to be a coach. I taught and coached in Wynne, Arkansas, and then in Memphis, Tennessee, where I worked my way up to being a principal. Mrs. Strong taught me by her own example to treat everybody at all levels with respect. When I was talking to a teacher or someone who worked in housekeeping or food service, that person was important. We had a shared purpose. We were all there for the children.

Had it not been for Mrs. Strong and a few other important people in my life, I never would have been able to do all I have accomplished. Without her influence, I would have been nothing.

Mrs. Strong stayed in Marianna all her life. During her tenure, Moton changed from a three-room training school in the middle of a cotton field to a fourteen-room brick building with an auditorium and a separate vocational agriculture building. She was a noted educator. In 1934, she represented Arkansas in Washington DC at the first national Conference on Fundamental Problems in the Education of Negroes. She shared the stage with Eleanor Roosevelt at the 1942 meeting of the American Teachers Association, which Mrs. Strong helped establish.

Frustrated with School

Because I started school when I was five, I was not as mature as my classmates, and I think that affected me. This maturity thing is very substantial when you are young, so I was always frustrated and had some difficulty. To prove myself, I would do plenty of things that I shouldn't have done. When I started going to Moton, I was uncomfortable because everyone in my grade was eight or nine, which seemed like a lot older. Sometimes I would have to fight. There was a kind of initiation practice in the high school to rough up the kids who came in from the country in the ninth grade. So, I guess the younger boys tried to do the same thing.

One time, a third-grade boy named George Crawford slapped me around. I came back at him the next day with a homemade weapon. It was a piece of a curtain rod. I scratched him up a little and he never bothered me anymore. The other boys left me alone after that too. That is the kind of thing you'd get expelled for today.

But being younger wasn't a giant deal controlling my life. I didn't spend much time thinking about it. I had good friends. Aaron Oliver and Bill Stewart were my friends. They were two and three years older, and we stayed friends until they died in 2012 and 2009.

My sister Gloria knew how to be quiet and sit still, and Momma had been taking her to school since she was four years old. After Gloria was at Moton, she was put ahead a grade too. I don't think that Gloria had a hard time being younger. She just seemed to have a better level of maturity than I did. She knew how to be respectful and quiet. Gloria and Rowan both tell me that I was just crazy, and I could have started school two years later and still been crazy. That may be true. I don't know.

Pretty Girls, Science, and Math

Moton had things that I had never seen in New Hope's two-room school. It was a better school. There is no question about that. But all the pretty girls made the biggest impression on me. There were pretty girls at New Hope, but there were more pretty girls at Moton. There were all those pretty teachers too, and my Momma wasn't my teacher anymore. I found it all much more enjoyable.

In the eleventh or twelfth grade, when I was dreaming or something, I thought about being a doctor, but I didn't tell anybody. My style was whenever I told somebody about something, that meant I had to do it. Becoming a doctor looked impossible, so I didn't talk about it. The only person I might have told would have been Gloria because she kept my secrets pretty good. It never got to the point of finding out how to do it either.

In high school, we didn't have physics and we didn't have much of a lab, but whenever there was a course in the sciences I took it. I took chemistry and biology. I came to like chemistry and math because of the notion that if you did the exact same thing twice and didn't get the same result, you knew you had goofed up somewhere. In chemistry, we worked in milliliters, and a milliliter is a little bit smaller than a spoonful, so you had to be careful to get it exactly right. That required some skills and I liked that.

My grades helped me. I wasn't a star student, but I had better grades than most, especially in science and math. I remember one girl, Ora Dee Barnes, who was considered to be the prettiest. She used to give me a little bit of attention because I would help her with her math homework. But I didn't read anything then, so I hadn't learned much from books. I know Momma understood that kids had to read, but she had too many children to push reading with us.

Mr. Elmer C. Burnett and Vocational Agriculture

My first regular male teacher was in the ninth grade when I was active in something called vocational agriculture. His name was Mr. Burnett, and he was one of my best teachers—unsung. He was a great guy, and he taught us math in relevant ways.

As the vocational ag teacher, Mr. Burnett taught us how to survive on the farm. We had iron-wheel wagons until sometime in the mid-1950s when Daddy bought a rubber-tire wagon frame. Mr. Burnett had me build the bed for that wagon. I must have been about thirteen or fourteen, but Daddy trusted that I could do it and let me do the whole job. I put it all together. Of course, I was doing what I learned from Mr. Burnett in shop. He taught us all kinds of useful things. He taught us the math necessary to do a job. We learned a little bit about trigonometry because we had to do angles when building something. My brother Donnie built the shed we had at the back of our house in Marianna. Granville built a brooder for the chickens. We all had to build something.

This was when our teachers were really part of the community. We lived in the little shotgun house in Marianna, and Mr. Burnett had built his own house around the corner only about 300 feet away. So, he was a neighbor. His wife was secretary to Mrs. Strong, and that made her somebody important too.

In Marianna, we had kerosene lamps for light until 1953 or 1954 when Donnie and Mr. Burnett wired our house for electricity. Mr. Burnett would tell Donnie what to do like a homework assignment. Donnie would do it on his own and then Mr. Burnett would come over, check his work, and give him his next assignment. They got the whole job done that way. Back in 1951 or early 1952, Donnie had been Mr. Burnett's helper when he wired the MacDonald house in Warrior Bottoms. That way he had learned what to do.

There was a lot of trust between Mr. Burnett and all the parents. If our parents had to file income tax, Mr. Burnett had us bring in all their bills and records, and he worked with us to fill out their tax forms. Momma and Daddy had to file income tax because Momma was a schoolteacher. I filled out their tax form and took it home for them to sign. A lot of the boys did that. Daddy thought that I was insane, but he did have confidence in me with this kind of thing and believed that I would do it right. He was extremely pleased. Momma thought that I would probably screw up because I was so hard to keep in line, but in the end she was happy too.

Staying Out of Jail

The Blue Goose was a joint out on Highway 79 about four and a half miles west of Marianna. It was considered very rough because somebody got killed out there about once or twice a year. There were more knives than pistols, so the fights were usually knife fights. When the Blue Goose closed down in the early 2000s, some folks said that it was the oldest business in Lee County. The building is still out there. The city of Marianna had joints too where drinking and some fighting took place. All of these were places where Momma didn't allow any of us to go. But after we moved to town and when I got to be fourteen or fifteen, I did start going to joints in Marianna with my friend Aaron Oliver. There were two where we would go. The Swing Inn was owned by Joe Cole, who also drove Moton's only school bus. This is where most of the high school kids went. The Duck Inn was probably the worst of all. We went there when we wanted to be wild. It was owned by Lucius Jefferson, who had been to prison for killing someone. He had two wives and they both worked at his joint.

When I was fourteen, I got caught stealing. I worked before school each morning cleaning up a store, and I took some stuff because I was trying to keep up with the boys. I wanted to have matching socks and belt or whatever was matching at the time. I think I was trying to make up for my immaturity, and I don't blame anybody for that. As soon as school started, the police came to arrest me and take me to jail, but Mrs. Strong stopped them. She told them, "Our boys don't go to jail!" I don't know how it was that those white policemen listened to her, but they did. She could only protect me until school was out. Daddy was out in the field, and she had me send word for him to come right away. He got there at about two o'clock and arranged for me to pay off what I had stolen. Then he took me home. That was in the spring and Daddy kept me out on the farm all through that summer. I was out cutting timbers for railroad ties to pay it off. He didn't let me come to town at all.

Play Football or Milk the Cow

I am not that well-coordinated for sports and never had any athletic ability. I couldn't hit the ball or catch it very well, and even though I have long legs I run clumsy so I couldn't play baseball. When I was in high school I went out for basketball and football. I made the football team because I played up in the line and was strong enough and had enough nerve to stand there and block and not let somebody come through. They took twenty-two players to away games, and I was sufficient to travel on the bus to those games. I kind of enjoyed football—the camaraderie was great, being among the boys, hollering, and talking back and forth. I did a lot of talk—more talk than playing. I was not a good player and didn't play much. I only lettered one year.

We had a milk cow out in our backyard and during the day we staked her out in the grass across the street. One of my chores was to milk her twice a day, and I was still milking that cow in the eleventh grade when I was trying to play football. I remember because Momma told me that she didn't care where I went to play football, I had to milk the cow. So, one time I hired a man, Mr. Aaron Crenshaw, to milk her. He charged me a dime or something.

Stealing Minutes

In my junior and senior years, I was 6'2" and that was pretty tall, so I tried to go out for basketball, but I didn't make the team because I was too clumsy. For a time, they let me go with them because I had enough sense to run the time clock and keep the score. I did that for a while until one night in my senior year, I got in trouble.

We were playing Forrest City in Marianna and there was a big rivalry between Moton and Lincoln schools. Forrest City's Coach Livingston was really tall, and we weren't supposed to call him "Tree," but we did. I was running the clock. It was a really tight game, and when it got down to the final seconds, we were leading by just a little. So, I tried to run the clock out a second or two when nobody was looking. Now how could I expect to do that with a gymnasium full of people watching? It was dumb.

Tree saw the clock move and went crazy, and of course me and my ignorant friends came out of the stands and were ready to fight. The test of manhood was if you were ready to fight. Fortunately, cooler heads prevailed. Our coach took me off the clock and I never ran it again. He just said, "Neal, get off the clock."

Stealing Cars

Momma bought a new dark-blue and sky-blue Delray Chevrolet in March 1958 when I was in the twelfth grade. Donnie was in his third year of a four-year "hitch" in the Air Force and still single. When he came home on leave that time, he gave her the down payment. I had a key made that she didn't know about, and after Momma would go to sleep my friends Aaron Oliver and Billy Stewart and I would push her car out of the driveway. We'd start it when we got down the street. We just wanted to let the boys see us driving. We called the car a Short. We were in a Short. That doesn't make any sense. We called it Wheels too. We had all kinds of names for automobiles. We only took her car a couple of times in the spring before graduation. We'd be nervous until we got home. When we got back, we'd turn it off in front of the house and then roll it up the driveway. I don't think my Momma ever knew about any of that.

In 1996, my son Nic did the same thing to me one time. After we had moved to Little Rock, I gave my wife Karen a new car. It was our first new Mercedes. When I had to go to St. Louis for a hearing, Karen came with me. We left on Thursday night and my son Nic convinced my sister-in-law that I had told him to get the keys. So, he took the car and drove it to Marianna and then back to Little Rock that Thursday night. On Friday morning, he took the car to his school in Little Rock and drove around the school campus there too. He didn't go to class at all. I checked and verified that with the teachers. He drove over to Marianna again and drove around the Lee High School campus a second time. The whole idea was just to be seen. Karen didn't understand any of that, but I fully understand. I punished him for it though. He was not very smart about covering what he had done. He didn't fill the car back up with gas and that is what made me notice. So that's it. When boys are fifteen or sixteen, they just have these stupid notions. My son and I wanted to be seen doing well. Wanted to look cool.

Stealing Books

Moton Training School had some teachers who were really good at helping those of us who were not trying to be our best. And today, my most important memories of Moton have to do with being tricked into reading. These memories ring in my mind. But I didn't learn the whole story of what happened until years later.

Mrs. Mildred Stubblefield Grady was my high school English teacher, and she had taught three of my older brothers too. All of them were relatively calm, and my brother Donnie always acted really decent.

I had Mrs. Grady for the first time in the ninth grade. One day she made the mistake of comparing me to Donnie and I told her "MY NAME IS OLLY." I was telling her that I wasn't going to be like him. And I said it so rough that tears welled up in her eyes. I think she started to cry because I hurt her feelings. She thought that I had some potential, and she was frustrated that she couldn't reach me. That wasn't the only conflict we had.

Every day it was something.

Mrs. Grady was an excellent teacher, and she knew the things that should be in a school. She wasn't paid to be a librarian, but she knew her students should have a library, so she took it upon herself to make a library. Our principal Mrs. Strong made space available. When I was in the elementary grades, the library was on a little balcony. And in 1954–55, when the school got money to build a new lunchroom, the old lunchroom that was in an old military barracks building was converted. One half became the library and the other half was where we had to go for supervised study hall.

Moton required some of us to take a foreign language. French was the one they offered so we all took French. I took it for two years. Mrs. Saunders was our French teacher. She never seemed like a southern black person. She might have been from some other country. I'm not sure. But Mrs. Saunders and Mrs. Grady were friends.

Mrs. Carolyn Frazier was another teacher I admired. She had just graduated from college, and this was her first year of teaching. I don't remember what she taught. All I remember is that she was pretty. At that time, I was in love with her. She was a teacher, but she was so pretty. She was so pretty it made your knees weak.

One day Mrs. Frazier said something like this to me: "Olly, can I talk to you after class?" And I said, "Yes, Carolyn." And she didn't react to me using her first name. She just said, "Olly, you always cause trouble in my class and I thought you liked me." And I said, "I do!" So, she told me, "Don't you understand that if I can't manage my class, I'm going to get a bad evaluation from the principal?" Well, from that point on she didn't have any trouble from me! And I didn't let anybody else act the fool in her class either.

I had Mrs. Frazier for study hall sometimes and didn't want to upset her study hall either. On a rainy afternoon I was in Mrs. Frazier's study hall and didn't want to be there, but since it was raining outside I couldn't just walk out and go someplace. So, I eased on over to the library. I was just looking around and saw a book by Frank Yerby that had a cover done so that any sexual vision you saw was in your head. It had a drawing of a slim woman who appeared to be wearing a sheer gown. I glanced at it and saw a few hot lines and said to myself, "I'm going to read that." I slipped it under my jacket and took it.

I brought it back a week or two later after I read it. I didn't need it and I didn't want to keep it around for my brothers to see and find out that I was reading. I put it back in the same place, and when I put it back, I saw another book by the same author, so I thought what the hell, and I took it too. I didn't notice that the second Frank Yerby book hadn't been there the week before. And when I brought it back a week or so later, there was another Frank Yerby book and I stole it too.

On our place in Marianna, we had a little shed out in the backyard where Daddy could store stuff. We called it the smokehouse, but it wasn't a smokehouse at all. It got to be a kind of junk house, and that was where I would go to read those books. I only could read in the daytime because the shed didn't have electricity or a kerosene lamp. I hid the book out there until I was finished with it. In the eleventh and twelfth grade, I used to tell my sister Gloria a lot of what I was doing, but I don't think even Gloria knew that I was reading those books.

The Book Thief Learns the Whole Story

The book stealing occurred in the winter of 1957 and the spring of 1958. I didn't find out the whole story until 1971 when we had our first class reunion. We invited some of our teachers to the reunion, and Mrs. Grady was one of them. She had retired by this time. I thought that Mrs. Grady was all right. She tolerated me after all.

We didn't call roll at the reunion until midnight. My buddies Aaron Oliver and Alvin Campbell came in just before the roll was called. That was their style to always be late. We talked about how Aaron had to get a ride to a football game in Forrest City one time because he missed the bus taking us up there. That night we all laughed at that, but Mrs. Grady kept on laughing, so I asked her what else happened that I didn't know about. And she said to me, "I was thinking about you." This is when she told me the full story.

She had seen me take those library books. And when she saw me, her first thought was to tell me that I didn't need to steal the books. They were free. I could check them out and read them for free. Then, she realized that Mildred and Bernice were at the checkout desk, and I didn't want them to check a book out to me because they might tell my friends. Reading a library book would not be consistent with my need for a tough reputation.

She decided if one of her boys would read some books, she would supply them. That was her theory. If he will read it, he can take it and keep it. In case I came back for another one, she wanted to make certain it was there. So, she and her friend Mrs. Saunders talked it over and decided to drive over to Memphis and find another Frank Yerby book for me. I guess they made that trip a few times. Mrs. Grady had been trying to get us to read since the ninth grade, and I was in the twelfth grade when all this happened. I really should have caught on to something... The rest of my night at the reunion was colored by hearing this story.

After that, Mrs. Grady and I grew to be friends. When I applied to law school, she was the person I asked to write my letter to the bar association attesting to my good character, and she was proud to do it. When she died, her son came to me and said, "Momma told me the story about you stealing those books and she wants you to tell it at her funeral." So, I did.

When I think about some of my experiences like this, I smile. So many folks have helped me along the way. I was talking with a group of college students one evening not long ago, and I don't think they have had the kind of breaks I had. I just don't think that they received the coverage given to me. I've had a helluva life thanks to a lot of help.

Mrs. Grady stayed at Moton until she retired in the late 1960s. Mrs. Frazier left Moton after a few years, got married, and went to work at her alma mater, the University of Arkansas at Pine Bluff. The Honors Program over there is named for her. It's the Dr. Carolyn F. Blakely Honors Program. In more recent years, we have attended some of the same banquets and laughed about the old days. She told me one time that when she was at Moton, she used to go home and practice how to look mean in front of the mirror. She still is pretty.

I Could Do Better

For me school was never smooth. I was always into something. In high school, it wasn't a "playful, having-a-good-time feeling," but I don't think I was terribly unhappy either. I don't know how to put it. I certainly wasn't going around mad at the world all the time and I wasn't depressed. I was more frustrated than happy. I was always frustrated about something not going how I wished it could go. I just thought that eventually I could do more.

I used to try to compete with Sterling King in our classes. He always had his homework done. He always did the thing that was supposed to be done, but I didn't want to do all that. He was really organized, so I didn't like him too much, but I don't think he knew it. Oh, I did homework from time to time because I did not want to be dumb, but I wanted to have a good relationship with the boys who could be damn fools too. I'd try to keep up with the good students like Sterling, but at the same time I wanted the other boys to say that Olly Neal is a crazy son of a bitch. I wanted both worlds.

My senior class at Moton put on a play called "Smiling Through," and it was the big production of the year. I was in it, but I can't really tell you what that play was all about. I do remember some parts. Sterling King and I were the stars on the male side. I played Uncle John, and Ora Dee Barnes played the niece of my deceased wife or something. She looked just like the wife, and that is supposed to be romantic you know. For about five or six years after that when I would come back to Marianna, kids who had seen it would call me Uncle John. They said we did a heck of a job.

"When You're Black Get Back"

We used to have a saying that went, "When you're black get back. When you're brown stick around. If you're white you're all right." So, when I grew up I never thought I was good looking, 'cause I have a big nose; I have very nappy hair; and I am black.

There was a little club I was associated with later—in the early 1960s. All the girls who came there had to be "paper sack." You know how tan a paper sack is? They had to be that color or lighter to get into that club. It was a built-in damn thing. They called themselves The Paper Sack something Club. I can't remember exactly. And there was a club in Memphis called the Black and Tan. This was when I was at LeMoyne. I wasn't a member of that club because it was for sophisticated black people. The Black and Tan was clearly designed for the Tan. It was for tan or lighter.

I'll tell you something else that was really profound. I don't know if I really want this out there, but I'm going to tell it to you anyway because I'm trying to be straight here. In January 1979 when I asked Mrs. Grady to write that letter so I could take the bar exam, she said, "I'd be glad to," and she asked, "Can I put it in my own handwriting?" She wrote beautifully so I told her yes. And she said, "Just stay a minute. Let me start writing it right now." Mrs. Grady was a so-called "high-yellow" woman. She started crying and then she told me, "I didn't treat you as well as I should have when you were in high school. You had a lot of potential and I just didn't push you hard enough like I did with some of the other boys." It was clear to me that she was talking about some of the boys like Cleaster Jackson and Bobby Dean Walton, who were real light skinned.

I knew a couple of things. I knew she had been upset when her son Connor Grady Jr. married a girl from Marianna who was a pretty woman but as dark as I am. That was back when I was in high school. This really was a built-in reaction. It was the normal order. I know it's hard for anybody outside to understand, but it was just built into us that if you were light you were a little bit better. And the worst were those real dark, big-nosed people like me. It was so common. You just knew it was going on. You rejected it personally, but you knew how folks operated. It just was THE thing. If you were light you were probably better suited was the thinking.

So, in 1979 when Mrs. Grady said that she knew she didn't treat me as well as she should have, I understood what she was crying about, and it just blew my mind. By then, she had gotten past the idea that you are only smart if you are light, and she felt guilty about it. I told her that she should not feel guilty because she really had done a lot for me. And she said, "I could have done so much more."

But for me, my book stealing episode and how Mrs. Grady handled it was the most exceptional thing that happened to me in high school. Frank Yerby was a black author. Mrs. Grady and Mrs. Saunders must have had to look hard for those books. We didn't have Amazon back then. And I lived in Memphis a little later during 1960 and 1961, so I know that they couldn't have just gone to a black bookstore because there weren't any. Or maybe they found it funny. Maybe they were laughing a little bit at how smart this crazy boy thought he was stealing books and getting away with it.

Mrs. Grady later said this to me too: "I did not think very much of the author. I was just pleased to see a young man reading. I thought if you read Frank Yerby, you might eventually go on to read something better." And she was right. I went from reading Frank Yerby novels in high school to reading Kierkegaard, Dostoevsky, and Camus in college.

Chapter 3
Hard Times

When I graduated from Moton High School in 1958 my mind was torn between two things: I wanted to go to Chicago where I could get a job, make a pocketful of money, and come back home driving a big car to impress my friends; on the other hand, I realized that there was a good chance I wouldn't be able to do that because I was only sixteen. So, I also thought about going to college, at least for a while. I went up to Chicago and stayed with my brother Granville (now Agin Muhammad), but I wasn't able to get a job other than flipping hamburgers and washing dishes.

Ignorant and Afraid of Momma

While I was in Chicago, I went to Pepper's Lounge one night with a couple of my friends to hear the blues singer Howlin' Wolf. He was singing a song about a woman who done him wrong when this drunk boy who was sitting there yelled out, "Yeah, mine done me wrong too!" And he pulled out his pistol and started shooting up through the ceiling. It was stupid. We got out of there and kept running for twenty-three blocks to a friend's place where we stayed the night. I wasn't running because I was afraid of getting shot by that son of a bitch. I was running because I didn't want Momma to find out that I had been drinking whiskey. I don't know what she could have done to me because she was in Marianna and I was in Chicago, but she had that kind of hold on me.

LeMoyne College

I enrolled in LeMoyne College for the fall semester. I chose LeMoyne because it had a good academic reputation and I saw it as a miniature Harvard for black students. In the back of my mind, I really wanted to stop being the foolish clown. I wanted to give myself a chance to be different. I wanted to do well and be somebody. That was deep down. I didn't want to go to AM&N in Pine Bluff because all the guys who used to do all the crazy stuff with me went there.

Another factor was that LeMoyne was in Memphis and my Great-Uncle James Maclin lived in Memphis. He and his wife Roxy offered to let me stay with them without having to pay anything. They just acted like I was their son. I got a place to sleep and two meals a day—one in the morning and one in the evening. This was a big part of my decision because I came back from Chicago with only $100 in my pocket, and I wasn't going to ask my parents for any money. My parents had a hard enough time. I was my own man and they didn't need to pay my expenses anymore. LeMoyne did not cost much either. I think my first semester tuition was less than $100. Books were high though. They could cost $10, $12, or $15 each.

LeMoyne right away provided me a window on what was out there—what was possible in a bigger world. The college required you to get a physical health examination to enter, and we got to choose between two black physicians. I had never seen a black doctor before. One of the two was real light skinned with straight hair, but the other one was a dark-skinned guy with hair like mine. I was impressed with that because I could identify with him. And once or twice when I was in high school, I had thought that maybe I ought to be a doctor. But I always suppressed that idea. It never seemed possible.

LeMoyne was one of those liberal arts schools that wanted to broaden your horizons. All of us had to take a class in philosophy and religion, and the professor, Dr. Arnold, insisted that we read. So, in the second semester of my freshman year, I joined a Great Books Discussion Club that was led in part by Dr. Arnold. I was in it with Charles Nichols from Tunica, Mississippi, and T. C. Herd from West Point, Mississippi. We joined the club because we thought of ourselves as sophisticated, independent thinkers. I was seventeen.

The books we read by Dostoevsky, Nietzsche, and Camus were pretty heavy stuff. One of the books was Camus's *The Stranger* and the protagonist was a young guy named Meursault, who didn't cry at his mother's funeral. He didn't do what other people expected him to do. That was the theme. I also had picked up *The Outsider*, a book by Richard Wright, and it was about Cross Damon, who rebelled against all that was culturally acceptable. I remember these characters because the idea of being on the outside and resisting the norm attracted me, and it became part of my learning.

Memphis Sit-Ins

During my sophomore year when I was eighteen, we were beginning to think about black and white issues a little bit. We were talking about what was wrong in the system and how to make things right. Then, four black students in North Carolina started the famous Woolworth's lunch counter sit-ins. It was February 1960 and the news was everywhere. Even though we had not really thought about sit-ins before, students at LeMoyne got inspired. When we discussed what was going on in North Carolina, we discovered that we were really mad about our limited use of public facilities in Memphis: the zoo, the museum, and the libraries. So, much of our sit-in conversations at LeMoyne were about the public facilities rather than the lunch counters in the downtown department stores.

I was particularly upset about not being able to use the Memphis technical library. I was taking biology and chemistry courses. When Dr. Gibson gave us some research papers to write, the books in LeMoyne's library were not what I needed. Nearby on Vance Avenue there was a little "colored" branch of the main library where if you needed a book you had to tell the librarian and he would order it from the big library. I never could get a book very fast or keep it long enough to do decent work on my assignments. It was not conducive to doing the kind of college study we were supposed to be doing.

Starting the Memphis sit-ins was a profound thing for all of us. And I got very much involved. Students from Owens Junior College went down to sit-in at the Woolworth's lunch counter on a Friday evening, but they left when requested and were not arrested. The next day, Saturday, March 19, some of those Owens students came over to LeMoyne, and we had a big meeting together in the C. Arthur Bruce Hall gymnasium. I think it started at ten o'clock.

Dr. Hollis Freeman Price, president of LeMoyne College, and some of the faculty tried to talk us out of a protest. They did talk us out of going to the lunch counters but not out of going to the two libraries, the zoo, and the museum. We left at about noon to go into those places, and we did not leave them until we were arrested. A TV crew filmed us being arrested at the technical library, and my brother Rowan saw me on TV. The NAACP gave the money to bail us out, so we were back in our classes on Monday morning. I think that there were about fifty of us all together, but I can't remember the exact number. I just remember there were three or four students who went to jail with me from the technical library.

Non-Violent and Alert for Danger

Jim Lawson, Marion Barry, and somebody else met with us the next week to help us figure out how to make what we were doing most effective. They did not push us to do anything we didn't want to do. They just talked to us about the pitfalls of activism and about nonviolence. Nonviolence was the key. Nonviolence was everything. It was acceptable to me and everyone because it made sense. And it still makes sense because folks who are protesting generally don't have the resources to win a physical battle, so you have to figure out another way to get into your opponent's head. That is what nonviolence is really about.

When I was a kid I had always wanted to be with the big boys—to be a "big man." For me, it was like that with practicing nonviolence. If you wanted to test your manhood, you could stand there and let somebody slap you and take it to prove your toughness. The test was not whether you could knock your opponent down but whether you could stand there and take it. So that is what they taught us, and I accepted it. We all were with it.

We also were told that we should never go anywhere by ourselves after dark because it was just too dangerous. I lived about three miles from LeMoyne College. By now I could ride the bus to school because I had a little pocket money from a carhop job. But the bus stopped running early and after our late meetings, it was a lot of trouble getting home. Sometimes someone would borrow a car, but I walked home in the dark many times. I'd walk on the sidewalk facing the traffic, so I could see what was coming at me. And I'd stay aware of everything around me so I would know if there was anything unusual or out of place. Always alert for danger.

Fire and Inspire

Our student meetings were about three or four times a week at Mt. Olive CME in downtown Memphis. I was a loud talker, but I was consciously and purposefully pleased not to be our lead spokesman. Our spokesman was a much quieter guy named Evander Ford, who later stayed in Memphis. He was a little-bitty guy who always dressed well and acted dignified, and we thought that we needed somebody kind of dignified when we had to talk to the college president or someone like that. So, Evander was our calm lead person, and I was the loudmouth runoff always taking the chance to make a speech. I was haranguing; I was loud and not always as logical as I ought to have been. But the students liked me. My role really was to fire and inspire. And Evander, as a more thoughtful person, was our public representative (this setup was similar to me and Sterling King later).

Frustrated, Successful, and Discouraged

The sit-ins branched out during the next six months, and by the time school was out that summer we were boycotting in downtown Memphis too. We were sitting at the lunch counters in the department stores like

Goldsmith's, Kresge, and Woolworth's. I cannot tell you how the decision to expand was made. I just remember that it morphed into more than just public facilities. And we continued sit-ins and picketing to stop black folks from shopping at the downtown stores all through the summer of 1960. But it was frustrating because older black folks were not joining us in the boycotts like I thought they should.

We also decided to sit in the front of the buses on our way to school starting on our first day of classes right after Labor Day. Integrating the Memphis buses turned out to be one of our major accomplishments. We also were successful in integrating the technical and other downtown libraries, the zoo, and the museum, but our boycott of the stores owned by the white power structure was a big failure and disappointment. We never got the level of community involvement that we expected to be automatic.

I was overly intense, as you sometimes are when you are eighteen and nineteen, and I couldn't understand why black folks were still shopping downtown. It just didn't make sense to me. I had an inflated notion about how right we were. Now, I see that our group of passionate students had some right on our side, but the older black folks had their reasons to do business in the downtown stores too. Anyway, by October or November 1960, I was so discouraged that I started thinking about dropping out of school. I finished the fall semester and left in January 1961. That is when I went to Chicago, took the civil service exam, and got a secure job at the post office.

Post Office Exam

A little later, one of my older brothers, Thaddeus, who lived in Chicago, wanted to get a job at the post office too. He already worked at Air King, but he had a family and needed another job. Thad couldn't seem to pass the civil service exam, and I wanted to help him by taking it for him.

I've always been pretty good at taking exams. I probably score better on tests than many people whose knowledge base is superior to mine because tests don't excite me. I knew how to be calm and not get caught up in being nervous, and I had a systematic approach that worked particularly well on a test like the post office used to have. Plus, I had already taken it two times before: once in Memphis and again in Chicago.

I didn't care all that much about myself, but my brother had a lot of children to support and I didn't want him to get in trouble. So, I decided to try taking the test for a friend of mine first. I told my friend that we ran the risk of being prosecuted or something if we were caught but he said, "Let's do it. I need the job." So, I took the exam for him and it worked out just like I thought it would. I was doing what I thought I should do at the time, and I got to be kind of an expert at taking the civil service exam. Both my friend and my brother got post office jobs and ended up doing really well there. My brother worked his two jobs until he retired. He delivered mail and then went over to Air King to work another four-hour shift each day.

The Worst Time of My Life

When I was doing these things, it was a time when nothing made much difference to me. It was cheating. That is what I'm talking about. But I didn't care because I was going through the hardest thing that ever happened to me in my personal life. I can't describe how hard it was.

Cleola Davis and I had started seeing each other when we were in high school. She was a pretty girl from an extremely poor family. She graduated from Moton High School two years behind me in June 1960 and enrolled at LeMoyne for the fall semester. And our relationship continued.

Cleola stayed at LeMoyne for another year and a half after I left. When I dropped out and went to Chicago, she would come up to visit me occasionally, and we used to talk on the phone a lot. At that time, you paid for long-distance calls, and my phone bill would be off the page. I worked as a letter carrier, a decent job for a country boy, so we decided to get married.

We got married on June 17, 1962, and Cleola died eight days later on Monday, June 25. This was the beginning of the worst days, months, and years of my life. My brother Granville and his wife June had hosted a party for us on Sunday evening, and the next day was my first day back to work. When I got out of bed that morning, Cleola said she had a headache, but she didn't say it in a way to make me worry. I told her something like, "Don't get up. It will go away."

Our apartment was on the third floor and when I came in that evening after work, I remember going up the stairs. I opened the door, walked in, and found her still lying in bed—already stiff. She must have died not long after I left that morning. I just started to scream. That's all I could do. I screamed and screamed, and that made the people across the hall come over. This was Chicago and you didn't know your neighbors, but they helped anyway. They called whoever needed to be called. I think it was the fire department that came. They took her away and I followed. I had three brothers living in Chicago—Donnie, Granville, and Thaddeus—and I called Donnie. He brought Granville and they were quietly supportive. Eventually I realized that I had to get control of myself. We found a funeral director, and he told me to take her rings off her fingers before she was buried, so I did that. I knew she would want her sorority colors, pink and green, so that is what I chose for inside her casket.

I was in a fog. There was a wake in Chicago with some friends and family on Thursday, and on Friday Cleola's body rode in a train to Marianna, Arkansas, where we had her funeral. I rode home with one of my brothers. I don't remember which one. Marianna's black mortician Lacey Kennedy met Cleola's train and collected her casket. My plan was to have the viewing and close the casket before the funeral ceremony. But Cleola's mother was too upset and did not want it closed. She wasn't ready to let her daughter go, so I told them to leave it open as long as she wanted. She stood there and cried and cried. It was June 30. Cleola's funeral was at Walnut Grove Missionary Baptist Church, where we had been married thirteen days before. It all happened in June. She was my high school sweetheart.

I think Cleola had a cerebral aneurism, but she was so young there was no reason to know she might have had a special condition. She was a cheerleader during her two years at LeMoyne. Cheerleaders had to have a physical at least once a year, and she had passed both of those. In 1962 the medical world was not so advanced as it is now, but it's possible that the same thing could still happen today.

I was twenty-one and fell into a deep, deep funk. When I was a little boy, I wanted to be big and now I thought I was a big man like I had always wanted. I couldn't ever admit to anybody that I was having any difficulty. I could not talk about it. That was not possible. I was supposed to be able to handle it myself. I went back to work at the post office and stayed intoxicated pretty much every day. This was a time (and maybe it still is for some people) that you didn't admit mental illness or go to a psychiatrist. It's too bad, but saying you might have a mental problem can limit your job opportunities and options. But, I have to admit that there have been times in my life when I would have done well to get a little counseling or even long-term therapy. This was one of them.

My Daddy was a strong believer. He really had absolute confidence in the Lord, who was always in control of everything and made no mistakes. When Cleola died so soon after we got married, I was about insane. I mean, I was never perfectly sane anyway, but this pushed me over the edge. I've always questioned conventional religion. But I had a deep respect for my Daddy, so I never wanted to say anything about religion that would make him feel uncomfortable. After we buried Cleola I was at my Daddy's house in Marianna just sitting around and wrestling with this shit. Daddy was coming at me talking like this, "The Lord is going to bless you, son. The Lord giveth and the Lord taketh away. It's the Lord's will. It's all for the best."

When he was talking I would find a convenient time to walk out of the room. But he kept following me into whatever room I'd go into. We had a six-room house, so there was a lot of walking into rooms. He kept following me and talking at me. Finally I put it out to him because this is the way I felt. "Daddy, if the Lord came down here right now, I would choke him! I don't know why he took my wife!" But that was not the right thing to say. I knew it was unfair, and after that I had to apologize. A month or so later I went back to him and apologized not as a matter of feeling but as a matter of propriety or correctness. I said that I was sorry even though I kind of lied in my apology.

I was having difficulty with myself. I was acting crazy and I was drinking too damn much. Soon after Cleola died, I got into a dispute with my supervisor at the post office. Neely Marshall, my co-worker and drinking friend, and I were in the station. He sort of kept me from getting killed when we were drinking and out on the streets, but he would get pretty good drunk too. When I got too drunk to work, Neely would call and tell the supervisor that we both had to take some time off. We also were known at the post office for doing extra work. We delivered mail to the houses and if the station had a carrier who didn't come in, me and Neely would cover the extra route. We would divide it and get ours and the other one done during our regular hours. At this time, we had a new under-supervisor named Al Weiderwerth. Because we had been drinking, Neely and I got very loud at the station that Saturday evening, and Weiderwerth told us to clock out and go home.

Well, the whiskey told me, "You are not going to take that shit off this little punk supervisor," and I said to him, "*You* clock me out, goddamn it." I know it sounds stupid now. He got mad when I talked back to him that way and there probably was some racial prejudice in him too. But I certainly can't blame him for what I was doing. He was so mad that he went up and clocked me out! And that made me mad so I slammed him hard with a stool. But when he hit that time clock he did something that he wasn't allowed to do.

One of the old timers, who had been in the post office for about twenty-five years, was in the back and heard all this. So when I came down, he said, "Neal, read this." And he handed me our contract with the U.S. Post Office Department. It must have been about 150 pages. I took it home and read all of it because I knew that Weiderwerth was going to write me up. I stumbled upon a section that said it was a termination offense for anybody to hit someone else's time clock. If a supervisor wants you out, he has to write in the time he wants you out and put his initials by it. He cannot hit the clock itself. That was a termination offense.

When I came in on Monday morning, I wrote Weiderwerth up for hitting my time clock. The big boss looked at everything and decided he wanted it all to go away. Nothing happened to either of us. Nothing. The big boss didn't want to fire Weiderwerth, and he would have had to fire him in order to fire me.

The truth of the matter is that the post office incident was just one of many. I was just out there. I was not following a path. I was wallowing. I was angry all the time. Some people who experience a death like I did are sad, but I was angry. My Daddy tried to help me when he said, "The Lord don't make no mistakes, son." But I couldn't accept that the Lord took my wife and I was having great difficulty. Looking back it seems that part of my way of showing how I felt was running the streets real hard. When I say running the streets, I mean drinking too much whiskey and trying to have too many girlfriends.

One night the cops pulled me over for DWI. I was so drunk that I must have run fifteen traffic lights. It was in the wintertime, and before I managed to walk back to the patrol car, I slipped and almost fell under my car. This is an indictment of the Chicago police department too. In those days when you got stopped for speeding, you handed your driver's license to the cop with $2 under it, and he would give you a warning. If you got stopped for DWI, to get out of it you gave him the driver's license with $5. This particular night I didn't have any money.

I was twenty-two years old and drunk. I was with this woman who outdrank me, and this was the first time I had been out with a woman who could do that. I was out of control drunk, but she was still in control. When I got up to the patrol car, the whiskey told me to talk to them. I leaned in the window and the officer said, "Get your head out of here. With all that whiskey on your breath you'll make us drunk too." Finally, when I was sitting in the backseat of the police car, it came around to this. He asked,

"What you going to do for us?" And I said, "Man, I can't go to jail." He re-peated, "What you going to do for us?" I didn't have any money so I went back to my car and asked the woman if she had any money. She only had a ten-dollar bill, and I told her, "I don't want to give them $10." She said, "Go on and give them the $10." So, I went back, got in the backseat of the police car again, and set the $10 on the console between the seats. I don't know why but I told him, "I want $5 back in change." The cop started cussin' and said, "We don't have cash change up there." Then, I started crying and act-ing the fool, and they shoved a $5 bill in my jacket pocket and pushed me back out into the snow.

I kept on living a depraved life. My draft notice came in January and about two weeks before I was to report, I wrecked my little Volkswagen. They had already taken my driver's license for speeding. I didn't have a driver's license, so I got arrested for the accident and the cops took me to jail. But when I was there I actually worked out a deal with one of the jail-ers. He had some kind of connection up the line. I called my brother Don-nie to come down and bring me $150. I gave it to the jailer and he made those charges disappear. These were the kind of things that were routine for me before I went into the Army. This was how I was living.

Chapter 4
The Army and Vietnam

I did all that drinking and running the streets for a year and a half after Cleola died and got away with it. I think that folks felt sorry for my crazy ass. Anyway, I survived. When I had been drafted, I didn't think the Army would take me because I had asthma and flat feet. But I reported to the Army in February 1964, and this was when they were getting ready for a big push in Vietnam. The Army was taking anyone who could walk. One old boy had a leg that had been broken when he was a little kid and it was three inches shorter than the other one. They drafted him. They only kept him three months, but they did draft him. If you could breathe, they drafted you.

I knew that a lot of people were protesting the Vietnam War, but I hadn't paid much attention because I just didn't care. My main reason for not wanting to go into the Army was because I couldn't stand the idea of someone telling me what to do all the time. I was so immature that's all I thought about it, and I went in resisting being told what to do.

Saved by Sergeant Chavira

When I was in basic training, my platoon sergeant's name was Alfonso Chavira. He told us more than once that he was Cuban. I'll never forget him. He knew how to deal with me, and he probably wasn't working at it very hard either. I sure as hell wasn't a good trainee. In my third week, I got crossways with a captain who was running the firing range and he put me on KP duty. Chavira called me aside and told me, "Neal, I've been in the Army nineteen years and six months and I can retire in six months at full pay. The Army's been all right for me. You may not like it, but you can't beat the Army. It is bigger than you are. If you soldier for me, I'll cover for you. But if you don't, we're going to have to break you because I've got to do what is best for the rest of the troops."

I didn't sleep that night because I was thinking about what he said. I knew that I couldn't get them to let me out. And I knew that I couldn't change the Army, so all I could do was try to survive. I thought to myself, "Hell, you can do this for two years and then you won't have trouble for yourself." When I got out of bed the next day I had changed. For the rest of basic camp, of the 1,400 men in training, I was the top-rated trainee.

I really credit Sergeant Chavira for saving me from self-destruction even though he probably didn't know what he had done. He didn't get my attention by slamming me. He got my attention by talking straight with me. Maybe somebody could have helped me earlier, I don't know. But I didn't have enough sense to ask for help.

After basic training, they sent me to Fort Lewis near Tacoma, Washington, for gunner training. I think I arrived out there in June. I was assigned to a small 105mm Howitzer, a cannon-like gun that could be carried in the back of a pickup. I had to do a little math to calculate where the round would land based on the elevation and the force of the charge. It wasn't very hard.

I was assigned to a unit called 266 Big Gun. The gun I was training on could be dropped out of an airplane. I didn't realize it at the time but they were preparing us for jungle combat in Vietnam. Then, sometime in the summer of 1965, the Army created a new unit called the 140 Quartermaster and made the decision to send all of us to Vietnam. I was reassigned to the 140 Quartermaster with about 200 men. We were sent to Vietnam in September 1965. I was there for only six months.

When I was in Vietnam, the fighting was pretty rough but it was not the worst. The roughest time was probably in 1968 and 1969, but the Viet Cong were killing us pretty good in 1965 and 1966 too. There was a unit over there called the 1st Division Big Red One. Because so many men were getting killed, it was commonly referred to as the Bloody Red One. My quartermaster unit was in charge of supplying the fighting units with repair parts for all their equipment, including the big guns. My job was to keep track of repair parts and store them in such a way that we could find them quick and ship them all over Vietnam. We supported the 101st Airborne Division.

My Friend Paul Fielder Got Hit

The 140 Quartermaster was supposed to have been in a safe area, but my unit got hit one night. It was Christmas 1965. There was a young boy in my barracks tent named Paul Fielder, and he was from Hattiesburg, Mississippi. He was just eighteen. First, he went almost crazy at Thanksgiving because he had never been away from home on Thanksgiving and then when Christmas came, he got drunk. Unfortunately, I aided him. I wasn't in charge or anything, but I was twenty-four and older and I kept a little liquor in my locker. Vodka was all you could get over there. He took the bottle I gave him and got drunk, and he must have passed out. Nobody was there to wake him up and get him back to the tent.

That night, ten or twelve Viet Cong slashed the throats of the two guards on the gate and came into our unit at about one or two o'clock in the morning. Then they started dropping explosive charges on the tents, and they dropped one near the place where Paul lay passed out. He got it real bad and never recovered from his injuries. Paul Fielder only lived another four or five years.

I didn't make any longtime friendships in the military, but after Paul came back home, I went down to Hattiesburg to visit him a couple of times. He had become an alcoholic and was still drinking the same stuff I had taught him to drink in Vietnam. He died in 1972 or 1973.

That was my most profound experience in Vietnam. I had taken Paul on like a little brother. Maybe if I hadn't had the vodka to give him, he wouldn't have gotten drunk and been hurt. You suppress this shit and don't really get over it. I still get sad when I think about him. He was a young guy and he thought that I was big. I was from Chicago and drank whiskey and talked about girls.

When I was there, the Army was integrated. The troops were maybe 70% black, but nearly all the officers were white. In Vietnam, I saw one black captain and I always gave him an enthusiastic salute. He was not assigned to my unit and we never spoke. But he was important to me because he was an officer. He was someone in charge.

An Encounter with My Friend Van der Mead

There was one little old white boy named Van der Mead (I can't remember his first name) in my unit, who I considered a friend. He was from Minnesota, and I remember that he told me he was Jewish. He clerked for the commanding officer and he would keep me informed on what they were getting ready to do. In the 101st, an airborne division on the fighting lines, guys were getting killed pretty regular, and they were sending replacements up there from my unit. I think that Van der Mead might have kept me from getting sent to the front lines.

The night we got hit, Van der Mead was standing up in the middle of our big tent crying because he was scheduled to go home in January and he thought that he was going to get killed just ten days before he got out. I was not afraid of dying there. When I say it now I don't know if this makes sense, but I feel the same today. Hell, I don't want to suffer or have it be so that I can't get to the bathroom by myself, but dying, that's just another step. Anyway, I went up to Van der Mead and got in his face because he was going into a tizzy. I slapped him and told him to put on his steel pot (that's what we called our helmets) because that's the first thing you are supposed to do so the shrapnel won't go into your head. He calmed down a little bit, and we went into the foxholes out on the perimeter of the compound. I never saw anybody to fire at. When I was in that foxhole, I was not worrying that the Viet Cong were going to blow us out of there. The only thing I was thinking about was that I was getting my boots muddy and I was going to have to polish them again. I realized this wasn't exactly sane thinking, but it was on my mind the whole time.

In the Army, you have enlisted men and officers. The enlisted men like me could go from E1 when you first went in to E10 or sergeant major at the top. I made the rank of Specialist E5 in January, a month and a half before I got out. E4 is a corporal and E5 is a sergeant, so I made sergeant in less than two years. My title was specialist E5, the same level as buck sergeant. E6 is a staff sergeant. Later on when so many were getting killed, guys were making E5 pretty fast, but I was in there when the death rate was not so high.

I was encouraged to stay in the Army, and they would have promoted me to E6. But I never had an interest in staying, because I couldn't ever get used to the military structure. For example, I was not allowed to go to my company commander without first talking with my platoon sergeant. I wasn't fighting it all the time, but I was always thinking that kind of thing was stupid. While I was satisfied that I could handle the Army short term since I needed to, it was not something I ever wanted long term. I would have had to reenlist for three years, and I couldn't do three more years.

Learning to Deal with Difficulties

Some people from my era were disappointed when I told them that the Army helped me. But I just have to be truthful. I didn't want to go in, but the military did plenty of good for me. I needed some order in my life and the Army gave me that. The Army forced me to think about what I was doing instead of just doing whatever I felt like. It provided me the structure that helped me get control of my anger—not to get rid of it but get control of it.

For me the impact of the Army was big mainly because of the things I learned from Chavira, my drill sergeant in basic training. I learned that when things were bad, I didn't have to let it destroy me. Chavira taught me to take the hard stuff and figure out the best way to deal with it. I learned to ask myself, "Can I fight to make a difference, or do I have to bide my time until I can get away from it?" In the Army, I could see an end point, and it was best to just bide my time. I really did learn some important stuff during those two years. But there were other things I hadn't learned.

Still High Flying

In mid-March 1966 when I came out of the Army, I went back to Chicago and worked at the post office again. I met my second wife not too long after that. We both worked sorting mail on the eighth floor of the post office. Her name was Margaret Cooper (I called her Cooper), and she was an aspiring model. We worked the same shift and after work we would go out with her friends and my friends all together. We got off at eleven o'clock and would party until two or three o'clock in the morning just about every night. She was kind of high flying and I called myself high flying at the time too. The guys I knew said she looked too hot for me, and her friends told her that she couldn't keep up with Olly Neal. They kind of egged us on.

Chapter 5
Back to Memphis

After I came out of the Army and was at the post office again, I wanted to push myself to do more than drink and chase women. The University of Illinois campus in Chicago had just been built on Halstead, and I registered there to continue work on my undergraduate degree in chemistry. I also thought that if I was trying to get a degree in chemistry, I ought to get some experience in that field to make sure it was something I really wanted to do. The Glidden Paint Company made paint and other chemical coatings, and they had a quality control technician opening. The technician job offered the possibility of moving into research and development, so I applied. I got the job and started working in June 1966. I worked there for a year and a half.

At first, things didn't go smoothly for me in school. My advisor put me in a couple of math classes that could be considered honors classes and I was not prepared at all. Hell, I'd been out of school for four or five years. Why he put me in there, I don't know. Anyway, it probably was my fault. I should have told him no. I was working full time, keeping all these different hours running the streets, and trying to go to school. I flunked out after two quarters. That made me discouraged, and I felt that college was probably not for me. But then my brother Donnie, who was getting a degree in electrical engineering at the Illinois Institute of Technology (IIT), convinced me to try over there. IIT is a technical school with a pretty rigorous curriculum. I took a calculus class and got a B. I thought, "Hell, that is pretty good. Maybe I'm not as dumb as I thought I was."

Glidden Coatings Job

I don't know for sure, but I suspect that Glidden was looking for a black person in particular to move up in the organization. I only worked in quality control for a month and was promoted to research and development, where I was the only black person. I worked in the appliance coatings lab. We made the product that covered washers and dryers. My section chief Gene Strang was a big, slow-talking white guy with a size 14 or 15 shoe—bigger than mine.

Gene Strang was a good guy to work with. He was very supportive. He had me and two white guys working for him, and he always treated us the same. I was a good employee, and he liked my work. When a problem came up in the lab, he would say, "What do you think we can do about that, Olly?"

While I worked with him in the appliance coatings lab, I created a new color you may remember called harvest gold. It was yellow with dark around the edges. When his section developed something new like this, it went out under his name. Somewhere in the report it mentioned that he had a young assistant named Olly Neal working with him, but the official report went out from Gene Strang. That was all right with me. I would never say anything bad about Gene Strang.

So as the only black person working in the research lab, I was doing okay. My work had not embarrassed them or myself. They were not displeased with me going to college either. They might have helped with the tuition, but I don't remember for sure. Based on an entirely good relationship, I think that, had I finished my degree in chemistry at IIT, I could have worked for Glidden long term.

I did something else while at Glidden that was thoroughly embarrassing to me, though. They took me with them on their annual retreat to Lake Geneva, Wisconsin. It was a golf outing with all the company big shots. We played golf that morning and I had never held a golf stick in my hand. But I lied. I lied. I told them that I could hit that ball pretty good. Then, when I swung, I missed it—again and again. To be truthful, I have never been very coordinated or athletic. Anyway, I struggled through it.

At dinner, there were no black folks in the dining room except the serving people and me. Our two black servers gave me special attention. I was at the same table with my boss and he said to me, "Olly, what are you going to have?" I had never tasted lobster, but I knew it was supposed to be wonderful. And you always act big when you're insecure and trying to show yourself to be equal, right? So, I said, "Gene, I want the biggest damn lobster tail they've got back there." When they came out with a lobster tail on a big old platter, I didn't know how to eat the damn thing. I don't know how I got through that meal. All I know is that when it was over I said to myself, "Never again. From now on, it's filet mignon for me."

So yes, at Glidden I felt inferior. I felt like I had to prove myself all the time. I was a stranger in a white world, and I never could make it be any other way. Looking back, I probably went to work at Glidden for two reasons. One is that since high school, I had found chemistry to be mentally challenging, and I liked that. The other is that my mother had made me understand that I was supposed to be a college man with a respectable college man's job. I grew up with this. You didn't need a college degree to work at the post office, so when I went to work at Glidden, part of it was that I was looking for a way to please Momma. But somehow this place wasn't for me. I liked the work because of the mental challenge, but I wasn't personally invested. It was just another job. And I was still staying out until one or two o'clock in the morning most days.

Lane College

When my younger brother Rowan graduated from Lane College, a little black Methodist school in Jackson, Tennessee, he came up to live with me in Chicago. He got a job teaching high school biology real quick, and we shared an apartment. Rowan always had more sense than I did, but after he got to Chicago, he started acting like me. During the week, we would go out and drink and carouse after work, and on Saturday, it was sort of like an all-day drinking orgy. On Sunday, we'd play basketball starting about ten o'clock in the morning until we got tired at four or five in the evening and then we'd shoot craps until somebody was broke and the game broke up.

One Sunday night in January 1968, we were shooting craps in our apartment and after most of the boys had gone home, I was tired and started thinking, "I expect to be plodding along doing stupid stuff the rest of my life. But Rowan has always been much better and now he has a college degree. I am taking him down the wrong path." So, I said to him, "Goddamn it, Rowan, you need to do better than me and stop this shit." And he said, "Hell, how come you aren't supposed to do better too?" Then, I said, "I don't have a damn college degree." Rowan's friend James Richards, who was one of those Cum Laudes—Summa or Magna, I don't remember which, was still there and he said, "We can get you in college, Olly. You can get yourself a degree at Lane, where we went."

So, we argued about that for a while and then Richards said, "If I can get you in, will you go?" And I said, "Ya, I'll go." I didn't think that he could do it because of my reputation from arrests during the Memphis sit-ins. Richards called the dean of the school at about nine o'clock at night. He talked to him and the registrar. The dean was a superstar chemist Herman Stone, and the registrar was a guy named George Thacker. By eleven o'clock that Sunday night they both had agreed to take me!

First thing Monday morning I gave my notice at Glidden. Two weeks later, I was a student at Lane. We had just been sitting around drinking and shooting craps, and then I was enrolled in college. They had put the muscle on me. I don't want to suggest to you that I was following a logical plan to make my life better. Hell, I was just doing the routine that I usually did. I was responding to whatever hit me in the face. I wish that I could say it was thoughtful, but there is no way in hell that I can say that. I got an apartment in Jackson and went back to college full time. I had VA benefits, so I was in better shape financially than most students on campus and I wanted my degree.

Martin Luther King's Assassination

I was at Lane only three months when on April 4, 1968, Martin Luther King was shot and killed at the Lorraine Motel in Memphis. Lane College is only ninety miles from there. My best memory is that the school held an assembly for him and that some classes were canceled. The assassination really upset the student body and if one person had been out there to stir things up just a little, something could have happened. But at Lane there was no real student outbreak, and no outsiders came in because they were too busy in other places.

Personally, I felt mad as hell, but I was committed to getting my degree, and that kept me in check. I did not want to do anything that would put my degree at risk. I remember thinking of specific things that we might do to express our displeasure, but I talked myself out of it. I just told myself, "Get your ass home to study some physics." I was taking physics, and it was giving me a rough time. I hadn't had a strong background in differential equations, and I was struggling. So, I did not do anything of substance after Martin Luther King was assassinated. I wanted my degree.

When Momma Died

Momma died in April 1968 too. She used to always tell me, "Whatever age you get to be, I will always be the same age over you, and I am still your Momma." And when I was pretty much grown and would do something that was downright insane, Momma would say, "I want you to hurry up and get married and have two sons and I want them to be just like you."

We never got along, but I didn't stay mad at Momma or feel deeply hurt by any of her actions. When she was hard on me I always thought that she was doing what she had to do. With all her children, she had a hell of a row to hoe, and she just took it up and bowed her back and did what she had to. Of course, when I was young and she was my teacher and my Momma, I didn't like that she made me learn to spell words that other kids didn't have to learn. But later I realized that she just wanted me to be better than I was.

The big hospital in Memphis where black people would go when they were real sick was a charity hospital called John Gaston. That's where Momma went when she got the colon cancer. My brother Donnie still lived in Chicago, and he didn't like Gaston. He came down and made arrangements to fly her up to Chicago. This was when I was at Lane College in Jackson. When I got out of school for Easter, I drove up to see her in the Chicago hospital. (Cooper and I were still dating but not yet married, and I saw her too.) Anyway, Momma started in, telling me that I needed to stop running the streets and settle down and get married again. I couldn't help myself, and I acted up toward her as I have always been prone to do. I called her "Dub," a name some of her friends would use, but a name she never tolerated from us kids. She picked up that water pitcher she had on a little table by her hospital bed and threw the whole thing at me. I still needed to be put in my place, and she had to do it. Momma only spent six or seven days in that hospital before she died. I needed her to live longer so she could have seen me be something other than foolish. It would had to have been another ten or fifteen years though. It took me quite a while to accomplish anything she could respect.

Another Huge Disappointment

When I was at Lane, my baby brother Prentiss was going to school at AM&N in Pine Bluff, Arkansas, and we were competing for who got the best grades. Rowan was "the graduate," and after Momma died, he was acting like our parent. All our grades were sent to him. He was the referee, and I was making sure I stayed on the honor roll.

Lane was an extremely conservative black school. For example, they didn't allow women students to wear pants until six o'clock in the evening or something like that. Neither men nor women students could have big Afros. (Cooper had a big Afro, and when she came down to visit me one time, she got plenty of attention.) Men had to wear a shirt and tie to convocation on Wednesdays. None of this bothered me because I was twenty-seven and had been in the Army, but some younger students started a little protest. I was not involved and did not care about the protest at all. But I had a girlfriend, Brenda Coggs, who was involved, and girlfriends can turn out to be dangerous. I advised her that they needed to talk to the dean with some respect and lay out what they wanted. So, they went and talked to the dean but nothing came of it. Then, Brenda convinced me to go talk to him and I did. With that, I suddenly was seen as the leader, and soon the whole thing got out of hand, no question about it.

A black high school was less than three blocks from the Lane campus and there was a real rivalry between the college guys and the high school guys. They competed for the girls. The high school had a semi-gang group, and the college guys looked down on them. When Lane's science building burned down one night, I immediately thought and still do believe that it was those high school boys that did it. But even though I was across the river in West Memphis that night at my Great-Uncle James Maclin's funeral, I got blamed for it.

I don't know what kind of arson it was, but it must have been something big because the inside of that science building was destroyed and the whole building had to be replaced. This was when black activist groups were moving about the country holding rallies and stirring up action, especially by young people on college campuses. I had come down to Lane from Chicago where one of my brothers was a Black Panther and I had spoken up on behalf of the student protest, so it was easy for the college president Chester Arthur Kirkendoll to identify me as an "outside agitator." There was absolutely no evidence that I was involved, but Kirkendoll was convinced that I was responsible, and he put me out of the school. I knew that I hadn't done anything, so I insisted on a hearing. At the hearing, I was charged with inciting a riot and arrested. I spent ten or twelve days in jail before my attorney Otis Higgs worked out a deal. The charge was reduced to disorderly conduct, so I paid a $50 fine plus $30 court costs and was released.

That was April 1969, and I was only two months short of graduating! I was a serious student then and should have stayed far away from those protests because I didn't care very much about the whole thing. It was the first time in my life that I had really good grades—well above a B average, and I wanted that degree. All this was a huge disappointment. When I was at Lane, I had an idea in the back of my mind that after I graduated, I would go to Knoxville, get a job at the Tennessee Valley Authority, and go for my PhD at the University of Tennessee. But after I was expelled instead of graduating, I went to Memphis.

My Damn-Fool Second Marriage

It was during this period that Cooper and I started talking about getting married. I would go up to Chicago and she would come down to Memphis.

It doesn't make any sense, but for our different reasons we ended up getting married in July. She moved to Memphis and stayed with me until Thanksgiving. That was our final separation in the sense that we never lived together again. (Later at a low point in Marianna, I asked her to come stay with me, but she said, "I would like to be with you, Olly, but it is too dark down there." She was a city girl.)

The day she left, Rowan was coming down from Chicago for the holiday and he had car trouble up near Blytheville. I told Cooper I was going to get him and drove my truck up there. We didn't have a great, warm relationship, but Cooper and I were not fighting. I don't know what was going on. I do know that I was not exactly what you would call a perfect husband. And at the time maybe she was trying to do too much. She was going to Memphis State to get her BA degree, and she was working full time for Southwestern Bell. I had no inkling that we were about to separate. I left to get Rowan at about nine o'clock in the morning. After I picked him up, we got a fifth of vodka and a quart of orange juice and didn't get back to our apartment until five o'clock in the evening. I assumed that I was coming home to a Thanksgiving dinner, but the apartment was quiet. No turkey smells were coming from the kitchen, and then I noticed that her trunk wasn't there either. She was gone.

Neither of us was ready for marriage. We were both damn fools. Based on our conversations we had similar views and we liked each other, but she preferred Chicago and I was in Memphis. Cooper and I have talked about this since then. She became a Methodist preacher. The last time I talked to her was in 1990 and she was Director of Pastoral Care at the University of Illinois Hospital, a big facility in Chicago.

Supplemental Food Program

When I came back to Memphis, Eddie Charles Meacham, my best friend from the student sit-in days, was still there. He was working for Audrey Parker, a quiet, straight-talking person who ran a community action agency called Memphis Area Project-South (MAPS). Parker knew of my community-organizing skills and that I needed a job. He was someone who could overlook my reputation from Lane. I hadn't been in Memphis very long when Meacham told me that Parker wanted to talk to me. I went over there, and he offered me a job managing the supplemental food program they had in partnership with St. Jude's Children's Hospital. The U.S. Department of Agriculture (USDA) was about to cut them off because their records had not been kept accurately. He put me over that warehouse, and he said, "Olly Neal is a damn fool, but if anybody can straighten this thing out, he can."

The pressure was on, and those first two or three months were hectic trying to get the books straight and to document everything we were doing. This was a special supplemental program for lactating mothers in the Memphis ghetto neighborhoods. We had 2,200 families, and I had to make sure they got their food each month. USDA supplied the commodities, MAPS paid me and my staff of three women to run the warehouse, and the St. Jude's nurse-practitioner nuns provided well-baby counseling. The nuns did home visits, and if they found an infant with a serious problem, they could put the mother and her baby on a fast track to be admitted into St. Jude's Children's Hospital. While I was there I got to know Dr. Donald Pinkel, the very first director of St. Jude's. I did a good job and saved that program, so he was pleased to have me work with him. And when we met again later, he remembered me.

My belief in community action and social change never wavered, and being with my old friends and people I admired from the Memphis sit-ins put this stuff back in my life. I guess it made me ready for the next step. I worked that warehouse job about ten months, and this was where the Marianna VISTAs found me.

Part Two: The Clinic and Civil Rights

Picture taken in Marianna during the 1971 economic boycott for an article in the New York Times *written by Roy Reed.*

Chapter 6
The Lee County Cooperative Clinic

You never know when a small decision is going to change the rest of your life. It happened to me in February 1970. Moving back home when I was twenty-eight put me on a new path. Before that, I had no direction. After I came back to Marianna, my life found purpose.

The Lee County Cooperative Clinic (LCCC or the Clinic) was the beginning. It came to mean a whole lot more than just better health for the black folks of Lee County, and I found my way because of it.

You might wonder if a small community health clinic could actually be the spark that ignited a civil rights fire in a sleepy Delta town. It was. Or you might not believe that an inexperienced health center director could become a civil rights bogeyman or hero (depending whether you were talking to someone from the white or the black community). I was. And it all happened in a flash.

What happened to me was profound. As I witnessed more and more success, my mind opened up to more and more possibilities. I changed from somebody who thought, "Just fight the damn shit and when you die you die," to somebody who said, "Wait a minute, we can do it! We can make something positive happen right here, right now."

Going Home

I had heard a rumor about a new community health center in my hometown. Then one day two VISTAs (Volunteers in Service to America) turned up, and they told me, "The new clinic in Marianna needs a director, and you are the person they are looking for." Marianna is only about sixty miles from Memphis, so I went over there to check it out and learned that the Clinic was getting a $39,000 federal start-up grant from the Office of Economic Opportunity (OEO). I certainly was interested in the job, but to be honest, I mainly wanted to get back home to be with Daddy for a while. He was there by himself. Momma was only fifty-five when she died, and he was seventy-two. If Daddy hadn't been there with his need, I wouldn't have been as interested in the job at the Clinic. And even though Daddy needed somebody, I couldn't have come back to Marianna if there hadn't been a job. All of this stuff came together, and it felt like something I had to do.

VISTA Sparked Change

VISTA started during President Johnson's administration to help poor people overcome poverty, and it was VISTA volunteers who started the Clinic. In January 1969, two VISTA Health Advocates were sent to Lee County because it was one of the poorest counties in the country. I've also heard that Winthrop Rockefeller, Arkansas's Republican governor at that time, was especially interested in sending some outsiders into the Arkansas Delta, where the Democratic Party had a stronghold. He thought the VISTAs might stir things up. And they did. According to Marvin Schwartz in his 1988 book about VISTA, *In Service to America*, "The most dramatic events in the total history of anti-poverty efforts in Arkansas occurred in the quiet, Lee County town of Marianna. Quiet does not always mean peaceful, and the status quo which Marianna had always maintained disintegrated soon after the first Health Advocate Volunteers arrived in 1969."

The Beginning

Corinne Cass and Jan Wrede were the first VISTAs assigned to Lee County. Corinne was an LPN and Jan was a science teacher. A profound experience for them came when a young black woman died (of eclampsia) during childbirth. She died at home less than a week after she had been turned away from a Marianna doctor's office because she couldn't pay an old bill. Her death drove home the obvious: poor black folks in Lee County needed reliable health care. When they heard that a doctor would be in the next group of VISTA Health Advocates, they lobbied their program officer, Joe Bruch. He and Ron Erickson of the national OEO office had the doctor assigned to Lee County. The plan was to establish an outpatient clinic run by the people it served. In preparation for the doctor's arrival and for Clinic management, Corinne and Jan organized four Neighborhood Action Councils (NACs), in Marianna, Brickeys, Moro, and Rondo/Aubrey. We soon added a fifth NAC in Haynes.

The Clinic started with almost a religious fervor, a feeling that came from the VISTAs. All our early VISTA workers were white and came from outside Arkansas. Black folks could see that they were trying to do more than just a good job. And my Daddy was watching too. No matter how often I tried to correct him and spell it out as Volunteers in Service to America, Daddy called the VISTAs "Vision Workers." And Daddy was right. They saw the future of our Clinic in a way no one in Marianna could have dreamed before their arrival.

The patients were poor people (black and white) who did not have access to decent health care. Each NAC elected two representatives to the board of directors. They were inexperienced, but the directors were dedicated. They governed our major initiatives, policies, budget, hiring, and firing. They were highly motivated because they knew that they were independent of the traditional white power structure. They understood, "It is up to us to make this work."

When I arrived, the board of directors believed more in the Clinic's long-term survival than I did. Somehow the VISTAs had convinced them that they could be successful. But me? I was not confident the Clinic would make it at all. I thought, "This is a fluke. The Clinic might last two or three years. We'll only make it until the federal official who approved our startup grant moves on. The next person won't want to work with us."

Dr. Dan Blumenthal Faced Challenges

The Clinic never would have gotten off the ground if it weren't for our first VISTA doctor, Dan Blumenthal. He was young and completely dedicated to his patients. And just as important, he remained calm in the face of the endless and unexpected challenges he met in Lee County. The NACs were organized, but we did not have a building. He was not automatically a member of the local medical society, and no one had notified the local officials of his arrival. Dr. Blumenthal had to apply for membership in the Lee County Medical Society. And until we found a building to rent, he had to see his patients where they lived—in shotgun shacks with holes in the floors and the walls insulated with newspaper. These homes usually had wood heaters made out of fifty-five-gallon barrels. In the winter his patients inhaled smoky air 24/7, and the children got burns when they fell against the hot metal. (That happened to me once when I was four or five years old.)

Sick children had skin rashes from ringworm and diarrhea from internal parasites, and some were badly malnourished. It was common for pregnant women (including my mother) to eat dirt or clay they dug from the edge of cotton fields. I am not sure why they ate it, but I think it had something to do with nutrients absent in their regular diet. Old folks had untreated high blood pressure and other heart conditions. Some patients were blind or had amputations due to long-term untreated diabetes. Cancers related to a high-fat diet were common.

Making Health Improvements

The Clinic taught new health care attitudes, and our patients became really interested in making improvements. During those early days, Corinne Cass was especially important. It seemed like she lived in the black community. She talked to everyone about taking care of themselves, and she trained local outpatient health aides.

Harry Conard was another VISTA Health Advocate. He arrived with Dr. Blumenthal and was all about improving sanitation. At night, Harry went to meetings and taught people about sanitation. This was something none of us had ever thought about before. He taught me a lot about it too. Harry started our sanitation program. This project was modeled after what they did over at the Delta Health Center in Mound Bayou, Mississippi. He built new outhouses for families whose children had been diagnosed with parasites. These families were too poor to be in a position to help with the construction, but he engaged the older children as much as possible so they would be proud and help maintain their new facility. Harry and his team always tried to place a new outhouse downhill from the hand-pumped water well. But this could be difficult on flat delta land, so sometimes they would just build the new outhouse as far away from the well as possible. During Harry's years at the Clinic, he was responsible for constructing about twenty outhouses. After he left, more were built, but I don't know how many.

Folks were learning that there was more to good health than taking their pills. It got so that you just had to do some new things to take care of yourself. I don't mean to suggest that suddenly everything was perfect. Not at all. But improving sanitation and providing clean well-water proved to be an excellent way to prevent intestinal parasites. Black families were proud that their children no longer had worms, and they spoke up. They would stop me on the street to tell me about the outhouse that was now far away from their water pump thanks to "that boy I had sent out to them." Also, folks were realizing that things like eating fatback all the time were not good for their blood pressure. Women were actually starting to say, "I'm trying to cut down on all those ham hocks, but the trouble is my husband wants 'em in his greens. It's hard."

Sterling King, a community health professional and son of a Lee County minister and farmer, said in a 2016 phone interview, "Overall, African American churches have been and remain the foundational platform from which we have launched our activities for community development and social action. However, I think the Clinic was the most important institution for facilitating social change in Lee County. It allowed the African American community to come together and begin to pool our concerns, ideas, and information around something that was needed. The Clinic was designed to meet a real genuine human need."

MoPac Depot Offer

The first major obstacle from Lee County's white establishment came in late 1969 shortly before I was hired. When the board and the VISTAs were trying to find a suitable building, the abandoned Missouri Pacific (MoPac) railroad depot seemed perfect. It was in the center of town and had stood empty for years. It was the right size and was a handsome brick structure that would lend an aura of respectability and permanence. The MoPac representative offered to rent it to the Clinic for only $50 a month, but before the rental agreement could be signed, MoPac abruptly withdrew their offer—with no explanation.

No Meaningful Communication

When I first came back home, I thought that white racism mostly had to do with whites not wanting their sisters and daughters to be around blacks. I certainly did not see how a small clinic serving the poor could upset anyone, and I hoped for a spirit of understanding from the local white community. I thought that by simply wanting to do what was right, whites would see that black folks ought to have some control over what happened in our lives. It was health care! How could health care be a problem to anyone? But the white community did not see it that way. They were threatened. And this led to an almost total lack of understanding or meaningful communication between the black and white communities.

VISTA Health Advocate Harry Conard understood what happened this way, as stated in a phone conversation in 2017: "I think that many members of Lee County's white community were suspicious because we worked on an even footing with black folks and they saw this as unnatural. They felt threatened because we were different and could not be controlled. Many in the white community saw all the VISTAs as outside agitators who were there to upset the status quo and create unwanted expectations among black folks. And for some, all the poverty in their own community must have been just plain embarrassing."

Medical Society Vote and MoPac Offer

Initially, I knew that the KKK was active in St. Francis County, but I didn't know about the white Citizens Council in Lee County. And I had no idea how effective they were at spreading their brand of what I have to call extreme racism. I came to understand that they hated the Clinic just because it was ours. They feared black independence and they wanted to shut us down.

As we began to gain some control over our lives by running the Clinic, the larger white community became uncomfortable too because we were changing the status quo. The Lee County Medical Society decided by a 3 to 1 vote to reject Dr. Blumenthal's membership. Consequently, he and his patients were denied access to the Lee Memorial Hospital. That meant the nearest hospitals for our patients were sixty or 100 miles away in Memphis or Little Rock. The one vote to accept Dr. Blumenthal was from Dr. Elizabeth Fields, who never had a segregated waiting room and later helped out at the Clinic by working with us part time.

The conflict between the Clinic and the medical society was in all the newspapers, so everyone knew of our problem getting admitting privileges for the Clinic doctor. At the same time, the white Citizens Council did a really good job of selling their opinion that the VISTAs were communist troublemakers, and much of the white community bought it. It was soon after the Lee County doctors voted to exclude Dr. Blumenthal that MoPac withdrew their offer. Later, we learned that MoPac rented that property to Lon Mann, who was prominent in Lee County's white power structure. He owned a cotton gin across from the depot. After that, during ginning season, they parked the cotton wagons all over the depot parking lot, but the building stayed empty for quite a while.

Clinic Opening, March 1970

When we couldn't rent the old depot, Marianna's black mortician, Lacey Kennedy, stepped forward and offered a little building he owned at 35 S. Liberty next to his mortuary. We received our grant from OEO, and the Clinic opened on March 2, 1970. Our VISTA staff was Dr. Blumenthal; Mrs. Janet Blumenthal, a child psychologist who wrote our patients' social service reports; Corinne Cass, our first nurse; and Jan Wrede, who did administrative work as well as performing the Clinic's rudimentary lab tests. The paid staff was me, the chief administrator; Pauline Bracy (and then Joyce Hooks Savage) as secretary; and four health aides: JoAnn Johnson,

Annie Mae (Baby Sister) Green, Cora Holden, and Frances Fields. Dr. Blumenthal saw about thirty-five patients a day, 90% black and 10% white.

My Gratitude for Mrs. Collier

When I first came home to Marianna I have to admit that I wasn't completely accepted by the black community. After my application for the Clinic director job, I had to be approved by the board, and my reputation from the Memphis sit-ins and the trouble at Lane College was well known. Some of the directors just didn't think too much of me. I had been kind of a "hellhound," and, looking back, I'm not sure that I would have wanted to hire someone like me either. Fortunately, one board member, Mrs. Willie Mae Collier, spoke up for me, saying that she had known my grandfather David Maclin and he had been a good man. She said, "I think we should give Olly a chance." And they did. I give credit to Mrs. Collier. She was a strong woman, and she is the reason I was hired.

First Board of Directors

Our initial success came from community organizing, excellent doctors, a capable accountant, and tremendous outreach by the VISTA Health Advocates. Ted Wilson, a VISTA supervisor at the CAP agency in Forrest City, said in Marvin Schwartz's history of VISTA: "It was a natural fit of volunteers and community people working together. Impressive to see community people being trained to take on roles within the clinic, learning to be health professionals and paraprofessionals under the tutelage of the volunteers who had the skills."

But the LCCC board also was exceptionally important. They were a cohesive and supportive group for the Clinic, and they helped hold the whole thing together. That is an absolute truth. They knew that our people needed better health care, and they always did their best to help the Clinic succeed. This first board of directors was an interesting collection of folks and they all were different.

Marianna NAC:
- Willie Mae Collier was on the Lane College board of directors, where I got put out. She would read a lot of stuff, and she had the global view. She trusted me and understood the Clinic's larger impact for the black community.
- Maurice Harmon was the only white person on our board. He was

an active UAW union member at the Douglas & Lomason plant that made automobile parts in Lee County, and he was an outspoken supporter of the Clinic.

Moro NAC:

- Eddie Foster was head deacon at the Springfield Church and served as the Clinic board chairman for three or four important years. He always did his best, but he did not have the educational background or experience outside Lee County that would have made things easier for him.
- Theressa Ramey was proud of the Clinic, pragmatic, and always looking for a way to make things happen. She was a great detail person and served as secretary. I think that Mrs. Ramey always looked at me with a little bit of suspicion.

Brickeys NAC:

- Donell Linton was really good at selling the Clinic in his community. He didn't do a lot of deep thinking and looked to me for leadership.
- Honey Moore was very active in her church and traveled all over the country with her church work. She was a good lady who was independent and a strong supporter of the Clinic.

Rondo/Aubrey NAC:

- Sarah Sauls was a midwife in the black community. Based on her own professional experience, she truly understood the need for health services. She was fully committed to making the Clinic work and was not fearful.
- Willie Gordon owned and rented land out in Rondo. He farmed over 500 acres and had become a successful farmer during hard times. He brought stability to the board but was not a talker. He did not think stuff up. He was an "If you want to do it, let's do it" kind of guy.

Haynes NAC:

- Emma Glaspy was very active in her church, going on missions all over the country. She looked to me for leadership. Although she may not have understood the depth of what we were doing, Mrs. Glaspy believed in the Clinic and was a strong supporter.
- John Lee Wilson was a dynamic leader in his little community and instrumental in getting Haynes involved. He could not read or write very well, so that was a disadvantage for him. But because he understood the big picture so well, he became an outstanding board member.

What did I do to make these people trust me? I did not have a college degree. I had no training. I was not a health professional. I did not treat one single patient. I was ignorant of sanitation. But everyone on that board worked with me. I still don't fully understand it, but I have to believe it was because they knew that my heart was in the right place. They knew that they could pull me back in line if I went too far wrong. And if I had ever done anything to truly harm the Clinic, they would have run me off. I believe that. Later, the NACs might sometimes elect board members who were a little bit softer because they just didn't have the same strength of character, but they always supported the Clinic in the best way they knew how.

Finding the Limits

The board members certainly did have some real limitations. Outside of the churches, there were few opportunities for black folks in Lee County to develop leadership skills. They lacked experience. They didn't know how to do a lot of things, but they were the final authority for Clinic decisions. How was I going to run the Clinic under the direction of these people? Then, I realized that they had managed to hang on to their little piece of land, they had done well in their churches, and they were leaders in their own small communities. So, my attitude was that they had meaningful knowhow. I just needed to figure out how to turn it in the direction of supervising the Clinic's business. This wasn't always easy.

I can tell about a situation that seriously tested my belief in their knowhow. I fired someone who was not doing her job. She went to the board and contested it. They sided with her and she was reinstated. As I walked out of that meeting I was upset and I wanted to quit. But after I cooled down, I reminded myself that I had to abide by the board's decisions and I let it go. Much later, when I talked to one of the board members, he told me, "We made a mistake, but we learn from our mistakes don't we?"

The Deep Divide and My FBI Record

After Jan Wrede left in July 1970, I had to handle all the Clinic's administrative work. My way is to avoid getting tied up in details, so I went to Dr. Jack Geiger at the Delta Health Center in Mound Bayou, Mississippi. They had been providing rural community health services since 1965. Dr. Geiger was their co-founder, and he was at the very top of the rural health center field. We visited regularly, and Dr. Geiger helped me learn standard practices and made it easy for me to get copies of the various documents we needed. We became colleagues and friends. I believe that the Delta Health Center's new building is named in his honor—the Dr. H. Jack Geiger Medical Center. They still do great work over there.

As I discovered, the black and white communities in Lee County were deeply divided, and it was a harsh divide. Black folks generally believed what I said and saw me as a leader, and white folks generally disbelieved everything I said and saw me as a troublemaker. Someone (I don't know who) had gotten a copy of my FBI record and sent it to Dr. Geiger, probably in an effort to stop him from working with me. I learned about it from Ollie Brantley, who was the first black deputy in Lee County. He was the friendliest guy I've ever known in law enforcement. Everybody liked him. He always had time to stop and talk, but suddenly he seemed distant and maybe even scared of me. I asked him what was going on, and Deputy Brantley finally told me that the people in the sheriff's department were saying, "Olly Neal has an FBI record as long as your arm."

When I found out about all this, I called Dr. Geiger and asked him to send me a copy. It was one page and showed that I had been arrested seven times during the Memphis sit-ins and once at Lane for disturbing the peace. So yes, I did have a record from my civil rights activities when I was in college. Dr. Geiger was not troubled by any of this. He understood. I gave Deputy Brantley a copy of it too. When he saw that my arrests were only for resisting segregation, that was the end of Brantley's concerns about me.

I made about 300 copies of that piece of paper, so we could pass them around the county, and I gave one to the Clinic board chairman, who needed to see it too. When I applied, Eddie Foster had gone along with Mrs. Collier, but I knew he still held some doubts about me. Seeing the FBI record of my involvement in the Memphis sit-ins helped him and the other board members understand that my only arrests had been for trying to break up segregation. Since by this time everyone in the black community believed it was time for segregation to end, I never had any problem being accepted by my community again.

Keeping Control of Myself

But I had other problems to deal with. Sterling used to tell me the two things that could most easily destroy our organization were spending the money the wrong way and having sex or even appearing to have a sexual relationship with the wrong person. Sexual tension is unavoidable, but it has to be controlled. Back when I was in my twenties and thirties, if a woman was sexually attractive enough, I would have a hard time. I would have to run. A situation happened after we got that first big chunk of money, and I knew that I couldn't mess up.

There was a woman on staff at the Clinic who used to come into my office to talk about work, and she would sit on the edge of my desk. My management style was casual and it wasn't unusual for staff to be in my office. But it was the early 1970s and this woman didn't wear a bra and she was attractive and I would have trouble. She was a very profound person for making good things happen for children at the Clinic, and I knew I had to control myself. So…I'm sorry, but this is crude… I had a little bathroom in the old building and I used to go in there and masturbate, so I could pay attention and talk normal. Now that is stupid, isn't it? Son of a bitch, I just had to fight it off. But looking back, I can say, "We made it! We survived." I also have to add in this woman's defense that I don't believe she realized the effect she was having on me, and we never had anything other than a professional relationship.

Dr. Robbie Wolf

Our doctors had some difficulties too, especially in dealing with patients who were inexperienced with health care. Dr. Robbie Wolf was our second VISTA doctor, and one day he had a female patient who needed a gynecological examination. There was a nurse in the room with him during the exam, but the woman still misunderstood his intentions. The only time any man had ever touched her genital area was when he wanted to have sex with her. She assumed that Dr. Wolf was interested in her sexually, and he was tall and cute, so she started running after him and wrote him a letter. I know about this because Dr. Wolf had to bring me in to help. As you can imagine, it was kind of tricky. I called her into my office and tried to explain that doctors had to do certain things in an exam. But she never did get what I was trying to say. She just thought that I was blocking her, and she finally stopped coming to the Clinic.

Dr. Irwin Redlener

In those early years, since the Clinic doctors were VISTA volunteers and their VISTA service usually only lasted one year, we were always having to recruit new doctors and nurses too. While Dr. Wolf was with us, an MD in New York who none of us had ever met called me. Apparently, he had seen a poster advertising the Clinic. His name was Irwin Redlener, and he wanted to visit the Clinic and meet everyone. When I got his call, I put Dr. Wolf on the phone to talk to him. After they hung up, Dr. Wolf told me to arrange to get Dr. Redlener out here, so I bought him a flight.

Dr. Redlener was not a VISTA, and we did not have money in our budget to pay him. But I believed in doing what was most important, so I cut something else out of our budget, and we offered him a small salary. Dr. Redlener was a pediatrician. He worked at the Clinic for two years during some of our roughest times, and he proved to be tough enough. He was a very good doctor and had a big influence on me. He changed the entire future of the Clinic.

Improving Rural Sanitation

Back in 1970 and 1971, there were outhouses all over the county and before VISTA Health Advocate Harry Conard got going nobody knew anything about sanitation. His program got us started addressing this issue. Then, Dr. Redlener took it a big step further. He treated little kids all the time with intestinal problems caused by contaminated drinking water and with sores on their faces from playing in filthy dirt contaminated with feces.

The National Demonstration Water Project (NDWP) was a new national program that helped poor rural communities qualify for loan money to put in water and sewer systems. When Dr. Redlener heard about NDWP, he got excited. He knew that if we could do something to improve the purity of people's water supply and the effectiveness of their waste disposal on a large scale, two common pediatric health problems could be prevented altogether.

At first, I was reluctant. I didn't want to do the damn thing because it would be too much work, and I had more than enough work already, but Redlener was a strong person and forceful as hell. He pushed this thing hard, so I had to do it, and we ended up involved for six years: 1971 through 1978. I was the director, but Wilbur Peer and R. C. Henry did most of the work. We helped put in sewer and water projects all over the Arkansas Delta—in communities including Birdsong, Haynes, Lexa, LaGrange, Moro, Poplar Grove (sewer), Marvell and Long Lake, Goodwin, Madison and Colt, and Brickeys—and in a couple of poor white towns in north-central Arkansas too.

When we worked with these rural communities up and down the Arkansas Delta from the Missouri border to the Louisiana border, nearly every place had somebody white in charge. And I realized that what we were doing could help both white and black folks think differently. Each area included a substantial number of black residents, so we always insisted on bringing in black participants commensurate to their population. And in these circumstances, we could say things concerning race out loud and be heard. For example, Marvell Rural Water Association had a white president, John Wesley Hall, who came to us wanting to be part of our project because he needed our help with a water system for the white folks out where he farmed. When we were getting ready to put together what turned out to be a large system with 1,600 connections, we told him, "Mr. Hall, the Zachary (black) community is over here too, and we can't do this project unless they are included." And he responded, "Oh, I gotcha." He then brought in strong black folks who represented their community. And shit, the next time we went down there, they were at the meeting. They were speaking up and witnessing who was making it all happen.

Wilbur Peer, R. C. Henry, and I made a good NDWP team. Wilbur Peer was only twenty-three or twenty-four and little reckless, but he was dedicated, energetic, and focused. R. C. Henry was a little selfish and never fully understood the importance of what we were doing, but he knew all the regulations and was well prepared. I had way too much work but could see that these water and sewer projects improved public health—and blacks were in charge! What was happening was unexpected because initially we were just trying to make life for our rural folks safe and healthy. Who would have thought there was a path to equality through sewage? As we helped poor rural communities improve sanitation, the old racial dynamic was changing, and Peer was essential because he learned fast and could get things done.

This is what Peer said about those days in a 2016 interview:

> The NDWP water projects were more complicated than sewer systems. A water system required meters and usage billing, and a community had to be incorporated so it could have an administration to handle billing and payments, etc. Initially we had a problem because in Arkansas for a community to incorporate, it had to have a "qualified electorate" of 150 voters. Well, that was way too many for most of our rural communities.

In 1979, R. C. Henry and I went to Bill Clinton, who was governor of

Arkansas at this time, and told him that we needed legislation to lower the "qualified electorate" for incorporation to seventy-five voters. He said it would be no problem and he got it done. We were proud of this accomplishment. To be part of getting a state regulation changed and making life safer and easier for residents of small rural Arkansas towns was a big deal for us. It gave us some noteworthy publicity too.

Many of the rural sanitation projects were instigated by white people. They wanted our help! I didn't realize it too much at the time, but seeing blacks in a position of leadership for the first time was changing the mentality of both whites and blacks in these places. It was all new. You see, in the Arkansas Delta, blacks were not seen as anywhere near equal to whites. And I can tell you a story about whiskey in deer camps to show what I mean. A lot of black guys used to cook for white hunters at their deer camps, and my Daddy was one of them. His friend Mr. Kelly Wilson used to go cook at a deer camp too and when those white men got to drinking out there, they would shoot at his feet to make him dance. He could have gotten killed!

Old Man Lipsky, a rich, white landowner in Brickeys, wanted a water system and he asked me to help him. He owned about 6,500 acres. He chewed tobacco and spit. Any time you saw him, it was all over his khakis. Anyway, I was working with him, and Brickeys was close enough to Hughes to be included in their water association.

Sheriff Bobby May's Daddy was a member of the Hughes Rural Water Association, and we had a meeting out at his deer camp. There were just five or six white men and me. It was a fine place way out in the woods. I didn't know they even had facilities like that. After our meeting, they asked me to stay around and have a drink with them. But my Momma had always told me never to go drinking with white people by myself. So, I told them to pour me a cup of whiskey and I took it with me.

The Clinic's Major Impacts

Throughout my time as the Clinic's chief executive officer, my most important work was sharing the vision and keeping everyone on track with regular board meetings and staff meetings and a lot of one-on-one talks. I gave guidance. I was constantly urging and encouraging. I had to keep everybody focused on the big picture and on what was most needed from them. Through the years, the board and staff members requiring my attention varied, but they always looked to me to guide and inspire. They saw that I made some sacrifices too. I never made any money off of anything that came my way. I never wanted anybody to be able to say that I had ever taken advantage of anyone.

But were we successful? Were we having an impact? Were we improving the health of poor people in Lee County? Today, I can answer with a resounding YES. Our success came in many forms and some of it was unexpected. Our pediatricians were excellent, and after the Clinic was established there was a significant decrease in infant mortality. We improved environmental sanitation through education, outreach, and especially the NDWP projects.

The LCCC also had another profound effect on the black community, as the Clinic influenced a number of our folks to go into the health professions. When I was there we gave financial support to the schooling of a few of our promising staff members. Frances Fields and Barbara Hooks became LPNs. Rosemary Long became a dental hygienist, and her sister-in-law Joanne Long became an RN. Young people who grew up getting their regular health care at the Clinic were inspired by the professionals who treated them. I can name a few I know personally. Dr. Phyllis Eason is now a psychiatrist in LaGrange, Georgia. Her sister Dr. Anita Eason-Jones practices family medicine in Huntsville, Alabama. Dr. Holli Banks-Giles specializes in family medicine at the East Arkansas Family Health Center of West Memphis. Nyerere Billups works on the clinical research and development of pharmaceutical drugs. And Dr. Kellee Farris, the daughter of our longtime dentist Dr. Louis Mitchell, became the LCCC CEO who was directing the Clinic at the time of its fiftieth anniversary.

Besides improving health care and sanitation and inspiring students to become health professionals, there was one more major impact the Clinic had on the black community. We showed everyone that in the face of intense scrutiny, black management could successfully handle a substantial budget. This actually changed the attitude of many hold-outs. My cousin Buddy Mac (Albert Jones) was one of those hold-outs. He was a prominent farmer who owned over 500 acres, and he was the kind who never gave white folks any trouble. When Senator John McClellan sent auditors down from Washington DC to try to catch the Clinic doing something wrong, it was well known in both the black and the white communities. And when the auditors found that we were doing nothing wrong, people like Buddy Mac changed. He spoke up in favor of the Clinic and even supported a black candidate, Pitson Brady, when he ran for public office in 1972.

Chapter 7
Stolen Election of November 1970

Every one of us at the Clinic had a lot to learn, and we had serious pressure from the white community. But even with the controversy and uncertainty, we were not just surviving—the Clinic was thriving. Along the way, our achievements were having a wider and deeper impact on black folks. Our community was becoming stronger. We were gaining confidence and beginning to speak up and to see change. We decided it was time to become active in local politics. But I can tell you we were ignorant, and it was not easy.

Black folks who were there call the election of November 1970 the stolen election. White folks who were there don't remember. In Lee County, the number of voters who participated in the 1970 election was huge. The Lee County population was about 61% black and 37% white. Both black and white voters turned out in record numbers, and 86.5% of Lee County's registered voters voted! That kind of turnout is rare, and in Lee County I don't think it was ever that high before or after. BUT the record shows that both of our black candidates for countywide office lost.

Sterling King, my friend and Lee County native who was there, told me in 2016, "They didn't beat us at the ballot box! I believe to this day that in a fair and square manner we got more votes for our county judge candidate Thomas Ishmael and our county treasurer candidate Spaniard Butler. They were on top. They were beaten at the absentee ballot box because the absentee ballot box was stuffed. It was a stolen election!"

None of us were there to make trouble. We were not yet troublemakers. In the electoral process, you have observers present to see that everything is done above board and who can make challenges if necessary. In the courthouse when the votes were being counted, both white and black observers were present, but our black representatives were prevented from seeing the ballots counted as they came in. When Sheriff Langston and one or two of his deputies arrived with the regular and absentee ballot boxes, none of our observers were allowed around the table with them or anywhere in the proximity. Our people were kept so far away that they couldn't have seen what the counters were doing even if they had had binoculars.

We knew that something irregular was happening. We knew that we were being treated unfairly, but that night we were unprepared. Our representatives didn't have the knowhow or leverage to resist and say, "This is not the way this should be done. You are not handling these boxes properly." Our black candidates had run as Republicans and the Republican Party was a legitimate party in the state of Arkansas. But we were totally ignored! Those in control made no attempt to do what the electoral process required. And, there was a mob of ANGRY black folks outside the courthouse, looking for something to set them off. The situation presented an imminent threat of violence.

Getting Started

Sterling and I were high school classmates and had kept in touch. In the spring of 1970, we talked about political change in Lee County. There had been more blacks than whites in Lee County for a very long time, but the black community had not been involved in politics or shared any part of running the county since Reconstruction—far beyond anyone's memory.

We knew that black folks were rising up, and change was happening all over the country. One of the most profound stories for us came from rural, black-majority Greene County, Alabama, where a black guy was elected probate judge. That is the same as county judge in Arkansas. He was the chief executive officer. He was in charge of that county! If a black candidate could win in Greene County, Alabama, a black candidate should be able to win in Lee County, Arkansas, too.

In the beginning, we were not a sophisticated group writing out plans. We had some grandiose thoughts. When we felt confident of success, we thought we could move on into St. Francis County too. We were in our twenties—young, energized, and not narrowly focused. We had some thoughts larger than life and could be almost braggadocios. We were so convinced that we would succeed. We were the majority! We wanted to undo the complete white control we had always known. We started to think, "Hey, we could run this county." When our sensible outlook took over, our conversations led to the notion of government that truly reflected the desires and wishes of both the majority and the minority.

Both then and now, it is clear that we were pushed into politics by the actions of the white community against the LCCC. During the spring of 1970, it seemed that none of the people involved with the Clinic could resolve our problem in getting hospital admitting privileges for Dr. Blumenthal. When we discovered that the county judge appointed members to the hospital board, it was obvious. We needed a new county judge! If we could get our own guy elected, he could use his position and countywide influence to help the Clinic. He could appoint new hospital board members who would vote to accept our doctor. It only made sense. The bottom line was that as we focused on this practical concern, we planned deliberate actions. This was the source of the first serious political challenge from the black community in Lee County.

Concerned Citizens Organization

After coming home, I was living with my Daddy in Marianna. Sterling was enrolled in graduate school at UCLA for the fall semester, and he lived with his parents all that summer. We brought together a group of like-minded people, and we started having a lot of what Sterling called "skull sessions." At first it was Sterling, myself, and Antony Hobbs. Very soon Rabon Cheeks joined us. And although he was not a big part of the decision-making process, Cheeks provided essential support. We were the central leadership group during the 1970 campaign. We talked about what would work and what was possible. And we formed the Concerned Citizens of Lee County as the umbrella organization under which we would conduct our activities.

If the Concerned Citizens wanted to get some blacks elected, we needed our headquarters in a place where Lee County's black folks could feel comfortable. As owner of the black funeral home in Marianna, Lacey Kennedy was independent of the white power structure. He made space in one of his buildings available to us when we were just getting started. This proved to be vital because it was in an area that was a hub of activity for the black community. Once we got that office, Rabon Cheeks took it over and assembled old and current copies of *Jet* and *Ebony*. They were the magazines that everyone wanted to read because they covered the issues of the day. He spread them around so that anyone who was there had a chance to read what was going on in other parts of the country. We had all the magazines, a desk, a file cabinet, a typewriter, and eventually an old duplicating machine. Our place became a kind of little club where folks came by and where we had our meetings. It felt like a safe place.

Lee County Republicans

Since Lee County didn't have a history of blacks being elected to public office, our candidates needed to start out strong. We made sure that everyone knew our candidates had not volunteered themselves but had been chosen. We believed that if they had been selected by the Concerned

Citizens, it would make their campaign easier. Candidates for county judge and treasurer would have to make speeches all over the county. Being "chosen to run" gave them a foundation on which to stand when speaking to the public.

The governor of Arkansas at this time was Winthrop Rockefeller, and he was a Republican. He had been elected governor in 1966 and in 1968, and now in 1970 he was running again. Dale Bumpers was the Democrat running against him. A Republican governor may have been in office for four years, but in Delta counties the Republican Party was still just a name. It had no standing. The Delta was run by Democrats. In Lee County, Hack Adams, the incumbent county judge, was the face of the white power structure, but he was not the source of power. The big people in Lee County were Lon Mann, Dan Felton, Jimason Daggett, and the Turners, all Democrats. They came from the white families that had exercised complete control in Lee County for generations. And, of course, none of them would give us the time of day.

A few folks in Lee County, including Thomas Ishmael, knew Governor Rockefeller and were active supporters. Mr. Ishmael said, "A. C. Sisk is chairman of the Republican committee in Lee County. We will just go to him and ask how to do the filing." Mr. Ishmael put us in touch with Sisk, who was white, and when Sisk became aware of what we were trying to do, he made his party apparatus available to us and paid the filing fees for our black candidates. He and his father were solid Rockefeller Republicans. They were business people and had done some farming too, so they also had standing in Lee County's white community. Sisk did not go out campaigning for black candidates, but he didn't put any roadblocks in our way either. We found him to be reasonable and cooperative.

Sterling King recently reminded me of the problems we had convincing black folks to vote Republican and how we used some history to help us: "Our candidates running as Republicans certainly confused some black folks. They said, 'Hey, we have been voting Democrat all this time.' So, we told our people, 'We don't care how you vote in the national election, we are just trying to get some black people elected here in Lee County.' We had to remind them that Abraham Lincoln was a Republican and that we didn't have any permanent issues with either party."

The 1970 filing deadline was in May, and I think the primary was the second Tuesday in July. Anyway, on the last filing day, Rockefeller's office sent a black guy, Johnny Lang, to Lee County with the intention of getting black preacher Armstead Slater to run in the Republican primary against one of our candidates. They thought this would be a good idea, but we didn't want a contested Republican primary. We didn't have much money and we needed to save what little we had for the general election. To convince the preacher to change his mind, I just got Big Daddy Herman Neal (no relation) to go with me, and we cut him off on the road as he was coming into town. We told him that he didn't need to be doing this. It would not be good for our people.

Some white people in Lee County were saying that the Concerned Citizens were an arm of Rockefeller's Republican cadre. They were saying that Rockefeller paid Sterling King and paid for the Concerned Citizens office. That is not true. Sterling was not employed by anyone, let alone Rockefeller, and he personally paid almost all of the rent, light, and telephone bills for our office. I helped some. We worked with the Rockefeller people, but none of us were paid by the Rockefeller office.

Strong Candidates for the County

Marianna city government is made up of a mayor elected citywide and eight aldermen who represent the district where they live but are also elected citywide. Each county in Arkansas is run by a Quorum Court with the county judge (chief executive) and the county treasurer elected countywide, and justices of the peace who represent and are elected by voters in the district where they live. In 1970, Lee County had seventeen justices of the peace.

We worked at finding candidates who were willing to run, who had a chance of being elected, and who could be successful in public office. We listened to respected older people in the black community. And because the Concerned Citizens core group had grown up in the county, we knew all the church leaders, the ministerial group members, and those active with the Lee County Clinic.

LaFayette "Son" O'Donnell and Landers Isom Sr. ran for city alderman positions in Marianna. O'Donnell owned some joints he had inherited from his Momma, and he made pretty good money running his business. Isom had been a barber for black folks at least since the 1940s and people were always lined up to get in his door. So, both of these candidates were financially independent of the white power structure. Pitson Brady ran for Quorum Court justice of the peace representing the Oak Forest district.

All of our candidates had to be independent, so they couldn't be living on a white man's plantation. Of course, the countywide offices of county judge and treasurer were the greatest challenge. These candidates had to have serious managerial experience, and Thomas Ishmael was an obvious choice for county judge. Mr. Ishmael was a solid citizen and a community leader who had the necessary skills. He farmed 160 acres near Gill in the northwest part of the county. Everyone out there went to him for guidance. He was a leader in his church and an active supporter of the Clinic. There were three or four other highly respected members of his community who also followed Mr. Ishmael's lead. He was a big man, 6'5" and about 275 lbs. We all agreed that Mr. Ishmael would be a good county judge.

The second countywide race was treasurer, and Spaniard Butler came to us because he wanted to run for this office. We were glad to have him as our candidate. He was a little-bitty old man who talked with a hoarse voice. Mr. Butler had over 500 acres and was as solid as a rock. He owned the land he farmed and had pulled himself up by his bootstraps. He could have run for a bigger office, but he wanted to be county treasurer and he was good for that job because he had plenty of experience managing money.

The reason I know Mr. Butler owned the land he farmed is because when he sold 160 acres of it in 1973 or 1974, I tried to buy it. But I didn't talk to him until he had already promised to sell it to a white man. And Mr. Butler said to me, "Well now, well now, Brother Neal, I didn't know nobody colored could raise that kind of money." Etheyln and I had married by then and I told him, "Mr. Butler, you know my wife is a doctor." And he said, "Yes, I believe you could raise it. But I done promised Mr. Herron and I can't go back on my word." Jess Herron was a white man who happened to be a key member of the Lee County white Citizens Council, and he was a terrible racist. But I didn't get upset with Mr. Butler for selling to him because Butler was always a man of his word. Maybe the Good Lord looked down on me and said, "Damn fool, you ain't got sense enough to farm. That line of work is not for you. I ain't going to let you worry yourself." But I really did want to farm.

Vulnerabilities and Limitations

Sterling King was the son of a respected Lee County farmer and preacher. Rabon Cheeks had just returned home after being administrative assistant to a dean at Howard University. Antony Hobbs Sr. was a popular Spanish teacher and respected member of the community. As the most outspoken of the school employees who supported what we were doing,

Hobbs was very important. However, school teachers were especially vulnerable because the school district was controlled by whites who opposed the Clinic and the Concerned Citizens. Hobbs had a wife and children to support, so he couldn't do anything to jeopardize his job. In September, he resigned from high school teaching to accept a position in Little Rock as director of the Arkansas Program on Food and Nutrition. With that move, he was able to remain an active member of the Concerned Citizens. His family stayed in Marianna and his children continued attending Marianna's public schools. Soon his daughters, with their father's support, would play a prominent role in the school boycott.

I had my own limitations because I worked at the Clinic, which was funded by federal money. As a federal employee, I had to live within the Hatch Act law that limited political activity by federal employees. Throughout this time, I remained a member of the Concerned Citizens but was not an officer. All those in an active leadership role protected me, including Reverend Spencer Brown and Reverend I. V. McKenzie, who was our chairman for a long time, and Reverend Andrew Williams, who succeeded him. The Marianna newspaper said that I ran the Concerned Citizens, but they could never tie that down because our official leaders would say, "No, he is a member, but he is not in a leadership role." The fact of the matter was that everyone worked diligently and with some degree of success to keep me separated from pronouncements that would endanger the Clinic's funding.

Black Folks Learned How to Register

We had to teach folks how to register to vote. You had to go to the county clerk's office in the courthouse and you had to tell the clerk your name, the address of where you lived, and your date of birth. I remember this one young woman from out in Brickeys, which was Donell Linton's area. Now, Donell was an interesting guy. He wouldn't be against you, but he would kind of smile and say, "You can't do that." Donell knew of this twenty-three- or twenty-four-year-old woman who he said would not be able to learn. To qualify she had to be able to answer the questions not necessarily in a certain sequence because they asked them in different ways.

Donell was trying to be helpful and was testing us too. He brought her into town on two different days for Sterling to teach. Sterling would say, "What's your name?" And she would say, "My name is..." and she'd say it. He'd say, "Where do you live?" She'd say, "I live at..." and would say the place. And he'd say, "What's your date of birth?" And she'd say, "I was born on…" Over and over and over. And Sterling was always patient. She got all that down and she got registered! After that Donell went to his church and said that these boys are GOOD. But he wouldn't say boy. He'd say, "This is a good man." They all were so proud of what Sterling and that woman had done. Nobody believed it possible. And I give Sterling all the credit. He was patient as hell. He worked with her. The result was profound. It gave us credibility in that community. Real credibility.

Getting our candidates elected in the 1970 campaign was an exciting time for all of us, and in 2016 Sterling King relayed his vivid memories of the campaign:

> We really took it very, very seriously. We got a lot of people from different parts of the county interested and involved. We helped get as many people as possible registered to vote. We talked in churches and had informal gatherings at homes. I remember one evening my family had a campaign meeting at our place. There were people that I couldn't call, so my mother invited them. She talked to her church friends, who would bring others too.
>
> Later during the boycott, some people were of a mind that the Concerned Citizens were trying to stir up something but not in the 1970 election campaign. We kept reminding our brothers and sisters of the gospel teaching that as members of the Christian community, "We are to render unto Caesar that which is Caesar's and unto God that which is God's." And Caesar was the government, so voting for government offices was something that we ought to do. By campaigning in this context, we were able to urge people to vote and remind them that there was nothing radical about coming out to vote.

Powerful Support from Black Preachers

Lee County preachers were our mainstay. During the 1970 election campaign, we had candidates of stature and good character, and we got out the black vote in Lee County like no one had ever seen before. But we never could have done it without the support of the black churches. And as I've said before, you can't separate the Clinic from all this either. The real leaders in the black communities, the ones who were respected countywide, were already out there showing their support for the Clinic. And when the Clinic was under attack by white folks, they didn't just lay back and say, "Well okay, I am with you." They stood up and spoke out in defense of the Clinic to prevent folks from believing the negative things that were going around.

Preachers have always taken leadership roles in the civil rights movement. After all, Martin Luther King Jr. was a preacher. And in Memphis
during the 1960s sit-ins, we had preachers in leadership roles too. But that
was only a few who were especially strong. It was different during the 1970
elections in Marianna. You could barely find any preachers (maybe one
or two) who did not support what we were doing. The kind of support for
raising up the black community that we had from those preachers in Lee
County was powerful.

We held most of our meetings and voter education sessions in different churches all around the county. The main ones were New Bethel Missionary Baptist and St. Luke African Methodist Episcopal in Marianna,
Spring Grove Missionary Baptist in Haynes, Seekwell Missionary Baptist
in Rondo, New Hope Missionary Baptist in the New Hope community, and
Freedonia Missionary Baptist in Moro. The ministers would announce our
campaign and the voter education meetings coming up at their churches.
After we got a duplicating machine, they could give out our handbills too.
Most of the churches had one main sanctuary where we would just sit on a
few benches. We would talk with six or eight or maybe ten people. It would
be like a small conversation.

On Sundays, we made speeches in the churches when they were full of
folks. At the very height of the campaign, we sometimes would talk in five
churches on a single Sunday. The pastors were so supportive that when we
came in they would interrupt the service and say, "I see we have Brother
King and Brother Neal with us. Let me get them up here." Reverend Mc-
Kenzie, Reverend Brown, and many others would do that. After speaking,
we would beg to be excused because we had more stops and would leave
and go to the next church.

Subsequent to the 1970 campaign, several churches in different communities around the county continued to be active and sponsored voting
seminars. They would make their buildings available for someone to talk
about voting and discuss which local issues were most important to support. Because the preachers were so critical to everything we were doing, I
also went to Lee County's Ministerial Alliance. They had a meeting every
Monday night. You would have thought I was a preacher because I was at
all their meetings. And I was probably the only non-preacher there.

When it came to speaking in the churches, Sterling was much better than
I was. As a little boy growing up, I went to church and Sunday school every
Sunday. So, I knew the Bible verses, but religion had not become as big a

part of my life as it was with Sterling. I am convinced that he was the most effective leader in that election campaign. When Sterling was not there during the later elections of 1972, 1973, and 1974, we didn't deliver nearly as many black votes. He wasn't the sole reason—but not having Sterling to speak in the churches definitely contributed to a much, much lower voter turnout.

Many Election Irregularities

We worked hard to get all our folks registered and as it got closer to election day, we had more and more difficulty. Davis Bullard was the county clerk, and he was cold to blacks coming in to register. He had all white women in his office, and it was a foreign place for black folks. Many of our people were fearful and easily intimidated, so it didn't take much to scare them off. They just didn't know what to do when anyone spoke rough to them.

In 1970 in Lee County, we did all we knew to do to get our election machinery in order. We consulted with Tom Glaze, who directed the newly organized Election Laws Institute, a nonprofit created to do Arkansas's election law education and provide public commentary on recommended election law improvements. Glaze was most interested in improving election policy, and he never talked to us about the prevention or correction of election fraud in our county. The Election Laws Institute continued to exist up until 1978. I know that because I spoke there one time. Later on, Glaze was elected to the Arkansas Supreme Court and he published a book on election fraud in Arkansas.

The local party chairmen chose the judges and clerks to represent their parties at each polling place. According to existing statewide rules, the Republican Party had at least one clerk and one judge at each polling place. We gave Mr. Sisk the names of strong and respectable people we wanted to represent us at the polls. But he just saw us as running some black candidates and not as part of the county's Republican Party leadership. Sisk's interest was in supporting Governor Rockefeller. He had little concern for our black candidates and did not choose a single one of our people to serve as a Republican judge or clerk. Some black judges and clerks were out there, but they were not strong people. They were not able to stand up and make a challenge when they saw something wrong.

In 2017, Bob Donovan, the person who taught everyone about the election rules, recalled, "County Judge Hack Adams asked me to teach the election classes. And they invited blacks to attend them. Blacks were probably the majority and they asked some hard questions. I remember that the county judge didn't like some of the answers I was giving. I just gave them truthful answers and he didn't like it."

We hired Robert Morehead to help us monitor the election. I don't know how much we paid him, but it wasn't much. He was one of our most important poll watchers on election day. He was a young black lawyer from Pine Bluff who had been a part-time assistant to the Arkansas attorney general. He was right there with us in Lee County on election day, and he knew the laws. When we had trouble at one of the polls, he would go out there and tell them what the law was.

Sterling King's sister Mae C. King was one of our unpaid poll watchers on November 3, 1970. She observed and wrote up a litany of election irregularities in an article she published in *The Black Politician*:

"The evening before election day, both Sheriff Courtney Langston and Judge Haskell Adams escorted Harvey Williams out of a meeting for election workers when he questioned the spokesperson for County Election Commissioners about his interpretation of a provision of the election code. The spokesperson said that poll watchers had to stay 6 feet away from the polling station. This meant that from 8 am to 7:30 pm on election day they had to remain outside in the cold (40° to 50° F) where they could not possibly do their job—check for irregularities. Then Sheriff Langston announced that he and his deputies would arrest any person (except those going in to vote) caught within 100 feet of the polling place. Judge Haskell, who was not in charge of the meeting, dismissed the meeting preventing any further questions from the blacks present." (Mae C. King, "Politics Southern Style," *The Black Politician*, July 1971)

It rained on election day. We had three polling places in Marianna. One was in the Ford Motor Company dealership on the corner of East Main and Alabama. They moved the cars out that day, and voting was in their showroom. This was a black ward and even though there was plenty of room inside, when the line of voters got to the door they wouldn't let folks come in and double around so they could be out of the rain. Everyone had to stay outside and get wet for a long time. I remember only black people were in those lines. There might have been three or four white people who came to that polling site to vote, and they were allowed to go directly inside. But all those black voters waiting out in the rain were determined. For them it was like, "You can make it hard for us, but we are going to stay and vote anyway." They stood strong.

Robert Morehead went over there and talked to the people running the poll on East Main and Alabama, but because there was no actual statute for this particular situation, he couldn't make them let the line of black voters come indoors. That was a memorable and major poll problem. But there were others too. Morehead had to go down to the courthouse because Sheriff Langston had put his deputy sheriffs at that polling place to intimidate black voters. The white deputies would stand too close to the voters and would go right in the voting booth with old, unsure black people to help them vote. Morehead talked to the deputies, but he couldn't get them to change anything there either.

Potential for Violence

The Marianna courthouse is on a hill at the end of Marianna's downtown park. You have to go up a bunch of wide steps to get in. After the election, two separate groups stood outside waiting for the election results. The white folks were thick all over those steps and spread out on the west side. The only thing I know about the white crowd was that they were waiting and ready for something. The black folks were close to the steps on the east side. People on both sides were armed. I'm pretty sure the number of white people was larger and I think that they were better armed too.

Late in the night when the announcement came that Mr. Ishmael and Mr. Butler had lost, black folks did not want to believe it and they did not want to leave. We had done something big that had never been done before, and everybody there was sure that our candidates had won. We had been peace-loving for so long, but there were black folks out there with weapons and they were ready for trouble. I saw a quiet preacher from one of the little churches outside Marianna with his folding knife open as he moved forward toward the front of the crowd. I believe he was ready to die that night. I could see it in him. He was different from how I had ever seen him before and I had never known he had that in him. Frank Allison, who had fought in the Vietnam war, was there. He was the same age and friends with my brother Rowan. Much later he told me, "Nobody cared about dying that night as long as we could take somebody with us." Mack Cleveland had his .38. He was quiet; not saying anything; waiting to see the direction we were going. Johnie C. Evans and Clyde McClendon were ready to fight. And I have to say that much of the leadership including me had our concealed pistols. I thought of it as being ready to protect myself.

I didn't see any of the white leadership outside to control the white mob. It was a threatening situation, no question about it. Our people and the white crowd were milling around. It only would take somebody accidentally bumping into the wrong person. At any provocation a fight could break out and spread out of control. Some of the Concerned Citizens leadership conferred and set our minds to keeping our people safe. Before anything happened, we had to break it up.

Reverend McKenzie was the master at dealing with a crowd and moving the people. He took the lead and as soon as he started speaking in his loud, unabusive tones, we all went to work convincing everyone to go on home. Big Daddy was there too. His size and force helped us move people. Clyde and Johnie calmed down and immediately reverted to their leadership roles, saying, "It's not time for that yet. We're not going to get into that now." Sterling was quiet and persistent. We moved through the crowd, saying, "Not tonight. Not tonight. Come on. Come on. Let's go home. We will figure out something to do with this tomorrow."

Our unity gave us the power to calm the crowd of black folks. We were a tight and cohesive group following McKenzie's lead. And we were very, very effective. I believe we made the right decision. Left alone in the heat of this moment, our people were heading for an explosion, a pitched battle that would not accomplish anything. That night would have made headlines but some of our people could have been killed out there.

More Trouble?

In Lee County, black folks had no experience standing up and voting for black candidates, and whites with all the political power had no experience with blacks winning elections either. A win in 1970 could have led to a complicated situation. On this same election day, up in Madison, a little town about twenty miles north of Marianna, a black man named Willard Whitaker won the mayor's race. In order to enter his office on January 1, he and his friends had to take their shotguns and run the white folks out. It was a hell of a situation. Whitaker must have been about fifty, which seemed old to me. I was twenty-nine, and hearing about this had a big effect. I thought, "Here is this old son-of-a-bitch who had the courage to go down there with shotguns and do what he had to do." I was impressed.

Looking back now, I realize that had Thomas Ishmael and Spaniard Butler's election not been undermined, there could have been this kind of conflict in Marianna too. And Sterling King agrees. In a 2017 conversation, he said, "I believe that if Thomas Ishmael and Spaniard Butler had officially won their elections and it had been acknowledged, they most likely would have had plenty of trouble assuming their offices. Would Hack Adams have willingly relinquished his office to Mr. Ishmael? No, I can't image him conceding gracefully. I believe that the long-existing power brokers in Lee County could not have allowed a smooth transition to these black men."

An Election Challenge?

On the day after the election, I couldn't get out of bed. As you can imagine, I was exhausted by the tension of the night before. I was crushed by the failure after all our excitement and work, and all I remember is feeling miserable. I was pitiful. At that point, I hadn't even considered being a lawyer. So even if Mr. Ishmael and Mr. Butler had the most votes, we failed to prevent election fraud and we failed to elect our most important candidates. We didn't do anything to challenge the election either. The truth of the matter was that none of us in a leadership role knew how to go about making a challenge. I know about that now. In 1970 none of us had that level of sophistication. We had done the best we could, but in truth we were ignorant and unprepared. Also, had our young lawyer Robert Morehead been able to go after them and help us make a challenge, we didn't have any money to pay him. I don't hold anything against the people who were helping us.

Robert Morehead shared this clear memory of election night in a March 2017 interview: "It was two hours before the ballots got to the courthouse. I was never granted access to the actual ballots, if you follow me. We all knew that most of the ballots never got counted in the first place. It was 1970. I also knew that there wasn't anything we could have filed anywhere in Arkansas that was going to get us any relief in Lee County."

Much later, we heard that Sheriff Courtney Langston did have something to do with what happened. Word came back to us anonymously from the white community indicating that Thomas Ishmael had gotten more votes than Hack Adams and Spaniard Butler had gotten more votes than the man he was running against. I think that those white people wanted us to know this, but they weren't willing to speak out in direct terms.

A Powerful Awakening

Despite the disheartening events, we cannot ignore what was positive in the 1970 Lee County election. For the first time in modern history, black candidates were overwhelmingly supported by the black community. And we did have some winners who had run for non-countywide offices. Son O'Donnell and Landers Isom were elected Marianna city aldermen. Pitson Brady was elected Oak Forest's justice of the peace on the Quorum Court, and he beat a white man named Ed Whitehead, who was a big farmer.

When Brady won, Dan Felton Jr., one of the white men who pretty much ran Lee County, sent for Brady. Felton told Brady that he had to decline the election and refuse to be sworn in. Fortunately, Brady was strong enough to handle it. He was not well educated, but he was someone who always found a way to do what he felt like he had to do. Basically, he said, "Yas sir, yas sir. Yas sir, Mr. Dan, but I told the people. Yas sir. Yas sir, but I promised my people." Brady never was disrespectful of the social mores between blacks and whites at the time, but he didn't back down either. He was sworn into office in January 1971.

Pitson Brady resisted Dan Felton's demand to withdraw, but he paid a personal price. Brady was a pretty good farmer with about 160 acres, and he owed about $18,000 on his land at a low interest rate of something like 6%. I can't prove that Felton was in on this, but after the election, the mortgage company called Brady and demanded full payment on his mortgage. Brady came and asked me if I had that kind of money to loan him. Unfortunately, I didn't, so to keep his land Brady had to go and get another bank loan, but the interest rate this time was 18%. For the next two years, except when he was serving on the Quorum Court, you did not see Pitson Brady in town. He was out on his farm making sure everything went well with all his crops, so he could pay off that loan. He paid it off in two years and he was reelected to the Quorum Court in 1972!

The 1970 election was a bitter experience and a powerful awakening for the black community of Lee County. After our candidates for county judge and county treasurer lost, tension in the black community was running high. People were on edge. And the Marianna economic boycott erupted out of this tension.

Chapter 8
Economic Boycott

Some people think it was just one, but there were two Marianna boycotts. The two boycotts were connected for sure, but they were different because the motivation and sacrifices made by members of the black community were very different. The economic boycott started on June 11, 1971, and the school boycott started seven months later on January 25, 1972. Both ended in July 1972.

Some consider these boycotts to be the greatest crisis in the history of Marianna. I'm not sure about that, but they did turn Marianna into what felt like a battleground. As a central player in the story, I'm going to tell you everything I know about the boycotts and give my opinions about what happened and why. You can decide for yourself who were the winners and who were the losers.

Quincy Tillman's Arrest

The incident that triggered the economic boycott started with a pizza. Quincy Tillman worked at Lee High School in Marianna, and she had an hour for lunch. On June 8, 1971, Ms. Tillman went to the Mug and Cone drive-in, owned by a white Marianna policeman, and ordered a pizza. When it took too long to get her order, she canceled it and went back to work. After she got home from work that day, she heard that the owner was looking for her, so she went over to the police department. She was arrested on the grounds of ordering a pizza on "false pretenses" or without intending to pay.

Quincy Tillman was a strong, no-nonsense woman. She had helped organize Lee County's welfare rights organization. At the high school, she was an outspoken and popular social worker committed to helping the kids and supporting the black community during a tough time. Public schools had just been integrated. Students and parents were unsettled. When Ms. Tillman got arrested, it was like all of us got a slap in the face.

Frustration and Anger

Racial tension in Lee County had been building under the surface as long as I can remember, and it rose to the surface in 1969 when the VISTA Health Advocates started working in Lee County.

Susan Daggett grew up in Marianna and was one of a few white students who attended Lee County's integrated schools in 1970. She is a graduate of Mount Holyoke College, and her 1986 senior thesis is titled "Marianna, Arkansas: A Study of Race Relations in a Small Southern Town." In it, she discussed the development of racial tensions during the early 1970s:

> Lon Mann, like so many other white people in Lee County, believed that VISTA had created a belligerence that could destroy the race relations of the county. He did not understand that VISTA had only uncovered and brought to the surface the hatreds that had been growing for over a century. The good relations that Mann thought he had with the black community often went no deeper than a surface civility: with the changing black expectations, a conflict was inevitable. The superficial amiability between the races was destined to erupt into hostility.
>
> In June of 1971, the feelings and frustrations that had been festering openly for over a year (and unconsciously, for over a century) reached a breaking point. Black people were extremely touchy about how they were treated, quick to interpret (sometimes unjustly) white attitudes as racist or discriminatory. White people were equally edgy. They feared the Clinic, the changing attitudes within the black community, and most importantly, the fact that the blacks constituted a majority of the population in Lee County. Paranoia corrupted their judgment and shaped their decisions.

The pizza incident was the final wrong that put the black community over the edge. Our frustration and anger, concealed until that time, came out all at once. Up to this point, the Concerned Citizens organization had been calm, but when we met to decide how to respond, the mood was hot and furious. The community immediately came up with a list of twenty-three demands. And Mamie Nelson, president of the Lee County NAACP chapter, presented these demands to the white leaders of Marianna. We wanted them to be published in Marianna's newspaper, the *Courier-Index*, for everyone to see, and we gave the newspaper two days to respond. We waited, but our demands never appeared in the paper. They didn't take us seriously, and I think that they laughed at us. They didn't know they were dealing with a new kind of organization and a deep desire for change.

Boycott of White-Owned Businesses

We answered their silence with a boycott of Marianna's white-owned businesses until our demands were met. On Friday, June 11, Rabon Cheeks and my brother Prentiss Neal, who were our designated boycott leaders, led a big group on the first day of picketing. They walked along Poplar Street carrying signs that said stuff like "Let's be free!" and "Keep your money in your pocket. No Shopping." They handed out flyers urging black folks to stay out of downtown stores and go elsewhere to shop. Concerned Citizens' members offered rides to other stores and pharmacies in Forrest City and helped folks pay their bills by mail, so they could avoid the downtown area altogether.

It wasn't like a small group decided to boycott and the rest were forced. This was a strong communitywide action. All the people involved in the Clinic were active, and that is why white people made the mistake of blaming the Clinic and the VISTAs for bad race relations. Through standing up to adversity at the Clinic and working together on the 1970 election campaign, the black community had become a united force. Rabon Cheeks and Prentiss Neal made the boycott really work, but my name was upfront associated with it because of my outspokenness and because in general black folks thought that I was the one who had brought in the VISTAs who were helping everyone. It all was connected.

Susan Daggett had a sound understanding of the situation when she wrote the following in her thesis:

> In their analysis of the situation, the "City Fathers" misinterpreted the true black sentiment towards the white community. Marianna did have an apparently good history of race relations: there had been no race riots or lurid tales of racial violence. However, this surface calm had little relationship to the subversive feelings that existed within the private black world. In the past, blacks had hidden their resentment, their genuine feelings, from white people in an act of self-preservation. Now, as a result of [Quincy] Tillman's arrest and the growing support groups of the Concerned Citizens, VISTA, and the Clinic, blacks were bursting with their emotions and their urge to strike back. They did not necessarily want to "avoid conflict"—instead, they encouraged it in order to avenge the years of repression and to finally accrue some local power. The white leaders, who thought they understood the black mind, attributed the unrest and dissatisfaction to the young radical "hotheads" and outsiders, not able to believe that the "good people" supported the movement.

The Defiance of Reverend Hinkle and Mrs. Clay

Very few black people flat out defied the boycott picket line. I only remember three or four who insisted that they were going to shop downtown, and it probably was a little more than that. Obviously, I wouldn't remember everybody who was against it, but Reverend J. H. Hinkle and Mrs. Vera Mae Clay stand out.

Reverend Hinkle was the worst black voice opposed to the boycott. He pastored a church in Marvell, a little town west and south of Marianna in Phillips County, and he would say all kinds of terrible things. To white people in private, he would say, "These niggers don't know what they are doing. They should leave white people's businesses alone." In public he would say something similar but a little less crude. During the first week of the boycott, Hinkle's house was firebombed and it burned internally. He left town, went up north to Chicago, and never returned.

Reverend Hinkle and Mrs. Clay thought that they had more sense than we did. They had been born with a way to get the necessities of life. They never needed anything like what the Clinic offered regular, less privileged black folks, and they did not see themselves as being part of the larger black community. They saw themselves as being above everybody else, better and more knowledgeable, but they were wrong just like the white folks were wrong. They didn't understand any of it.

The Efforts of Rabon Cheeks and Prentiss Neal

After the first week, when we had a lot of people downtown picketing the white-owned stores, Rabon Cheeks and my brother Prentiss were the ones who kept the boycott going. Sometimes other people would join them, but they were the ones who put our message out there every day. There was no time when they were not there. Neither one of them had another job. Prentiss stayed at the house with me and Daddy, so he had something to eat and a place to sleep. Rabon lived in Marianna with his grandmother and stayed with us sometimes too.

Prentiss was the most outspoken of the two and on July 2 he had a confrontation with Mrs. Clay as she was coming out of the Daggett Drug Store. Prentiss was talking to her about the boycott and in the conversation, he said to her, "Don't you understand anything?" She answered him, "I understand something. I'm a school teacher."

Prentiss's Arrests

As Prentiss talked to Mrs. Clay, someone came out of the drug store and told him he was harassing their customer. The drug store owner made a complaint, and Prentiss was arrested for the first time. It was for disturbing the peace, and he was given a $500 bond. When Daddy heard about it, he went down to talk to Sheriff Langston about getting Prentiss released. Daddy had always been a quiet, unpretentious citizen, and assumed he had a good relationship with the sheriff. But when he asked if he could take Prentiss home with him and promised to bring him back on July 12 for his hearing, the sheriff said, "NO, I'm not going to do that, Ollie. You got to pay the bond money." Daddy only had $200, so he walked the little way from the courthouse over to the Clinic to get the rest of the money from me, and he was HOT. I hadn't seen him like that in a long time. I got the rest of the money, and Prentiss was released.

Prentiss was arrested a second time on July 9 after a white woman motorist nearly ran him down as he crossed the street. She stopped the car and Prentiss mouthed off at her for almost hitting him. Then a guy came over from the Esso Station and they exchanged words. Prentiss was arrested and the bond was $25. His court appearance for both arrests was July 12.

Our Tactics

Around this time there was another incident that bothered me a lot more than the arrests. A white boy, Leroy Webb, punched Prentiss in the face when he was downtown picketing. Dr. Redlener stitched up the cut below his eye. The Concerned Citizens discussed the attack but ultimately decided that we couldn't spend time and risk going after Webb because he was nobody important. I had a hard time with that. I hated Leroy Webb and wanted to make him pay, but we did not go after white folks just because they were racist rednecks. I had to put my personal feelings aside to uphold our tactics. I made plans to get Leroy Webb later when he was unsuspecting.

Hack Adams Unified the Black Community

We were interested in fighting the power structure, and we didn't hesitate going after someone big like the county judge or the sheriff. So on July 14, when County Judge Hack Adams ran his truck up on the sidewalk where my brother and Cheeks were picketing, we were ready. It clearly was an attempt to hit them. Hack Adams's stupid hostility got worse and united the whole black community in anger. This was the real beginning of Marianna's long, hot summer of 1971. An article on July 8 in the *Arkansas Gazette* stated, "When Prentiss and Cheeks tried to file a complaint at the police station, they were told to go to the sheriff. And when they went over to the sheriff's office, Judge Adams rushed in behind them shouting curses. He pulled a pistol out of his pocket and threatened to kill them. Sheriff Langston tried to calm him down, but Adams ordered them out of the building with more profanity."

In an attempt to prevent the situation from dragging out and accelerating hostilities between the black and white communities, prosecuting attorney Gene Raff quickly set a hearing to decide whether or not to charge the county judge. Superficially, I'm sure this seemed like a good idea to Raff and the white community. But on July 17 when County Judge Hack Adams was charged with a misdemeanor assault and illegal possession of a weapon, this was seen as a huge victory throughout the black community. It gave us something to celebrate and strengthened our resolve.

Arson Fires

At the beginning of the boycott (on June 11), we had made our list of demands and by this time they had changed a little and expanded from twenty-three to forty-one. The next day, July 18, Concerned Citizens sent a letter to the Chamber of Commerce asking for a meeting to negotiate our boycott demands. The boycott had been going on over five weeks, but for the second time we did not receive an answer. What would it take for the white community to realize we were serious? How much disrespect could the black community tolerate? We found out nine days later.

Early in the morning of July 27, an arson fire destroyed the Main Dollar Store and damaged two adjacent white-owned downtown stores. Later that morning, someone shot at Deputy Sheriff Jimmy Burrows as he was driving through a black Marianna neighborhood. No injuries, no suspects, and no arrests. Concerned Citizens and our NAACP chapter issued a joint formal statement denouncing these incidents, but the fire was cheered in the black community. An interesting irony here is that the fire department was less than a block away and they didn't put out this fire (or another arson fire in January 1972 that burned the Concerned Citizens office and a whole block of black businesses). Marianna had a sorry volunteer fire department. They simply did not execute their duty on either property—white or black. At that time, there were no blacks in the fire department, and I never learned anything concrete about what was going on over there.

The next day, July 28, the white community leaders finally decided to meet with boycott leaders, and we agreed. Nearly all of our demands were about hiring blacks. We named stores, offices, and positions where a black person should be hired, and number forty-one on the list said that our "selective buying campaign will not stop during conferences or negotiations." This meeting went absolutely nowhere because the whites refused to negotiate until the boycott ended. We were at an impasse.

When the white business buildings burned, both sides hardened. There was no evidence, but it was pretty clear that somebody on our side had set the fire, and I think that some white folks were saying that it was time to take us on. I can tell you too that people in the black community were getting ready to defend themselves. That was the way it was. A low point. It was bad.

So, who set those fires? And who shot at Deputy Burrows? I don't know. I might have had some ideas, but I purposely never tried to confirm my thoughts. I have never wanted to know any specifics about that stuff. I can say that Burrows was not the one I would have chosen. He must have been rougher on others than he ever was on me. These incidents and especially the fires toughened both sides, including the ones who were inclined to say, "Let's not cause any trouble." We now had a widespread, forceful black resistance.

Nonviolence was never a way of life for me like it was for people like John Lewis. As students in the Memphis sit-ins, we practiced nonviolence, and I believed, as did many others in the movement, that nonviolence was the best way for black folks to fight. Memphis was a city with a big police force designed and trained to deal with us, and we could not win a physical battle.

In Marianna, the situation was different. It was a small town. We knew everybody and we knew where they lived: the white merchants, big white leaders, and individuals in the police force. Now, I agreed with what most of the black community was saying: "An eye for an eye." Could we win with open confrontational violence? No. Forces on both sides were never equal. We had adopted our version of insurgent defiance because the threat of violence was safer and might be useful—for example, when what was done caused Courtney Langston or Lon Mann to pause and think. We had their attention.

Damn Curfew and Protecting the Neal Brothers

On July 30, to prevent further violence, the Marianna City Council ordered what they called a day-to-day curfew. Some blacks were arrested on that weekend for curfew violation.

Prentiss and I were staying with Daddy. We were in our brick house on Moton Street across from the school. The house is gone now, but its foundation is still there. You have heard of "night riders"? They were white men going around protected by the dark of night and out to harm black folks. In Marianna some of the white Citizens Council were night riders, and we had heard that they were going to burn us out. So we talked Daddy into going up to Chicago to stay with our brother Rowan until things cooled down.

When the curfew started, the word was out that one of these white men was going to "get one of the Neal brothers." We heard that someone had put a $1,500 hit contract on each one of us, and we thought it was the white Citizens Council. I don't have any proof, but this is what we thought at the time. Their leadership was W. H. Barker, Harold Meins, and Jess Herron.

William Adler wrote about this in his book *Land of Opportunity*, pp. 210–211: "The logistics of killing Neal, the clinic administrator who whites suspected was the behind-the-scenes mastermind of the boycott, preoccupied the White Citizens Council. Once Meins attended a meeting at which he says 'a man from out of state' presented a plan to 'take out' Neal for twenty-five hundred dollars. 'They wanted me to write a local man a check; he could cash it and pay the contract guy.' Another time, Meins says he was shown bombs intended for Neal's house and the clinic. Both plans were aborted, Meins says, because 'we decided to wait until the niggers drew blood.'"

Robert Morehead and I kept in touch after the 1970 stolen election, and in March 2017 he still remembered the big picture at this time and the fact that we were in danger:

> Lee County was one of the poorest and one of the most racist counties in Arkansas. Helena and Marianna had a history for years and years of being just so. Suppressed people couldn't do anything and Olly Neal ended that. Olly Neal lifted them up and gave them a sense of community. He gained a lot of respect through his health clinic. He became the person to talk to. Those people had more confidence in Olly than any community organizer I have seen before or since in Arkansas. I mean they believed in him. I don't know how he was able to take those people

who I know had fear in their hearts and engender so much trust and faith. I still haven't figured it out.

I really worried about Olly a lot because he had no fear. None whatsoever. And I worried about his Daddy and his brother too. But he had people who had his back at times when he needed it. The worst thing that could have happened in Marianna at that time would have been if something had happened to Olly Neal.

I don't remember the hit man's name, but I still remember where he lived. It was south of Aubrey about a fourth of a mile. I got the word on a Saturday morning and called Mack Cleveland. He said that we should just go talk to him. Mack Cleveland worked out at the Douglas & Lomason (D&L) plant and was active in the union. Some of the redneck crackers out there thought pretty well of Mack because he didn't take any abuse off the supervisors. So Mack got his name and where he lived from D&L redneck "friends," and we went out there on that Saturday evening. When the guy came to the door, Mack got up in his face and threatened him, "Now you better listen. If you are not out of the county by tomorrow evening, we are coming after you." That was it. Nobody heard of him being around after that.

Mack was tough, but you know, I wasn't all that tough. I was never one who liked fist fighting or anything, but everybody knew Mack's reputation. He never finished high school, but he always figured out a way to make a living. He was not a troublemaker. He was not a bully. He didn't go out looking for anything. He had a joint where he did a little gambling and bootlegging, and everybody knew that you didn't come into his joint and cause trouble. (Much later, in the 1990s, an old boy who had moved away and become a deputy sheriff in Georgia was back home visiting. He came into Mack's joint wearing a pistol, and he was being overly proud of himself. Mack told him that he couldn't wear a pistol in his place and shot him. Mack didn't kill him or anything.)

Mack also put together a team for surveillance and protection. The ones I remember on the team were Mack, Ben Anthony Jr., Frank Allison, Leon "Main" Flannel, and Melvin Campbell. But I'm pretty sure there were six or eight all together. At least two men would be up watching all the time. We had several shotguns and several 30.06 rifles, and we all had .38s. Everybody brought their own weapons. I had my .38, my 30.06, and my 12-gauge.

In 2017 Mack Cleveland was willing to say only this much about those days:

Olly was a close friend. When they put that contract on him he called me. He wanted me to come up there and stay with him and watch out for them. I come up and brought six men and spent some nights with him. I was the type that just wasn't scared. I would stand up for right. I tried to do the right thing, and I wasn't scared. That is why Olly would always come to me for something like that. He knew that I would come to the rescue. He could count on me. He knew, no matter what, I was with him. I was Olly's man.

I done the same thing for Reverend I. V. McKenzie too. One time they got after him. They tried to cut him off...tried to block him off the road. They were trying to get him but somehow or other he got around the roadblock they had set up for him and he come straight to my store and woke me up in the night. He knocked on the door, and I had to get up out of the bed and follow him home. He was scared to death. I went around home with him to make sure he was okay. It was like one or two o'clock in the night.

On the first or second night of the curfew, some white boys in a white station wagon drove by Daddy's house. They drove down the street real slow, and as they came by our house, their car came almost to a stop. There were several in the car. Their car door opened, then closed, and they took off. I called the sheriff on the phone and said, "Sheriff Langston, this is Olly Neal." He asked me, "What is it, Olly?" I told him about the white boys out after curfew and described the white station wagon and told him, "If they drive by again, I'm going to call Hodge!" And the sheriff said, "I hear ya, Olly." Hodge was the funeral director for white folks. The sheriff understood my implication. I wouldn't say that now, but I meant it then. After that, for the rest of the curfew, we never saw any other white boys driving past the house. Nobody else come by. That was our plan, and it stayed that way until that damn curfew was lifted. It was on for about two weeks. And later when I asked Deputy Ollie Brantley about that incident, he told me that the sheriff actually told those boys to stay off the streets at night or he would put them in jail.

Angry White Mob Makes Threats

On August 5, the day of Judge Haskell Adams's trial, the Marianna courtroom was packed with about equal numbers of blacks and whites. Judge Adams had insisted that the incident in which he ran his truck up on the sidewalk where my brother and Rabon Cheeks were picketing was caused by his brakes failing, but at his trial, he pleaded no contest. He was fined $95 and released.

After the trial got out, the situation was tense. Groups of angry white men were hanging around the town square just down from the courthouse. Prentiss and Cheeks stopped on the sidewalk to talk to Bill Husted, who was a young white reporter covering the trial for the *Arkansas Democrat*, a statewide newspaper in Little Rock. Husted asked Prentiss something about being threatened, and Prentiss told him we had heard that the Ku Klux Klan had placed a price on his head. He called all those radical white people the same. As they were talking, about twenty white men surrounded them and threatened Husted, telling him, "It's not him we want. It's you. You reporters are the ones causing all the trouble." One of the men kicked Husted in the backside and told him to "get out of town fast." And he did.

A little later that morning, the same white mob beat up Al Daniels, the white attorney from Little Rock who represented my brother and Cheeks at the trial. Daniels had seen the white men carrying baseball bats and when he reported them to the police, he was told that there was no law against carrying a baseball bat on the street in Marianna. Daniels started taking Polaroid pictures of what was going on, and white guys surrounded him, kicking him and punching him in the head. He had to go to the Clinic for treatment.

That afternoon, a white Citizens Council bulletin appeared around town. It said:

> "If you want Marianna to be a battle ground, you Can get it. You can look for the same medicine as you got a taste of today every time leaflets are passed out. No more food stamps will be signed by white people as long as this is going on! THIS IS OUR LAST WARNING! All you Red-Blooded Whites Come to the Aid of Your Town."

The next day or so, they dropped another bulletin from a crop duster that was addressed to "The good black citizens of Lee County," and it said, "THE BOYCOTT IS OVER."

More TV and AP Reporters Harassed

On August 9, reporters from Little Rock's KATV were harassed by whites in downtown Marianna. The white mob blocked the reporters' car, grabbed a camera, and tried to drag one reporter out of the car. Police came, returned the camera, and dispersed the crowd. One person was taken into custody. No charges were filed.

On August 11, state troopers in Marianna were increased, and they escorted reporters wherever they went to do an interview. The next day, Robert G. Knox, a field technician for the Associated Press, was run out of town by four men when he stopped to get gas on the edge of town. Some white men grabbed him and put him back in his car and followed him several miles as he drove out of Marianna.

U.S. Justice Department's Effort to End the Boycott

The racial crisis in Marianna and all the press it attracted drew a lot of attention from people who thought that they could fix the situation. Ozell Sutton was a Philander Smith graduate who had been active in the 1960s sit-ins. The United States Department of Justice Community Relations Office sent him to Marianna to speak with leaders of both the white and black communities. I think that Sutton related to what we were doing, and we really had a decent thirty-minute talk. It wasn't that I was ragging his ass or nothing. He talked about the necessity of having peace in order to create a circumstance where you could reasonably negotiate. And I asked him if his role was simply to get peace, or if it was to negotiate with both sides for a reasonable solution. And I kept pushing that point until he finally acknowledged that his job was simply to get peace. He tried to sell it to us, but how could we stop the boycott with no benefit in it for us? To stop the boycott, the other side had to yield. They had to give us something. And he was not able to assure us that the other side was going to make any kind of concession.

The Boycott Continued

The curfew stayed in effect until August 17, and tempers gradually cooled. But the intense disturbance that had been boiling over was only turned down to simmer, and the conflict remained unresolved for the rest of 1971. The white community continued trying to beat us any way they could. On October 19, hundreds of Lee County's white citizens attended a meeting at which Bob Cunningham, a businessman of Cairo, Illinois, and George Shannon, an employee of the national white Citizens Council, talked about how to break a black boycott and prevent political takeover by black militants. They came up with a white Citizens Council Shoppers Guide listing more than twenty-five white-owned businesses that cooperated with them. Whatever that meant.

Prentiss and Cheeks pretty much stopped picketing or handing out flyers downtown. Throughout the fall, we kept the black community together with flyers distributed at church meetings around the county, and our people held firm. We had good support from the preachers and the churches and well-established black folks. But I can tell you that holding everyone together was difficult. After it was over, I didn't ever want to do anything like that again.

More Struggle and Unease

The economic boycott wasn't all that was going on in Lee County. Public school administrators, teachers, parents, and students struggled with court-ordered integration. While applying for a major grant to build a new building, the Clinic encountered fierce opposition. The black community continued to be unsettled by the 1970 "stolen" election. And there was a drive to register many new voters.

Difficult Integration of Lee County Schools

The 1970 integration of Lee County schools was a long time coming. It finally happened with a court order, but before that there were a few years of "freedom of choice." No one expected white families to send their children to a black school, so "freedom of choice" really meant that black children were supposed to choose to go to a white school. It didn't work. Black children were naturally reluctant to leave their friends and the familiarity of their own school to enter an all-white school where they knew they would not be welcome.

Forced integration added to the racial tensions. I remember being at a community information meeting for black folks right before the integrated schools opened. Lon Mann, president of the school board, was introducing the principals for each of the five public schools. All the principals were white except Mrs. Davis. He introduced the white principals as Mrs. Somebody or Mr. Somebody, but when he got to Mrs. Davis, he introduced her as "my friend Emma Davis." Well, I jumped up to complain about his disrespect and acted the damn fool until Sterling King finally pulled me off and went on to do the intelligent thing, saying, "Now, now, I know you don't like his method, but you have to agree he is right."

Clifton Collier was a senior in 1970, and during a 2017 interview he remembered that school year with clarity:

That was when nearly all the schools integrated throughout Arkansas. Strong High School, Marianna's black high school, always had the more successful football team and the year before integration we were 10 and 0. We were the Lions, and the white school had been the Porcupines. Coming up to integration, one of the things we thought about a lot was that we did not want to be called the Porcupines. And the whites didn't want to be called the Lions. So, we had a meeting and the football team came up with Trojans, and that's how we got a new name.

After integration, we had a white principal and our black principal became the assistant principal. The same thing happened with the coaches. The white coach, Charles Moore, became the head coach and our black coach, James Coleman, became his assistant. Coach Coleman had talked with us before school was out the year before, and he told us that we were going to stick together, so we looked to him for support and guidance. But things got off track with the football team. When Coach Moore gave the starting lineups, there were only three blacks on offense and three blacks on defense. That's all. In spite of this, the Trojans were undefeated in our first four games and we ranked highest in the state.

We had a black quarterback, James Williams, who was a senior and really good. But Coach Moore always started a white quarterback, who was a junior. James was a better athlete. He was faster and he had a stronger arm. He was clearly much better than the white quarterback. But the white quarterback started, and when the game got tight the coach would put James in.

Well, James always had a quick temper and we all knew he didn't like what was going on. Then, when we went to our game in Helena, there were some words between James and Coach Moore, and Coach Moore left James in Helena. He left him there! So, all the black players quit until James was reinstated. He was put back on the team, but after that we no longer had whatever it is that a team needs to win. We went downhill. We went from being undefeated to not winning another game.

Strong High School had always been known for our band, and York Wilborn had been our band director for probably thirty years. We were so good that we would get invited to parades in Little Rock, Memphis, and some other places. And when the schools integrated, a young white man just out of college became the band director instead of Mr. Wilborn. That just didn't seem right. And it happened all up and down. The whites got the top positions and the blacks became the assistants.

Andrea Hope Howard, a 1970 Lee High School junior, said of that year in a 2017 interview:

In the summer of 1970, a girlfriend and I were looking for a job. My mother told me that there was some voter registration work with Sterling King. So, I was able to do some voter registration with him. And I really got to admire Sterling because of some of the things he was doing. Through him I met some other people who helped to inspire me. This was also during the Black Panther movement, and I was coming to the point where I wanted to be a Black Panther so bad. I met this guy in Marianna who came from California and he told me he was a Black Panther. I sat and talked to him for two or three hours just reveling in what he was saying. Then came the school integration.

When we started the 1970–71 school year, I was a junior, and it was rough for me. So much was hard for me because of all that was going on that year. I just did not do well with integration. The white kids at school didn't like me because I was very outspoken. They were just constantly belittling me. They used to make all these cracks about me getting in trouble because I had some political material in my mailbox.

The year before at Strong High School, a teacher had told us that we would stick together, but that did not happen. The teachers ended up being so different from what they had promised. They didn't support us. That hurt too. My English teacher was black and really pathetic in what she allowed white students to get away with in her class. I will never forget one day when a white student said to her, "You are just a goddamn liar." And we all turned around to see what she would do. The next day he came back and apologized, but that was it. What would have happened if a black student had said that to her or a black student had said that to a white teacher? We used to have debates in that class. Helen Peer, Dolores Humbert (Hare), and I were the only ones to speak up and tell the white students why we would not stand for the Pledge of Allegiance.

By the end of that year, I was getting to the point of total frustration. And I wanted to get the hell out of there because if I didn't, me and these folks were going to have at it. Anyway, I decided to see how I could get out. I went to my counselor, and she told me that I only had to take English to graduate. So the summer of 1971 I took senior English as a correspondence course.

This was the summer the [economic] boycott started. All kinds of stuff started around that time. I had met Rabon Cheeks that year too, and I was listening to him and getting involved in some of the things he was saying. So, it was getting harder and harder for me to accept everything, and I decided I had to get out of Marianna. That correspondence course was difficult, but I was determined to get the hell out of there. And you know I was lucky because the school boycott started the next year and if I had stayed I probably wouldn't have graduated.

I went to Tennessee State in the fall and when I got there I was acting the same way. My girlfriend used to say to me, "You are just a militant." That is exactly how she would say it. There was a wave of activism going on across the country. Some people participated and some didn't. After that, in my sophomore year, I settled down and became a serious student. I graduated in three and a half years and came back to Marianna.

Continued Voter Registration Focused on Young Voters

As Reported by Arkansas Council on Human Relations, September 1971: "Our Concerned Citizens organization and the local NAACP continued to register as many black voters as possible. In the summer of 1971 the Arkansas Voter Registration Project received a special grant for summer interns and three of them Miss Alma Jones, Miss Winnie Kennedy, and Miss Bonita Hobbs were in Marianna. They received their training at the Atlanta Voter Education Project led by Julian Bond in Atlanta. Between July 1 and August 30 they registered 200-300 new voters in Lee County. A quarter of those registered were 18-21 year olds."

Fierce Opposition to the Clinic and VISTA Continued

On November 1, 1971, when the Clinic had its second annual meeting, over 800 people attended. The theme of that meeting was Working Together through the Cooperative Clinic. Our speaker, Dr. Randall Maxey of Howard University, told us that the community itself must make the changes that will solve health problems. And our board chairman, Mr. Eddie Foster, emphasized that we welcomed everyone to participate in Clinic activities.

At the same time, white community leaders continued to show their fierce opposition to the Clinic and the VISTAs. They went to Senator McClellan asking for and getting investigation of the Clinic and our personnel. They threatened economic reprisal against drug firms that gave us free medicine for indigent patients. They also asked Governor Bumpers to abolish the VISTA program. If that happened, we would lose all the services VISTA workers provided for our patients. It had become clear to everyone that most of the white community did not care that this would create a crisis for the county's poor families.

Resentment over 1970 Election Lingered

In November 1971, the Arkansas Advisory Committee to the U.S. Civil Rights Commission held a meeting in West Memphis to hear testimony from citizens. The black community was still unsettled over Thomas Ishmael's and Spaniard Butler's losses, and we worked hard to get our people there so our problems with that election could be heard. Mr. Ishmael testified about "instances of electoral irregularities in the conduct of the election by officials." Robert Morehead started by saying that he had observed the 1970 Lee County election closely because he had been retained as an attorney by the Lee County Concerned Citizens.

Morehead testified to the following facts:

1. black poll watchers were harassed,
2. the sheriff refused poll watchers admittance to the polling area,
3. the sheriff confiscated voting boxes before the votes had been properly counted, and
4. the FBI had ignored complaints submitted to them concerning the election.

I was there. I heard what he said and I read the committee's report. Nothing happened. These were hard times and people were hot.

Serious Proposals from White Leadership to End the Economic Boycott

In early December 1971, a more reasonable group of white leaders started meeting with representatives of the Concerned Citizens. Governor Bumpers sent someone from his office (I believe it was Thomas McRae) to talk to both sides about a settlement. These meetings took place in the basement of the Community House on Main in Marianna because where we met had to be a neutral location. The moderate white leadership eventually presented these sixteen proposals to end the boycott:

1. The Marianna School Board had voted to fill the first vacancy with Rev. Spencer Brown. Dr. Fred Rutledge will resign when the boycott is ended to provide this vacancy. (Rev. Brown will become the second negro member of the board.)
2. The County Judge has given his assurance that he will not oppose in any way the federal grant now being sought for operation of the Lee County Cooperative Clinic.
3. The City of Marianna will employ a second black policeman. Ad-

vice and council [*sic*] of the black organization will be sought in selecting an individual who is qualified for this position through Alderman F. M. Owens.

4. Sheriff Courtney Langston will add a black deputy sheriff to his staff.

5. Marvin Caldwell will resign from the Marianna City Planning Commission and recommend that a black citizen be appointed in his place.

6. Marianna banks have agreed, by resolution of their board of directors, to hire a black citizen.

7. The Marianna Water Commission has agreed to expand the office force at the Water Department and hire a black citizen.

8. A black citizen will be appointed to the school superintendent's Advisory Council to replace Rev. Brown when he becomes a member of the school board. (This committee had 7 blacks and 7 whites and has been meeting regularly once a month since Sept.)

9. The Arkansas National Guard rolls are open to qualified members of all races. Anyone interested should apply. Assurance has been given by Battalion Commander Colonel John B. Webb of Little Rock.

10. Ray Shillcutt is certain that the office force of Arkansas Power and Light Company in Marianna will be expanded in the near future. Mr. Shillcutt has agreed to hire a black office clerk. He points out that all employees hired by the local office must be approved by his district office, but he anticipates no problem in this respect. Applications will be accepted now.

11. Alderman F. M. Owens, chairman of the Police Commission, will discuss any problems relative to police work with black citizens at any time.

12. The Marianna Fire Department has no restrictions on race.

13. Notices of School Board and City Council meetings will be published in *The Courier-Index*. (This has been done regularly since Oct.—both meetings are held the 2nd Tues, night of each month—no change in last 15 years.)

14. The school administrative offices now employ three black secretaries.

15. At least two aldermen have pledged that they will work toward expanding the City Council so that it will include black aldermen.

16. It is suggested that a bi-racial committee be selected/elected to discuss any future problems and make every effort to work out misunderstandings. This committee would work in the interest

of employment for blacks and more representation on various boards.

Many Sources of Distrust

Looking at this now, it appears to be exactly what we were working for, and personally when I first read it, I liked what I saw in this list. But I can tell you that the rest of the black leadership was very suspicious. Prentiss and Cheeks had been physically assaulted while picketing, and they were against ending the boycott. Many of us felt loyal to them for all they had suffered out on the street, and just about everyone involved did not believe that these proposals were being made in good faith. They would tell me, "You can't trust them, that's all." And it wasn't just the naturally tough ones like Mack Cleveland, Leon Flannel, or Pitson Brady saying this hard line.

Current conditions contributed to distrust in the black community, and old hurts were still festering. Just a year before, Thomas Ishmael and Spaniard Butler had lost their elections under suspicious circumstances. Everyone involved felt that those elections had been stolen.

It was also the first year of school integration. Black children and parents were struggling as they went from the safety and familiarity of black schools to the hostility of white-controlled schools. Families of black students were experiencing more evidence that the white leadership did not understand or address their children's needs.

Based on bad experiences concerning land, farmers like Thomas Ishmael, Birben Griffen, Ben Anthony Jr., and Herman Jones felt a profound animosity toward white people. The Delta soil here is exceptionally fertile. At one time, about a third of the land in Lee County was owned by black farmers. Over and over again, when a white man came after their land, blacks had to fight hard to keep what they owned. Often an uneducated and uninformed black farmer didn't understand what was going on and had been cheated out of his land. If a black farmer hadn't had this happen to him, he had seen it happen to others around him. Under these circumstances, it was impossible for them to trust even the most reasonable white people in Lee County.

The hard work and difficulties of the Concerned Citizens' organized action against Marianna's white businesses were over. By late 1971 we had forced at least seven businesses to close, and there were more on the brink of closing. With the economic boycott, we had exercised black power, and black folks did not want to give it up. Deep in the black community was a bitter emotional drive—to keep punishing. Consequently, all sixteen proposals were rejected, and everything got worse.

Chapter 9
Integration and School Boycott

Before integration, black families in Lee County wanted their children to have more opportunities than they had in the segregated system. They knew a good education was the key to success. But black students and their families anticipated public school integration with uncertainty and anxiety. Some black students did not especially want to go to school with white students at all. They just wanted what white students had—the best available. And to get the best education in an integrated system, the black students (and the white students) needed to be safe and comfortable. They needed to feel supported and respected. This was going to be a tall order.

Even though both black and white leaders may have been doing their best to make integration work, the Lee County public school district experienced tension and strife, and there were a lot of mistakes. The result was that both white and black students, parents, teachers, and administrators suffered and paid a personal price. I have to wonder if the suffering was inevitable given the participants, our history, and the times.

First Year of Integration Was Not Easy

From a distance, the first year of integration appeared to go fairly smoothly. Nothing happened that attracted much attention beyond Lee County, but there were some incidents, and it wasn't easy for anyone involved. At the beginning of the second semester in January 1971, black students at Lee High School (eleventh and twelfth grades) were denied a school assembly to honor Dr. Martin Luther King's birthday. When they considered having an off-campus program, they were warned that any student who came to school and then walked off campus would be suspended for ten days.

On Friday, February 12, white students at Futrell, the tenth-grade building, protested a black history week sign saying, "To Be Black Is to Be Beautiful." It was hung in the cafeteria with principal Ronnie Austin's permission. When Austin changed his mind and asked a black teacher to take it down, the teacher refused, so Austin told a white teacher, Ben Williams, to take it down. A conflict ensued between Ben Williams and a black student, and the student was suspended from school. Just after noon of that same day, a majority of the white students at Futrell walked out, and later white students at Lee High School also walked out in support. They were not threatened with suspension, and as far as I know, the police were not called to intervene.

Over the next weekend, 500 Lee County residents, including thirty-five teachers, signed a petition demanding Principal Austin's resignation. They presented the petition at a special meeting of the school board on Sunday. At 8:00 a.m. the following Monday, February 15, Austin held an all-school assembly at Futrell. He introduced a new black assistant principal, Robert Scott, who was a librarian and had been selected for this new position at the Sunday school board meeting. Black school board member Connor Grady and Deputy Sheriff Ollie Brantley also spoke at the assembly, but the black students still were aggrieved, and they went to the principal's office. Before 3:00 p.m. that afternoon, Austin resigned.

The following summary is from a portion of Susan Daggett's 1986 college senior thesis, based on a 1986 interview with Lorraine Jones and referencing her personal files. During that same week, some white students at Lee High School who felt threatened by the school having a black history week, wore all white clothes to school. Following this incident, Lorraine Jones, a white psychology class teacher, conducted a student activity with the hope of reducing racial tensions. Of her white students she asked, "If you were black, what would you do differently?" Of her black students, she asked, "If you were white, what would you do differently?" Their answers show the stress and difficulties these young people were experiencing.

The white students revealed feeling intimidated, and they expressed some of their racial prejudices. They complained of blacks "grouping up in the bathrooms and threatening whites" as well as intentionally running into them in the halls. Also, one person said, "If I were black, I would try to understand the white people's position as a minority and try not to push them against the wall by taking all the advantage a majority has." Several complaints showed concerns about interracial flirtation, for example, "If I were black, I would teach the black boys to leave the white girls alone." In their list, the black students were disturbed by the attitudes of superiority by white students. For example, they wrote things like, "If I were white, I would do away with the old ideas that blacks are stupid, lazy, or inferior" and "I would stop...rolling my eyes at them and sneering down my nose" and "I would mix with the black race, carry on a conversation with them, not huddle in the hall right at the front door and look at them like they are some kind of strange and mysterious insect."

Daggett's thesis states with clarity, "Many of the grievances on both sides were the same. For instance, both groups complained of vulgar language, lack of respect for each other, and the exclusiveness of each race. One black student pinpointed the problem beautifully: 'The basic problem with our school is the lack of communication between the two groups. We need to talk freely and openly to one another with honesty and sincerity.'"

Black student Andrea Howard gave her perspective of her teacher and this class activity in a 2017 interview: "I was in Ms. Jones's psychology class. My impression was that she only pretended to care about the black students. I remember this assignment, but it didn't have a memorable impact on me. I just couldn't trust her or anyone else in that room."

Second Year of School Integration Grievances

In January 1972 of the second year of school integration, many black students at Lee High School still felt unsettled and unhappy. They wanted some changes and had put together a list of grievances for their principal. Just like in many other schools around the country, black students in Marianna pursued approval of a special program to honor Dr. Martin Luther King in their school.

On Thursday, January 13, 1972, two days before Reverend Martin Luther King's birthday, ten black students approached their principal, Bob Blankenship, with a list of fourteen demands that included a threat to boycott their school if their demands were not met. Here is a list of the topics covered in this list:

1. Dissatisfaction with Mrs. Burke, English department chairman,
2. Grades lowered because of too many tardies,
3. Poor quality of lunchroom food,
4. Not enough time (eighteen minutes) to eat lunch,
5. Not getting program to commemorate Rev. Martin Luther King's birthday,
6. School run like a military college,
7. High school students treated like children in Head Start,
8. School is dominated by white rules,
9. Mr. Blankenship is not qualified to be principal,
10. Don't need one white and one black student council president,
11. Remove white drum majorette,
12. Do not want white band director,
13. Not getting information from counselors about educational loans,
14. Want our civil rights.

Students Say They Did Not Walk Out

The ten student leaders went to their principal first thing in the morning, and many black students (somewhere between 200 and 400) did not go to their first period classes. Instead they sat in the hall outside of the principal's office in support of their leaders. They chose to be quiet so they would not be accused of interrupting the classes that were in session.

Lee High student Marguetta Wafford said that she watched the news on TV that night and was upset that they got it wrong. The TV reporters called it a student walk-out. She said, "We did not walk out. We were run out of school like dogs and beaten like rats."

What Happened, Step by Step

I was not at the school to witness exactly what happened on January 13, 1972. And I didn't know all of the details at the time, but recently I was able to put together the whole story after reading Governor Bumpers's papers, which have been archived by the University of Arkansas at Little Rock Center for Arkansas History and Culture and housed at the CALS Roberts Library in Little Rock. From those documents, it is clear to me that the students believed they had a right to speak to their principal. They were committed to being courteous and to being heard, but they were in his outer office only a few minutes before Blankenship said that he wouldn't listen to them, and he phoned Superintendent H. C. Dial. Then, Blankenship said that he would only talk to five students, and he wouldn't talk to anyone under the pressure of a sit-in. When the students insisted on having all of their leaders present, Blankenship went in the hall outside his office and told the sit-in students that they had ten minutes to get to their classes. At 8:31 a.m., after the ten minutes were up and the students stayed right where they were, Blankenship went on the intercom and told the teachers to lock their classroom doors.

Dr. Dial must have called Sheriff Courtney Langston immediately. Dial arrived at 8:35. Sheriff Langston and Deputy Ollie Brantley got there by 8:45. Deputy Brantley talked to both the principal and the students, and soon realized they were at an impasse. Brantley advised the students to leave, but they said no. At 9:03 the sheriff used his bullhorn and told the students that he would arrest them if they didn't get into their classrooms in the next five minutes. And he told them that there was a law that made it a misdemeanor to loiter on school property. Principal Blankenship got on the speaker system and told his teachers to admit their students during the next five minutes and then lock their doors, but nearly all of the students stayed right where they were. After the time was up, Sheriff Langston announced that all the sit-in students and their leaders were under arrest, and they had to get on the buses that were already waiting outside to take them to the courthouse.

At first, seven local law enforcement officers moved the students onto the buses. Two buses were almost full when the remaining students got anxious and refused to be moved. As the officers started having trouble getting students onto the buses, they grabbed some of the girls and were pretty rough with them. That's when the students already on the buses started coming off to join the group outside and Sheriff Langston overreacted. I'm not sure what he expected to accomplish, but he shot his gun up in the air! After that, law enforcement lost control. One boy got punched in the stomach as he jumped off the bus. Most of the students went to stand around the flagpole and started singing "We Shall Overcome."

The officers managed to keep the ten student leaders inside the school building, where they could see the mess that was going on outside, until Deputy Sheriff Brantley took them downtown to the courthouse to be arrested. Right after the student leaders left, a fire truck came up the driveway, and the rest of the students shifted away and around the corner of the building to a smoking area near the gym. But the fire truck followed them. It was a damn cold January day. The temperature was down near freezing, but that didn't keep the firemen from spraying high-pressure water on the students. They ran. And the fire truck chased them until the truck almost got stuck in a field. Then a farm tractor was used to chase after the students. Some students were hit by nightsticks or black jacks, I'm not sure which. A few injured students went to the Clinic for treatment. Juanita Wright was beaten on her head, and Dr. Redlener had to refer her to a hospital in Little Rock.

And at some point, state policemen arrived and joined in with the local law enforcement to chase the students. The state police stayed until all the remaining students were either caught or run off the school grounds. A State Department of Education Committee (SDEC) report stops at this point, but the students' descriptions of what they saw and what happened to them were also recorded.

What Students Saw and Reported

Anita Reeder was a student "locked" in a classroom, and she watched what was going on outside the window. She saw firemen and police pull out the water hose and spray it on the students. She saw the students "run like rabbits," and she saw the men catch them and pull them onto the buses. She saw students chased across a field, pushed down into the mud, and beaten with nightsticks.

Several students heard the men chasing them yell "run nigger run." Many students reported seeing Principal Blankenship holding a student while the student was beaten by a police officer. A boy on crutches got knocked down by fire hose water. When students running through a muddy field fell down, they were grabbed and dragged by the men chasing them. One girl lost her shoe and was hit on the head as she went back for it. Many students were chased even after they had been forced off school grounds. Students were looking for any place to hide. They ran to a nearby motor company. They ran across a field. They ran along an airport field. They ran through a peach orchard. A few made it to a friend's home looking for safety.

A small group of students running toward a road were picked up by the father of one of the students. He just happened to be driving by. One student mentioned seeing the fire department, state troopers, telephone men, and store keepers pursuing the students. This raises the question: Who exactly were the "officers" apprehending the students?

It Could Have Been Avoided

> "Following the trouble at Lee High School, there was a 7 pm to 6 am curfew in Marianna. But in spite of the curfew and the presence of numerous state troopers in Marianna that night, two rooms in Deputy Sheriff Jimmy Burrows's home were damaged by gasoline fire bombs. No one was injured." (*Commercial Appeal*, Friday, January 14, 1972)

Governor Bumpers's file on Marianna includes more than 150 letters written by Lee High School students within a few days of this event. Students were afraid to go back to school and begged Governor Bumpers for help. They expressed all kinds of strong emotions and a desire to return to school as soon as they could feel safe again. The Marianna file also contains a few letters written by the students' parents. Students and parents told their own stories with the conviction that this terrible day could have been avoided if only the high school principal had been willing to talk to the ten student leaders. They wrote that the fear and overreaction of the principal was so serious that he should be fired. Most also were critical of Superintendent Dial and State Trooper Captain Dwight Galloway, who were at the school that day, although there is one letter written by a white parent who had a completely different point of view.

As a result of what happened at Lee High School, Governor Bumpers immediately sent his executive aide Carl Agers (who was black) to Marianna. This is the text of the memo Mr. Agers submitted following that visit.

DATE: January 14, 1972
TO: Governor Bumpers
FROM: Carl Agers
RE: "Marianna Crisis."

The following statements were made by Black residents of Marianna whom I consider to be very credible.

1. The principal of Lee High School refused to talk with ten (10) Black students concerning thirteen (13) questions relevant to conditions of Blacks enrolled at the school. (Among these was a request for a vacation period and memorial celebration in honor of the late Dr. Martin Luther King, Jr.) The principal's stated reason for this refusal was that they (the 10 students) did not represent the entire student body.

2. The students decided that they would gather, peacefully, to show the principal that the 10 did, in fact, represent them when they went to meet with the principal. The principal stated he would speak with three (3) of the students, of his own choosing. The students, however, recognized this as a "divide and conquer" tactic often used by the principal heretofore and refused to accept it.

3. Somewhere around this time, the superintendent and law enforcement officials were called. The principal was instructed by the superintendent to notify the students that they had ten (10) minutes to disperse and return to class. This notification was made; however, the principal denies having called law enforcement officials. During this waiting time, city police, State Police, Sheriff's Department, fire department, and Prosecuting Attorney Gene [Raff] arrived on the scene.

4. Until the time of the arrival of law enforcement officials, students had remained peaceful and orderly. It seems as though some residents of the area had a two-way radio and heard a dispatched call to State Police to "come and help quell a riot at Lee High School." Keep in mind the Blacks contend that all was peaceful until authorities arrived.

5. When the authorities arrived, complications set in. Much of the turn of events can be attributed to a State Trooper, Bob Selph. Although

Courtney Langston fired the first shot, this trooper, upon arrival, reportedly went through the crowd of students "bumping and nudging" the children and saying, "hit me, hit me." (To the best of the knowledge of the persons with whom I spoke, nobody swung at Courtney Langston at any time during the crisis.)

6. Trooper Bob Selph beat, dragged, and kicked Juanita Wright, causing the necessity of sending her to the University of Arkansas Medical Center for treatment.

7. The fire department used high pressure water hoses to "spray down" kids who had not dispersed upon the department's arrival.

8. Captain Galloway, officer in charge of troopers in the area, threatened to beat a parent who came to pick up her child, "get your bigmouth black self on." The parent said to him, "don't talk to my child like that," to which he retorted, "I'll talk to you that way and whip your head too if you don't move along."

9. Principal Blankenship held a young lady, known to him to be pregnant, while she was whipped by a policeman. (It is not clear whether the policeman was local, state or from the Sheriff's office.) The principal also held a young man by the name of Bobby Manley while he was beaten by policemen.

10. Many students were "thrown" on buses to be "taken downtown to be put where you belong." The original 10 students were arrested and charged with "inciting to riot."

11. Law enforcement officials deputized members of the White Citizens Council, but no Black citizens were deputized.

12. A man, identified as an F.B.I. Agent from Forrest City, was reported to be wielding a night stick, although no one actually saw him hit one of the children.

13. People are always talking about how badly local authorities treat Blacks in that area, but the State Troopers are equally as bad. The reason this fact is "unknown" is that the reports are always made by the State Police.

Help must come from outside the area if justice is to prevail. More specifically, the Governor's Office must issue a mandate that State Police cease and desist actions such as those on Thursday, January 13, 1972.

Unanswered Questions

Carl Agers's report adds new information to the story. First of all, Blankenship's refusal to speak with more than three students was a "divide and conquer" tactic that the principal had used with the students in the past. It also is interesting to note that the prosecuting attorney arrived with the police when they were summoned by the school administrators. This is very unusual. Why was the prosecutor there? Does it indicate that the authorities knew of the sit-in plans and had planned their own response in advance? And the civil authorities were called in to quell a "riot", but the students were conducting an orderly sit-in. A gunshot fired by Sheriff Langston caused the students to flee in fear. Principal Blankenship, State Trooper Selph, and Captain Galloway actively threatened, restrained, beat, kicked, and dragged students who had heretofore been peaceful. Members of the white Citizens Council had been deputized, but most significant is that Agers states that help is needed from the outside. So, we have to ask what outside help did the students receive?

Black Parents Sought Help from Governor Bumpers

On the following Monday, January 17, about 150 black Lee County residents, led by Reverend I. V. McKenzie, drove to Little Rock with a list of their concerns and grievances. Governor Bumpers was out of town and the governor's closest aides, Archie Schaffer, Carl Agers, and Tom McRae, met with a committee representing the parents.

Here are a few more pieces of information contained in what they wrote.

The black community in Marianna believed that what was reported by the press was incorrect and incomplete. For example, the students had asked for a thirty-minute assembly to honor Dr. Martin Luther King, not a holiday.

In defense of so many students sitting in the hall to support the ten student leaders who went to speak with Principal Blankenship, they said that in the past he had dismissed a group of five as being too small and not representative of the student body, which is 80% black. The student delegation believed that they had to demonstrate strong support in order to get a hearing.

Witnesses, including the principal and superintendent, had stated that the students were non-violent. However, the students had broken school rules, and the parents felt that the students should be disciplined appropriately by the school system.

The delegation from Marianna was most upset by the beatings and the fact that the students were hit with water from firehoses. They requested a thorough investigation of what happened and wanted legal action taken against the state police officers who could be identified as having assaulted black students.

They also criticized the curfew set by the mayor of Marianna as applying only to blacks. They wanted to protect the rights and well-being of the children and had lost confidence in local officials. Thus, they wanted to know what the state Commissioner of Education could do to help.

Dr. Arch W. Ford, who was head of the State Department of Education (SDEC), and Arkansas State Police Colonel Miller met with the Marianna delegation. Dr. Ford told them that he had no police authority, but he would send a committee from the state education department to investigate the situation from an educational standpoint. Colonel Miller said that he would investigate allegations against the state troopers and take action if warranted.

The Semester-Long School Boycott Begins

When the parent delegation returned to Marianna, a spokesperson for the blacks said, "Marianna parents have agreed to keep black students out of class until 'racism' is ended in the schools. A large group of black parents demanded the resignations of the principal and superintendent of schools. Black teachers also requested that civil and criminal charges against some of the students be dropped, and that the three-day suspension of others be forgotten."

Dr. Ford acted promptly, and less than a week after the controversy, he sent a biracial SDEC committee of three blacks and three whites to Marianna. They came on January 19 and spent the entire day, from 9:05 a.m. to 7:00 p.m., listening to testimony from forty people "representative of the entire spectrum of thought on the matter."

Their report concurs that the student action was a sit-in and not a walk-out. It states, "On January 13, 1972, the morning of the protest, and immediately after the 8:15 bell, groups of students began to gather in the hall around the door of the principal's office."

What Should Have Happened?

I think the SDEC committee walked a narrow line and did a fairly good job under the circumstances. They were accomplished educational professionals from Dr. Ford's staff chosen because they were "moderates" and capable of arriving at consensus. The language and presentation of their report was measured and neither conciliatory nor an outright condemnation of the students. However, it is clear that this group came down in support of the traditional white establishment. The Marianna school administration and the civil authorities were satisfied, but the black community was disappointed. Many students faced criminal charges and many more lost a semester of school.

The SDEC's report rests on Principal Blankenship's inability to get the students to go to their classes. As I look back, I can say that he at least should have tried. He should have talked to all student leaders. When you have authority, you are bound and obligated to be fair and evenhanded to everybody even if you don't like them or are uncomfortable with what they are doing or saying. The record states that the students were orderly, and a reasonable person certainly could have talked to those kids (and their parents). I would have spent more time listening than talking. As long as they were orderly, it was the right time to listen to their complaints and figure out what was going on. I also would have let them know that we could work it out, but in the end that they probably would not all be perfectly happy with the results and I probably would not be perfectly happy either. They also needed to know that the school had to keep operating in order for the situation to be addressed and resolved.

Blankenship said that if he had talked to the students under the circumstances it would have been interpreted as a victory for the students and a loss of face for him. But, hell, he did not have to be concerned with loss of face. He was in charge. He had forgotten that *he was the principal*. I think that Blankenship's fatal flaw was being worried that he would lose face by talking with the students. You can't be a leader and operate that way. It meant that he cut himself off from those who could have helped him resolve the situation.

A principal's responsibility and obligation is to his students. When faced with a difficulty such as the student sit-in, he must be able to rise above the stressful circumstances and not let himself feel threatened. As leader of an educational institution, it is his duty to remember that his responsibility includes troublesome students and he has an obligation to do the right thing for them too. But I do have to acknowledge that this was a very difficult time with unsettling changes going on everywhere. Many people who are excellent in times of routine leadership are not cut out to handle the most serious and difficult situations. This apparently was true for Principal Blankenship. He failed the black students when he refused to listen to them. And he failed the parents when he refused to protect their children from the sheriff, state police, and fire department.

I agree with Mrs. Gertha Trice, who had two of her twelve children at the high school during the sit-in. She told Blankenship at the time, "We accuse you of running scared in a time when indeed straightforward empathy, warmth and genuineness was needed." This was absolutely true. Mrs. Trice was an aide at the Clinic, and she was one of the parents who went to seek help from the governor. I supported her involvement even when I was doubtful of success. Mrs. Trice did not have much schooling, but she used words that made her sound well educated and she was determined. All this made her a strong advocate.

Firebombs and Gunshots

Following the disastrous events at Lee High School, there were more incidents of violence in Marianna reported in statewide newspapers. The black community was outraged. It was an out-of-control anger at what had been done to our children. In the night after the students were attacked on school grounds, someone firebombed the home of Deputy Sheriff Jimmy Burrows.

On January 23, most of the black part of downtown including the Concerned Citizens' office was firebombed and burned out. Some of the hostility felt in the black community was a hardened undercurrent of bitterness from decades of white condescension and suppression. On top of that now was something new—a powerful, no discussion, we-got-to-get-even kind of anger. The Concerned Citizens had considerably less control than earlier when we were outside the courthouse waiting for election results in 1970 or downtown after Hack Adams tried to run over Prentiss and Cheeks in 1971. This time the kids were at the center. Superintendent Dial and his family were threatened in a phone call. A shot was fired and almost hit School Board Chairman Lon Mann as he was entering his house. Some black families that defied the school boycott had firebombs thrown at their houses or threatening signs put in their yards. The school boycott continued to the end of the school year. And what happened during these five months continued to affect the young black students for the rest of their lives.

Students Found Guilty of Inciting a Riot and Suspended

About 60% of the students enrolled in the school district joined the boycott and did not go to school for the rest of the year. A total of 117 students were charged with disrupting the high school, and they were tried in a series of municipal court trials held mostly on weekends from March through May. The presiding judge, Cecil Matthews, was from Stuttgart. Fifty students were found guilty, thirty-four students were found innocent, and thirty-three cases were dismissed for lack of evidence.

Superintendent Dial resigned at the end of the school year. He was quoted in the April 10, 1972, *Press-Scimitar*, a Memphis paper that included excellent coverage of east Arkansas, as saying, "I'm tired. I've been under a lot of duress. I've reached a point where I feel a new face will help the situation much better than I can."

Forty-Five Years Later

This is what four students who were active participants had to say decades later about the sit-in and boycott.

Lillie Perry, one of the ten student leaders, said this in a 2017 phone interview:

> I really saw how different they treated white and black students when I was in the tenth grade at Futrell. We had a little group whose parents were active in the movement and we hung out together. We would band together, and then more and more students started following with us. Whenever anyone had a problem they would call me. Pretty much all we wanted was to go to class and get a good education like everyone else. When we protested about some things, a lot of the white kids would call us "nigger." I had never been exposed to this before.
>
> Mrs. Warner was a good white math teacher, and she was fair to everyone. Mrs. Clark was black and she was fair too. She was a good teacher, and she tried to help us. Every time you turned around there was trouble in the hall with a white kid calling a black kid "nigger." That year at Futrell we had a really prejudiced principal, Ronnie Austin. Mr. Robert Scott was a librarian at Nunnelly Elementary School, and we suggested him to come to Futrell. Things got better with him there.
>
> The next year at Lee High School we had more problems. When it was time to go back to school they wanted a white queen and black queen on the football court, and we didn't want that. We put our foot down about that. There were meetings at night, and the adults were guiding us. We decided to take our grievances to the principal on January 13 with a sit-in. We were communicating by phone and had told everybody that when we got to school that morning to sit down, and they did. I was in that group of ten who stayed standing and got handcuffed and taken off to jail. Most of us were juniors. We were charged with inciting a riot. The police made the riot. Someone got a whiff of it, and the police and press

were there really fast.

During the boycott what happened was we ended up hanging out. But we weren't just sitting around. We were doing something positive. We formed the Lee County Community Youth Choir and went around to sing at the churches. My mom helped make our uniforms. Rabon Cheeks helped us with flyers and stuff. My parents owned their own land, and nobody could tell them to move. My dad went to the meetings, but we had so many people who lived on a "mr. sonny boy's" farm and worked in his fields. They could get kicked off and so they couldn't come and be with the movement like my dad. So I had a better advantage.

When we missed so much school during the boycott, my parents couldn't send me anywhere because I didn't have any relatives to go live with. And my parents couldn't afford to buy me correspondence courses. I ended up taking [both] eleventh- and twelfth-grade English my senior year and I took my math that year and also an elective, and I got enough credits to graduate on time with the class of 1973. Some of the 1972 class graduated with us too. They only needed a few classes to graduate, and after they took them, they could graduate. But some of the students in the class of 1972 never did graduate after the boycott. I mean, it was terrible for them.

Larry Smith, one of the ten student leaders, said this in a 2017 phone interview:

We started an organization called Junior Southern Christian Leadership Conference, and I was president. I was pushed into that spot. I was a soft-spoken person, and they said people would listen to me. I did pretty good. They told me I was a natural leader. I don't do outbursts. I weigh it out and make a decision after thinking, not on emotions. I was a hands-on leader. I was in the middle of it.

At a meeting after the sit-in, we decided Rodney Slater and Dennis Winston should go on back to school because they had a chance to get out and they needed to get their scholarships. The rest of us would boycott. Then during the boycott, different people would give us homework so we wouldn't be too far behind.

After the sit-in, the student leaders were suspended from school. I remember going before the judge…and we got a misdemeanor charge and I pleaded not guilty. I'm not sure about the others but I was suspended, so I couldn't graduate. When I got my suspension sentence, my

Momma was upset in the court and started acting the fool. She wanted me to graduate. I was kind of a Momma's boy. The judge had already pronounced his sentence. He didn't listen to her.

I ended up in St Louis with my sister [and] I went into the military. That was when too many were dying in Vietnam. My Momma didn't want me to go to Vietnam, so I volunteered for the Air Force to avoid the Army. She signed for me because I was only 17. I got my high school diploma while I was in the military.

I guess the boycott did have some bad effect on me. Before the boycott I was playing football, and I liked football. I had to give that up and I was separated from my friends. I expected some consequences, but I had to make a big life adjustment.

I don't put blame on anyone. I can't see anybody I would blame. I don't even blame the white people for this either. That was just how it was. I don't hate white people. And there was a good thing that came from the boycott. It helped us form unity. We are still friends and get together nearly every year.

After I was in the military, I came to back Marianna because I didn't know what else to do. And I have spent some time in prison.

Carolyn Brown Elliott was an excellent student, active in the band and student council, and she was Lee Senior High School student council president. Her father, Reverend Spencer Brown, was a leader in Marianna's black community. She said this in a 2017 phone interview:

In the black schools, we had student council and we were big on student government. But when we got to Futrell a group of citizens came to me and said, "We want you to relinquish your position as president of the student government and allow Billy Gerard Jr. to be the president because the white kids elected him. And of course, next year, you will win because there are more black students than white students."

I told them that I understood their concerns and felt now that we were in one school, the student with the most votes should be the president. But they did not want that. I am not going to name any names, but they decided that we should have co-chairs of the student council. Billy Gerard would chair the meeting one time and I would chair the meeting the next time. The problem was that in our community Robert's Rules of Order were a big thing. Billy Gerard was bright, but he didn't know any meeting procedure. His meetings were awful, and he was just eaten alive. Everybody saw him as privileged, and they really thought that he didn't deserve his position.

Things went downhill in the classrooms, social organizations, and athletics. It got so bad that when we tried to approach teachers about our concerns, they were very uncomfortable. In my mind, everything started to go crazy in the fall of 1971 when the white kids left to go to their all-white Lee Academy. We called it the "auction barn school" because it was a big metal building and that's what it looked like. It is still there.

We had a white counselor that put Rodney Slater, a high-level student, in special ed. I'm sure that counselor regrets it today because in 1980 Rodney got his law degree from the University of Arkansas and he was the first African American to serve as director of the Federal Highway Administration. There was a white woman put over the English department. She came to school intoxicated. She reeked of alcohol, and the kids knew that she was drinking. We experienced all kinds of discrepancies in the grading process. It was just not a fair shake.

We had been taught to respect our elders. Even if they were wrong, you were to respect them. But now the people in authority were our enemies. When we went to Mr. Blankenship to talk to him peacefully, he refused to talk to our representatives. When we were sitting on the floor, the thing that the cameras failed to capture was that it was an integrated group of students. It was not just black students protesting for Martin Luther King. Mark was white. He had long blond hair halfway down his back. He was not afraid of black kids, and he agreed with us. I can't think of his last name.

They ran us from the building and locked the doors on us so we couldn't go back in. They chased us and sprayed us with the fire hose. I had on my brand-new band blazer and my Christmas shoes. I got water hosed and was screaming. My cousin Charlotte and Frank Humbert were running out together. The police hit Charlotte with a billy club and put her in the bus. I was screaming at them, "How could you hit my cousin?" I didn't really know Frank at that time, but he pulled me out of the way, and we ran across the field and through the back of the cemetery.

Different people let children come into their homes. My dad had just gone to the lumber company because he was building a house, and he was driving west down 79 toward our home. He had already picked up a carload of kids who had gone through the electric wire where they had some Black Angus cows. Then, lo and behold, there is his own daughter covered with mud coming out from behind the cemetery. He took all of us to our home and told my mother to clean us up and feed everyone.

He went in to town to talk and she took care of us.

After the boycott, I would not go back to that school. I would never let anybody do that to me again. That was an awful experience. I was sitting on the floor because of injustice. I wasn't yelling. I wasn't screaming. I wasn't being disrespectful and neither was anyone else. We were NOT being disruptive. And those people sprayed us with a water hose. And then the good citizens, who my parents had taught me to respect, came and beat us up. FOR NO REASON!

Lee Ester Vaughn, one of the ten student leaders, said this in a 2017 phone interview:

I have older sisters and sisters under me. I was the outspoken one in my family, and I was a good student. My parents trusted me and what we were doing. We just wanted to get some things changed. When the principal wouldn't talk to us, students were locked out of the building and were sprayed with water from a fire truck. Guys stepped up to protect the girls.

Afterwards I did not return to school in Marianna. I went to Detroit to finish. If I could, I would go through it again. I would do it if it would help someone. I think it did a lot for Marianna. It helped the town because otherwise nothing would have changed. Looking back, I believe that I learned a lot about segregation and prejudice.

Community Leader Support

The Marianna boycotts were one of the hardest times of my life. The economic boycott was hard, but the school boycott was worse. While students and parents may choose to take the step of boycotting at the moment they are upset, this type of action is especially hard on them, and it can wear everyone down. I thought the school boycott would do that to us. I tried to resist it, but I couldn't, so I got credit for being very supportive and that was a hard thing. The school boycott just made awful anxiety and stress for the families. If they didn't go to school, those kids had no place to go but stay home. And because of all the trouble that would cause, I didn't think the parents could stand behind the boycott for very long.

When I talked to Sterling King at the time about the school boycott, he and I agreed that it was not the best thing. He was probably even more against it than I was, but I remember him saying, "You can't stop it. You have to try to guide it the best you can." I ended up going that route not because it made the best sense but because the community was enraged by what had happened to their children. And the preachers supported a boycott of the school too because that is what their church members wanted.

I felt it my duty as a leader in the black community to support the parents and the preachers when they said, "We got to keep our kids at home." But what was especially difficult for me was that I have never accepted that a school boycott can bring about substantial change in a hopelessly low-income community. As I see it, education is the only hope for young people. If children are going to school, they grow up with the possibility and hope of getting better jobs due to that education. When kids stay out of school, they have lost their only way out of the poverty of their birth. I believed this then, and I still do today.

Chapter 10
The Big Grant

T he school boycott erupted in January 1972, the economic boycott continued, and in April the Clinic applied for a big grant that had to be
approved by Governor Bumpers. Looking back, we can see and understand these as distinct and separate events, but at the time they were indel-
ibly connected in the minds of our white opposition. They saw the Clinic,
the economic boycott, and the school boycott as trouble, and they blamed
me and a few others for all the trouble they were having.

Fearless and Outspoken

I figured that I was a good average son of a gun with a little bit more
nerve than many. The biggest thing I brought to the black community was
a kind of fearlessness. I think this was important. I came to believe that,
more than anything else, my people needed someone to stand up and be
their voice. So, the fearlessness was essential. I don't mean that I always felt
no fear, but I acted fearless. I was a strong voice. I was outspoken. And I
was willing to go forward in spite of obstacles or difficulties.

One day I got a small envelope in the mail. It was addressed this way:

Olly Neal

Nigger

That's all. It had a postmark from Harrison, Arkansas, and the mailman
delivered it to me in Marianna. There was a one-page letter inside and I
remember it saying, *"you better get out of town or we got something for you."*
It showed some serious animosity and I guess the threat was supposed to
scare me, but I was just amused.

Racial tension shot through every interaction between black and white at
that time. I was riled up. I don't mean to say that I was the perfect person. I
didn't give a damn. I was carrying a gun. I thought I was going to be killed,
and I didn't want to die without at least fighting back. I didn't want to die
on my knees, so to speak.

My "Discussion" with Harold Meins

Harold Meins was an officer in the Lee County white Citizens Council,
and he was one of the three people who sued to stop the Clinic's grant
money. Harold started sitting in his station wagon across the street from
the Clinic building on Liberty Street. And when I saw him there, I didn't

know what he had, so I started bringing my shotgun to the Clinic. My office was upstairs in the attic. I brought my gun every day. When I went up the stairs, my briefcase was in one hand and that shotgun was in the other. No case.

I think some of the Clinic folks were concerned about it, but carrying that gun was a choice I made because I really did think I was going to be shot. And Dr. Redlener was also carrying. His doctor bag was a tool box. It held whatever stuff a doctor carries when making house calls, and his little .38 pistol was in there too. I remember one morning Meins was sitting out in front of the building and I had had enough. I decided to go down and run him off. As I was walking out, Redlener said, "Wait a minute, I can come too." He wanted me to know that he had my back. But I went out alone and walked up to Meins's car and told him that he was intimidating our staff and patients and he had to get on out of there. As I spoke, I sort of lifted the arm that was holding my shotgun to remind him that I had the gun. It was a public street and he had the right to park there, but he drove off and never came back again.

Dr. Redlener Designed the Clinic

Dr. Redlener thought big, and he played a critical role at the Clinic around this time. We had two doctors treating patients by then, so our little rented building was way too small. Dr. Redlener sold me and the board on the idea that we should build what we needed and some more for the future. He designed the entire building. We applied to the Office of Health Affairs (OHA) for a whopping $1.2 million grant—$600,000 for the land, material, and construction and $600,000 for the first fifteen months of Clinic operations in the new building. It was fifteen months rather than twelve because the federal government was changing the beginning of the next fiscal year from July 1 to October 1.

Dr. Leon Cooper Gave Me Confidence

In the meantime, the Clinic had some tricky hoops to jump through to get a new building. An OHA grant had to be approved in Washington, Governor Bumpers had to sign off on it at the state level, and we had to have a contract on the land where the new Clinic would be built. As the head of OHA, Dr. Leon Cooper liked us okay, but he was not a patient man, and the Clinic was giving him some headaches. Sonny Walker was a guy from Arkansas who I had known when he directed the Community Action

Agency in Little Rock. Now he was running the Southeast OEO in Atlanta, and he knew Dr. Cooper. One day Sonny called me and asked if I could get to his house in Atlanta by 7:00 that evening. I said, "Hell yes, I have a flight that will get me there at 5:30."

This is how Sonny Walker, Dr. Cooper, and I met to see if we could figure out how to convince Governor Bumpers to sign off on our OHA grant. From the days in Little Rock, Sonny knew that I could drink. After Cooper and I arrived, he set a fifth of Granddad 100 proof on the table, and we got good and comfortable. Not drunk but comfortable. Somewhere between 1:30 and 2:00 a.m., the three of us decided that it might be a good idea to call Bumpers. I had the inside number at the Governor's Mansion, so I dialed him up. And damn if he didn't answer the phone.

He got two of his aides on the line too, and we were on the phone for over an hour. We talked and they listened and asked questions. He didn't promise us that he was going to sign the thing, but we got the distinct impression that he did not want to veto it. That was a profound moment for me. Before that phone call, I would never have believed that a white person in a position of power was interested in anything except to be in charge. But Bumpers cared enough about the Clinic and the poor people we served to take my call and listen. And I know that Cooper was impressed too. He told me in no uncertain terms that if our grant did not get the governor's signature, there might be a way to override it, but Cooper also told me that this information was strictly private and could not be shared with anyone—no one, not even a solid friend of the Clinic.

The important thing that Dr. Cooper helped me understand was that I needed to be realistic, but I should not change course just because I was afraid of failure. And I was uncertain. I had all these black folks and some whites too in Lee County who believed, "Olly Neal will save our Clinic." But until this point I didn't know at all that I had a chance. Now, knowing that we had solid support in Washington gave me the confidence I needed. I felt damn lucky and I became more positive. And I needed to be more positive. In Lee County, the white community had organized intense opposition to the grant and the Clinic's credibility was being attacked. It really was the time I needed to be strong and confident.

Intense Opposition

On February 7, 1972, four Lee County doctors—F. S. Dozier, E. C. Fields, Dwight W. Gray, and Mac McLendon—signed a letter to OHA saying this about our grant and the Clinic: "the majority of the statistics quoted under General Information, I- Lee County Profile are inaccurate and falsified. Since the Lee County Co-operative Clinic or so called Vista has been in our Community, we experienced nothing but turmoil, chaos and upheaval amoung [*sic*] our citizens both black and white."

In early March, Governor Bumpers received a barrage of telegrams begging him not to allow the Clinic grant and in some cases threatening him with his political demise if he did. Here is a sampling, without any editing:

I AM STRENOUSLY OPPOSED TO THE FEDERAL GRANT FOR CONTINUATION OF THE LEE CO COOPERATIVE CLINIC AS THE WORKERS WERE INSTIGATORS OF THE BOYCOTTS HERE THE GRANT HAS BEEN HANDLED ILLEGALLY PLEASE TAKE ACTION AGAINST VISTA AND OEO.

EXPANSION OF LEE CO. CO-OP CLINIC SHOULD BE DELAYED UNTIL RESPONSIBLE SUPERVISION IS A REALITY. COMMUNITY AND SCHOOL SYSTEM ARE BEING WRECKED BY THE SAME PEOPLE WHO ARE BOOSTING THE CLINIC. THIS DOESN'T MAKE SENSE.

PLEASE FOR ONCE BE A WHITE MAN AND HELP US IN LEE COUNTY. REMEMBER VOTES PUT YOU IN OFFICE AND WHITE VOTES CAN PUT YOU OUT. DO YOU WISH TO BE A ONE TERM GOVERNOR

WE ARE SICK OF ILLS CAUSED BY LEE COOP CLINIC AND VISTA WE IMPLORE YOU TO STOP FUNDING THE SAME.

ALL POLARIZATION OF RACES CAUSED BY DIRECT PARTICIPATION OF STAFF MEMBERS OF LEE COUNTY COOP CLINIC MUST BE STOPPED – CLINIC STAFF NOT INTERESTED IN HEALTH AND WELFARE OF PEOPLE IN LEE COUNTY, ONLY INTERESTED IN FEDERAL MONEY TO SQUANDER AND POLITICAL POWER TO ABUSE

(Governor Bumpers's Papers, UA Little Rock Center for Arkansas History and Culture, CALS Roberts Library, Little Rock, Arkansas)

Pressure from the white community continued to intensify as the deadline for the governor's signature approached. White Citizens Council people wanted Governor Bumpers to shut us down altogether. They had already met with him and presented their position.

Some of the more reasonable white people in Lee County recognized that the Clinic offered important health services, but in a document sent to Governor Bumpers on March 4, 1972, they insisted that "the white community should be represented on the Clinic board." And they stated, "The Clinic must be forced to accept the White representation. They will not voluntarily accept this because of racial tension and distrust. This stipulation can be tied to the funds the Clinic expects to receive..."

Mrs. Sarah Sauls Speaks to Governor Bumpers

We did not know what the governor was going to do. At our regular board meeting in March 1972, Mrs. Sauls, our certified midwife from the Rondo/Aubrey NAC, asked me if the board could go meet with the governor too. And I thought, why not? I called the governor's office on a Tuesday, but the governor was out of town. He wouldn't be back until Saturday evening, so Sunday was the earliest he could see us. He actually agreed to meet with us on that Sunday evening.

At our meeting with the governor we were served tea and teacakes. The teacakes were good, and the tea came in little cups with handles too small for your fingers. Governor Bumpers kept directing his remarks to me and was peppering my ass with questions. He just wouldn't stop. He must have thought all the resistance against the plan to include white representatives on our board was coming from me.

Mrs. Sauls was born in 1907, so she was in her mid-sixties. She looked like a nice little church lady too and was a very shy woman who never said very much at all. But she spoke up to the governor, saying, "Mr. Bumpers, can I say something?" Now Bumpers was good with names and he said, "Yes, of course, Mrs. Sauls, you go right ahead." And she said, "We appreciate you letting us come up here and talk with you and we know you could be doing other things, and these are fine teacakes and we thank you. But we need the grant money and we want you to help us keep our Clinic. We understand that those people are asking us to change our board, but we have bylaws that tell us how to operate and we can't change how our board is set up without a special kind of meeting. We sure hope you will sign off on our grant so we can go ahead with our Clinic."

I had worked hard so the board would understand exactly what our by-laws said. And even though some of our board members could not read real well, they all understood that the bylaws required board members to be elected by the NACs. Mrs. Sauls had it right. She was a thoughtful woman. There was nothing I could have said that would have been better. Without her, Governor Bumpers could have looked at me and thought he was dealing with a hotshot rabble-rouser and turned his back on us. As a midwife, Mrs. Sauls knew first-hand how important our Clinic was to the black community. She chose just the right words and she spoke from her heart. I can't emphasize enough how important this was. I mean to tell you it was profound!

If Governor Bumpers had not signed off on the grant, Dr. Cooper had mentioned a way to request that our grant be funded over the governor's objection, but in truth this was a lengthy process and probably would take too long for us to make the current June 30 deadline. And we knew that Big John McClellan, Arkansas senator and chairman of the appropriations committee, did not support the Clinic. With the fierce white opposition coming down on us, we knew that, given more time, Senator McClellan would probably step in and make everything fall apart.

Revolutionaries?

Evidence of what I would call extreme opposition from the white community can be found in Governor Bumpers's papers. They include a number of identical petitions sent to him and signed by many residents mostly of counties near Lee but also from other parts of the state. The petition stated that the unrest in Marianna was of concern to residents of the surrounding area because "the tensions have grown to alarming proportions and now show signs of spreading." And then it got a little crazy... One petition ended: "The actions of the black militants have served to incite the whites who are in turn threatening counterviolence. This same tactic has been used before, not only in the United States but, in the Governmental takeover by Castro in Cuba, by Ben Bella in Algeria, and by Mao Tse Tung in China. It is our belief that the funds that were recently appropriated by the O.E.O. for the local V.I.S.T.A. Clinic have only added fuel to an already smoldering situation. For this reason we ask you, our Governor, to seek a suspension of said funds until credible and unbiased personnel can be found to work peacefully with the disadvantaged in Lee County without arousing the ire of either the black or the white community." (Governor

Bumpers's Papers, UA Little Rock Center for Arkansas History and Culture, CALS Roberts Library, Little Rock, Arkansas)

In other words, they considered us to be revolutionaries like Castro, Mao Tse Tung, and Ben Bella! And they wanted the Clinic funding to be stopped until the local revolutionaries—me and the others who spoke up for the black community—were somehow eliminated.

We did have the notion that changes for a better life in Lee County could spread into St. Francis and Phillips Counties too, but all we wanted was for black folks everywhere to have the same rights and benefits that white folks enjoyed.

Lon Mann's Influence

It seems that Governor Bumpers felt threatened by us too. He wrote, "I have felt that with the removal of one percent of the right people in Marianna, the problems could be solved." This was in response to a white Marianna resident's letter complaining about her "town being torn apart by racial strife."

In spite of this, I have to say that Governor Bumpers was a damn good politician. I did and still do admire him for that. He was in a nearly impossible situation handling the Clinic grant controversy, and he did his best to find common ground when there really wasn't much to stand on. Also, at the time, I was not aware of another fact, but since then have been told that Lon Mann ended up giving in and he worked behind the scenes playing a role in Bumpers's final decision to approve.

I don't think that Lon Mann "found religion," so to speak, and changed what he thought about us. I always felt that he did not like me and saw me as trouble. But Lon Mann was smart and practical. I believe that he assessed the situation and realized that absolute opposition wasn't going to cut it. His opposition slowed because he saw that it was not working. This is the only way I can understand what he did.

Bumpers's Conditional Approval

Bumpers finally announced his approval of an amended grant for the Lee County Cooperative Clinic in an April 6, 1972, press release. To summarize the most important points, it stated that after negotiations between the Office of Economic Opportunity in Washington and the Lee County Cooperative Clinic, the grant was amended to include three conditions. But there was *no change to the way the Clinic board of directors were elected*! This was a huge victory for the Clinic. This is what Mrs. Sauls and all of us had been requesting. It meant LCCC could continue operating under the control of the people it served. The amended grant required an advisory committee with representatives appointed from the following five agencies:

- State Comprehensive Health Planning
- Arkansas Regional Medical Program
- Arkansas Health Systems Foundation
- State Health Department
- Eastern Arkansas Planning and Development District

Governor Bumpers ended his announcement concerning the Clinic grant approval by saying: "From the beginning, my conscience has dictated that the moral issue be given precedence over any other issue. The moral issue in this instance is the undeniable fact that the clinic provides critically needed health care to many indigent individuals and families. In my mind, this outweighs all other considerations. However, it does not completely exclude them. My decision on this matter has been delayed as long as possible, not because I have been undecided, but because I had hoped the conditions I seek could be implemented prior to this announcement. I regret that this has not been possible. However, current negotiations are very favorable." (Governor Bumpers's Papers, UA Little Rock Center for Arkansas History and Culture, CALS Roberts Library, Little Rock, Arkansas)

As head of OHA, Dr. Cooper had assistants, who normally were the ones to talk to health center administrators like me, but in early 1972 he and I were talking regularly about our delicate situation. He convinced me that the Clinic should agree to have advisors with a bigger view of health care, and he pressed the governor to accept this in lieu of bringing in local people just because they were white.

The only advisory committee member of concern to me was the Eastern Arkansas Planning and Development District, which I knew to be an enemy of the Clinic. When I had gone to them asking for their support, they tried to block approval of our grant. Their board included a white guy, Mack Harbour from Paragould, who had major clout because he was a respected health professional. Harbour was articulate, and he was dead set against us. There were three blacks on that board, but only one, Leon Phillips Jr., was at this meeting. I knew the other two, John Clark and Lacey

Kennedy, and I was mad as hell at them for not showing up.

Phillips was a quiet person who was not particularly well-spoken, and I was shocked when he stood up and made a beautiful speech in support of the Clinic. In his slow and stumbling voice, he talked about how we were improving the health of the little children and made special mention of the water and sewer systems we were building in Arkansas's rural communities. When he wrapped it all up, he said, "The problem you folks have is that you can't stand to see a black man in charge." That was it!

His speech completely shut down any further discussion. While his talk was courageous and insightful, the Clinic did not get a vote of support. We just didn't have it. But what Phillips did was important. He could easily have sat there and said nothing. If he had just kept quiet, he surely would have gotten along better with those white people. So, I have always remembered his courage and admired him for trying.

Mr. Willie Gordon and Getting the Land

The Clinic's funding story doesn't end with Governor Bumpers's signature. Getting the grant money also hinged on having a contract for the land for our new building. And I was having a damn hard time with this too. Today, the Clinic buying some land in Marianna probably sounds straight-forward and simple, but it wasn't easy in 1972. I was an unpopular person with Marianna's landed gentry, and I could not find anyone who would sell us their land. I located two properties, but as soon as they learned that I was involved, the owners backed out. They did not want to deal with me.

After I enlisted the help of one of our board members, Mr. Willie Gordon, everything changed. For his entire life, Mr. Gordon had lived in Rondo, where he farmed 300 to 400 acres, and he was much more acceptable to the white community than I was. But Mr. Gordon never saw himself as being important. He always referred to himself as "Little Willie Gordon." One day I told him, "I am being dropped on this land thing. You know who owns what and who will do what and I need your help." He told me that he did know somebody with land for sale, and I asked him to negotiate for us. He said to me, "You think I can do that?" I said, "Yes, sir, Mr. Gordon, you're our man. You are farming all that land out there. You can just tell them what you want to do and see what they say." So, Mr. Gordon did that, and he is the reason the Clinic stands where it does today. He found the property and got those folks to agree to sell it to us.

After we found the land, all I had to do was complete the paperwork, but of course the paperwork put me straight into another problem. This property was part of the Foreman Estate, and the trustee was at a bank in Memphis. He had hired Jimason Daggett, head of the most prestigious law firm in Marianna, to handle the transaction. The folks selling the land didn't care a damn who was buying, but Daggett tried to block us by sitting on the deed and not getting it signed.

We had a deadline and we were at a stalemate. The situation was so sensitive that it was beyond me to figure out a way to get past Daggett. But I felt that I shouldn't be saying much about it to the Clinic board. I never went so far as to say that Daggett was balking. I might have told them that we were having a little trouble with the land. That's all.

When I look back on this I have to laugh because I didn't think it through and figure out what to do. I just got up one morning in late June, got in my car, and took the deed over to that trustee in Memphis myself. It may have been wrong of me, but I told the trustee that Mr. Daggett had looked at it and I needed to move this thing along. The trustee went ahead and signed the paper, and I carried that signed deed right back to Marianna. I drove straight to the courthouse, filed it, and sent a copy to Daggett. I just did it, and Jimason Daggett never once said anything to me about it. I had outfoxed him.

Chapter 11
Law School 1974–1978

Our Big Grant troubles hammered us in the first half of the year, but after that everything calmed down. With our land and the grant money in place, we got to work. The new building went up without any more conflict or any construction delays. We hired American Building Guild, Inc., from Milwaukee to be our architect and general contractor, and local craftsmen were included in the construction. We awarded the carpentry and plumbing subcontracts to locals Jesse Booker and Joe Dean. And our masonry subcontractor, who was not local, hired Marianna's best brick layer, Connor Grady, after Grady told us that he preferred this arrangement.

Suddenly, racist opposition to the Clinic became a non-issue. As the new 7,466-square-foot building went up, the opposition went down. Our position strengthened, and all the fight drained out of Lee County's white community. A good example is J. B. Smith, a prominent insurance agent in Marianna. Until then, J. B. had been an active opponent, but now the Clinic was a business opportunity, and he gave us a good deal on our building insurance.

The new building housed a pharmacy, a dental clinic, examination rooms, consultation rooms, an X-ray room, a laboratory, business offices, and a waiting room with a small play area for children. Our professional health providers included two physicians, one dentist, two pharmacists, three lab technicians, two physician's assistants, five registered nurses, one nutritionist, one childhood development specialist, and fourteen health aides. The Clinic was ready to provide comprehensive health care for the indigent of Lee County. And as our services improved and the Clinic was no longer controversial, our white patient population grew from near zero to something over 20%.

Me, Ethelyn, and the Clinic

I met Ethelyn in 1971 shortly after she completed her residency. She was a pediatrician working at the Mound Bayou community clinic, and Dr. Ben Hubby introduced us. Ben worked with Ethelyn in Mound Bayou, and he worked in our Clinic one day a week.

Ethelyn was a tall, lanky woman, and she had her style. It was a nice interlude. I would drive over to Mound Bayou, and we would get together in Memphis sometimes. Ethelyn was ready to get married, but I had been married twice already and marriage wasn't high on my agenda. Then sometime in 1972 Ethelyn told me she had been invited to go on a study in Paris the next summer. She made it clear to me that if I had any thoughts about our future, now was the time to express them.

I thought about it. I wasn't nineteen years old anymore, so it wasn't one of those situations where I couldn't sleep at night. But she was a good woman. She was solid in every way I could think of, and it seemed like the right time for me to settle down some. I believe that both of us were acting like reasonable adults, and we got married on March 3, 1973. This was about a year after the birth of my daughter Karama. Ethelyn was not her mother. Karama lived with her mother in Little Rock, where she was raised. I'll say much more about Karama later in the section on family. Some people think I married Ethelyn because she was a doctor, but that wasn't it. She was a fine person and we were married for twelve years. I knew it wouldn't hurt if she decided to come over to work at the Clinic. But I also thought that she might not want to stay indefinitely, and she might want to work in Memphis one day.

In a 2017 interview, Ethelyn had this to say:

> Ben Hubby lived in Mound Bayou and was trying to fix us up. He invited both of us to come to his house for dinner. I lived in an apartment right down the road and I could walk to his house. Olly and I knew some of the same people. He had gone to LeMoyne College in Memphis and he knew some of my high school friends who went there. We talked and we hit it off. To me it wasn't like we were being put together.
>
> Olly had invited me to come over to his Clinic in Marianna and he said that he would show me around, but the truth was that I didn't come for a long time. One day I was off, and I just decided to run over there. I called him and he said, "Come on." I think that he was especially proud to show a black doctor what they were doing. Dr. Redlener and all of the staff were very enthusiastic.
>
> My Momma and Daddy were living when we got married. We had a small wedding in Memphis. I didn't go to Marianna to work. I went to Marianna because I got married, but I think that Olly was expecting me to work there. All the doctors at the Clinic were only there on a temporary basis, and as soon as I arrived, Irwin Redlener left. When he left, the Clinic didn't have a pediatrician. Of course, the people in the community assumed that I was going to work there. I suspect that they thought, "We got a 'Momma' with us now. Olly got a wife and she

is a pediatrician!" I really don't know for sure what they thought. But anyway we just decided to get married. If Redlener had stayed, I might not have worked at the Clinic. I could have commuted someplace else. Redlener might just have waited to leave until after we got married, but I don't know. Anyway, they needed a doctor to see the children.

Ethelyn probably had a lot to do with keeping the Clinic together when she was here. She was a very good doctor and very patient with the other staff. We had these two doctors who were husband and wife: Charles and Renee Stringham. They were unrealistic and difficult to work with. For example, they insisted on putting money for a Selectric typewriter in the Clinic budget, and we never did extras like that. We had to budget our money for essential medical stuff. They even wrote a letter to the board demanding that we get that typewriter. I don't know how the hell Ethelyn could tolerate working with them every day. They were troublesome, and I have to give her credit. She was always calm and never, ever difficult to deal with herself. Every chance she had, she was supportive.

Ethelyn also has these memories of working at the Clinic:

> I was the Clinic's medical director, and I think that Olly and I worked well together. We had a relationship with the Medical School in Little Rock, and the Clinic referred a lot of our patients to be seen over there. Sometimes I would drive myself or ride the bus with our patients, so I could go on grand rounds with students at the medical school. This was a great connection for me. I was keeping up and not so isolated.
>
> I am diabetic and take particular interest in my diabetic patients. Dr. Joycelyn Elders was a pediatric endocrinology specialist at the medical school in Little Rock, and I sent some of my diabetic patients to her. She always encouraged me. She would tell me, "You're doing fine." Also, Dr. Elders was the first black woman to become the United States Surgeon General. She was appointed by President Clinton.
>
> The University of Arkansas gave me an unpaid faculty appointment. I supervised their medical students when they came to us for four to six weeks of clinical experience and training. I also made a similar connection with the University of Wisconsin medical school through Dr. Pinkel, who was a friend of Olly's and director of St. Jude's in Memphis.

Run for State Senate

The Clinic was moving forward, but I was restless in my routine job and looking for a new challenge. All my experiences after coming back home had kept me intensely interested in local politics. Then, in the summer of 1973, my district's state senator, who was a white boy, got convicted of income tax evasion and was removed from office. I just thought, "Here is my chance," and I decided to run for his seat.

The special election was in October. Back then they thought it improper for the Clinic's CEO to run for public office (later that changed), so I had to take a leave of absence. I talked it up and convinced Sterling King to drop out of graduate school for his fall semester so he could come home to direct the Clinic. I don't remember it being very difficult to convince him either. He was still connected to Lee County and happy to come back and help. I also had to convince the Clinic board of directors to agree to my plan. They all knew Sterling and liked him. They knew he could do everything I could do in terms of making the Clinic run properly, and they considered him to be a much nicer guy than I was.

I ran against Paul Benham, who was an insurance broker in Marianna and a planter. He owned some property, and his operation was out in the Jack Nash/Council area. Two ex-VISTAs, Earl Anthes and Jerry Cronin, helped me develop my campaign platform. They put the whole damn thing together for me. Earl took some photographs and was sort of like an advance man. I had a track record of being able to make things happen. But when I went to J. Bill Becker, longtime head of the AFL-CIO in Arkansas, he told me, "Folks aren't going to accept a black state senator, and we can't support you for that reason. You have the best platform, but they are going to put Paul Benham in office." Becker was a leading liberal activist of the 1960s and 1970s, and I didn't think that he was being a racist. It seemed like he was telling me the situation straight because he thought that I could take it. But I was hurt.

I went to all the black churches, but my campaign was not just directed at blacks. We didn't go to all the white churches, but we talked to some groups of white folks in Lee and Phillips Counties. Maurice Harmon, the local United Auto Workers' union representative at the Douglas & Lomason plant, campaigned for me in Lee County. I had an old-timer white man named Bankston Waters campaigning for me in Phillips. He wrote a good editorial in the newspaper asking white folks to give me a chance because I had shown that I could do something for the people I represented.

We worked hard. I think that I did as well as I could with the white voters considering my reputation from the recent racial conflicts, but I did not deliver the black vote I needed. Blacks had a slight majority of the electorate in my district, and I knew there were plenty of good people out there who would vote for me. But I didn't fire them up and they didn't come out. I didn't know how to switch from being a community organizer rallying folks to support a boycott to a Senate candidate campaigning for public office.

I got beat, but I learned a lot from the election. You can never assume that folks will vote for you just because they know you, and like you personally. A good example was a woman named Emily Williams at New Hope Church where I had been going since I was a baby. She and my Momma used to sing in the choir together, and they had been good friends. After the election, I was visiting with her and she told me that she was proud of me and I had done a good job. She also told me that she didn't vote for me because I never asked her. I guess she hadn't been to any of the meetings where I asked folks for support.

I was presumptive. I thought that the black community would support me because of my reputation, and that is a bad way for a politician to think. Plus, black folks didn't really know what the state Senate did, so they didn't know what I could do for them if I got elected. I didn't have a strong enough message. I failed to turn them on with a good reason to vote for me. All they knew was, "Olly Neal is trying to get that white man's job."

I had been fired up to break down a barrier and be the first black Arkansas state senator since the post-Reconstruction era in the 1890s. And I was invigorated by the campaign. Then when I lost the election that path didn't work out for me and I went back to the Clinic. But because I lacked an education in public health, I didn't have the necessary credentials or the experience for long-term health center management.

There were degree programs in public health for people in my type of position. I could have done one of them and still worked at the Clinic. I could have flown in to attend classes for only one week a month. I had at least three opportunities to get that kind of training, but I kept finding an excuse and putting it off. I wasn't happy with routine. I was a fighter, not an administrator. I was good at standing up and speaking out for my people. Somehow I felt that with the Clinic no longer facing opposition, there was no longer a need for an outspoken person like me.

Graduating from LeMoyne

I had to figure out what to do with the rest of my life. It was time for me to do something new, but what? One thing I knew for sure was that I wanted to stay in Marianna. I didn't ever have any solid logic about this. I just wanted to be in Marianna. People used to tell Ethelyn that she shared her husband with another woman named Marianna.

Working with the Clinic, I had met quite a few black doctors practicing in Arkansas, and I had become friends with some of them. Dr. Robert Smith, a surgeon from Pine Bluff, is especially memorable because every time I saw him he tried to convince me to go to medical school. It is true that being a doctor had been a long-ago childhood dream, and I thought about this real hard. But to become a doctor, I had to finish my college degree, go through four years of medical school, and complete another year of internship. That meant that I would not be in Marianna for a span of at least five years, and I just didn't want to be away from home that long.

Ethelyn thought that law school was a good idea. She talked about this in 2017: "When we got married, we rented a little house in Marianna and in a town like Marianna, you get involved in everything. I was on call a lot and even went over to the jail to treat some sick people. But Olly was THE MAN in the community, and they were always coming to the house knocking on the door for something. It was always Mr. Olly this and Mr. Olly that. I told him one time, 'You ought to go into law so you can really fix some of those people's problems.' He said, 'Well, you know, I have been thinking about that, but I have never finished college. I would have to go back to get my undergraduate degree.'"

One day I went over to LeMoyne College to see just how long it would take me to get my Bachelor of Arts degree. The college president at this time was retired federal judge Odell Horton, and I had known him in the early 1960s, when he was a lawyer representing students arrested in the Memphis sit-ins. It turned out that he had been keeping up with me. Since I had been a chemistry major, President Horton told me that if I could get Dr. John Beuler, head of the chemistry department, to approve, he would sign off on the graduation plan we put together.

I had taken chemistry classes with Dr. Beuler (a Holocaust survivor), and he seemed happy to help me. We worked out a plan where the college would count all the course work I had completed way back in 1958. That, certainly, was outside their policy, but both Dr. Beuler and President Horton agreed.

Since I could get credit for my previous course work, I only needed three more classes to graduate. They were a very tough physical chemistry course and two biology courses, but I could complete the whole thing in only one semester! I could do all my coursework on Tuesdays and Thursdays. Dr. Beuler gave me a key to the science lab, so I could do all of the lab work by myself on Saturdays from 8:30 or 9:00 in the morning to about 4:00 in the afternoon. This was amazing. It was a real shock to see how much they were willing to do for me. But it was tough going back to school. Horace Johnson, a medical student working at the Clinic, helped me study the physical chemistry, which was way out of my league. I managed to pass all three of those courses and finally got my degree.

University of Arkansas at Little Rock Law School

I set my sights on a new law school in Little Rock (now called UA Little Rock William H. Bowen School of Law) where all the classes were at night, so I could work all day at the Clinic and drive over there after work to go to school. For about five years it had been a semi-private night-school-only program. Then about a year before I was getting ready to start, it became a branch of the University of Arkansas law school. Later, in the fall of 1975, the Little Rock law school became full time and started offering day classes also, but I was only interested in being a night student.

Because the state bar association had been involved in developing the UALR law school, it did a good job of making sure students got courtroom experience. For example, in my last year, with my supervisor sitting quietly in the corner, I represented a woman who was the plaintiff in a domestic relations case. The lawyer who represented the defendant did not prepare adequately because he thought that, as a student, I wouldn't do a very good job. But I won and my client got what she wanted. On the short side, however, we didn't learn legal history, and we didn't get important background in the seminal cases that teach how the law developed and why it is the way it is today.

I took the LSAT in March 1974 and did pretty well, so I applied to law school. My name had been all over the Little Rock newspapers during the Marianna boycotts, and I had a hell of a reputation from all the trouble getting the Clinic started. The people in the admissions office must have known who I was, and they could have thought of me as trouble and passed over my application. But they didn't do that. I was accepted when I didn't even have my undergraduate degree yet!

They admitted me to the law school in Fayetteville, but I couldn't go all the way up there and still live in Marianna, so I called the dean's office and talked to an associate dean. I told him that I wanted to go to the law school in Little Rock. He contacted the administrator at that campus, and after only ten days, I was admitted. Everything had gone swift and smooth.

Law School, the Clinic, and the National Demonstration Water Project

I started classes in August 1974, and during my first semester, I only had to be in Little Rock three nights a week. I left Marianna at 4:30 p.m. My classes were from 6:00 to 10:00 p.m. It was a 100-mile drive and the speed limit was 80 mph, so I could get there in plenty of time. I was in my little blue Chevrolet SS Super Sport, and that thing would just run and run. I'd get in my car heading for school, turn off my work thoughts, and turn on a law tape. On my way home, I'd turn off law school thoughts, turn on my old portable recorder, and start dictating stuff for what I was going to do the next day at the Clinic. Looking back, that ability to work long and hard, to turn my brain on and off, and to keep a sharp focus was a beautiful thing. At the time I took it for granted.

When I was accepted to law school, I resigned my job as director of the Clinic, and they hired Ron McLean. But I kept working with the National Demonstration Water Project (NDWP) all during that time because Ron did not want responsibility for it. NDWP was a time-consuming job that required a lot of travel. I reported directly to the Clinic board, and I supervised a local NDWP staff of four, who organized most of the projects around Arkansas. We had expanded in Arkansas and were now also doing projects in north-central Arkansas. I also was active in the national NDWP organization that operated in twenty-eight states, but I was not yet president of the board of directors. That came later.

It turned out that McLean really wasn't up to the Clinic CEO job at all, and about a year after I resigned, he left unexpectedly. To make certain that the Clinic didn't fold, Pitson Brady prevailed on me to return. So in the fall of 1975, I took a leave of absence from law school for one semester to manage everything at the Clinic again. By the end of that semester, Brady had convinced our accountant, Clarence Coleman, to become CEO, and he worked in that position for a couple of years. But being a chief executive officer never was something Coleman wanted, and he went back to school to get his PhD in accounting.

McLean had all the credentials, but he didn't last. Coleman was all right, but he didn't relate to local folks like I did, and he had another career in mind. Brady believed that they needed to hire somebody from Lee County, and this is when he got the bright idea to recruit John Eason. But Eason had been with the school system for a long time, and nobody thought that he would leave the district. Pitson Brady led the charge and convinced him to come in, and Eason stayed with the Clinic for a long time.

NDWP had a working board and when I was their president from 1976 until I graduated in 1978, it was not just an administrative desk job. I had to travel all over the country. I had to go to a lot of meetings and was constantly promoting the program. One time when I was in Washington DC for a meeting, my flight home was due in Memphis at 5:15 p.m., and I had to make a connecting flight to Little Rock so I could get to my evening class. The professor had set a limit on how many classes we could miss without automatic failure, and I already had missed my limit. The flight from DC was so late that I missed my connection and had to pay $160 for a charter to fly me to Little Rock. I was desperate. This was my next-to-last semester, and I had to pass that class. I barely made the class that night and I barely passed the course with a D.

Another Failed Marriage

You could say that Ethelyn and I had an uneasy time together. I was not a responsible husband. I was commuting to law school a hundred miles away in Little Rock and did not make it home every night. I traveled all over the country for NDWP. I was still heavily involved in the community and was often called on to do things that kept me away from her. And then, I would do something that was just stupid like go out drinking and stay out all night. I was impossible to live with. No reasonable person could have done it. I don't know how Ethelyn stayed with me as long as she did.

I remember one night we went to a function down in Helena. When we left around 11:00 p.m., I said, "I'm going to Smale." Smale was a little community in Monroe County where they had a place you could shoot craps all night. I had never been a good gambler, and I can't tell you why I wanted to go there. She said, "I'm going too." Alright, so we both went over there. We went in and I was back where they were shooting dice, and there were two big pistols laid out on the table. I pulled out my pistol and put it on the table too. Ethelyn was standing nearby. I don't know how the hell she put up with me. She tolerated that shit for a long time but not forever.

One time I came home at 3:00 a.m. and when I went to open the bedroom door, it was locked. The whiskey told me to talk the fool, and I said, "Open the goddamn door, woman, or I'll kick it down." As I stepped back to kick, the door opened and there was Ethelyn standing with my long-barrel .38 pointed right at my face. As you can imagine, I got sober real fast. I went to sleep in the living room. Ethelyn was pushed to the wall and I don't blame her. There was no particular other woman who had a claim on me, but I was out of control and it was crazy. Around this time, Ethelyn also was feeling isolated professionally and wanted to go work in Memphis. We separated in 1977.

When Daddy Died

A year after we married, Ethelyn and I had bought a house around the corner from Daddy. When we separated, I continued to stay in that house and I was in and out of Daddy's house much of the time. Daddy and I got to be partners. We used to talk about all kinds of stuff. We'd talk about his golden days and who he courted. That is how I knew he liked skinny-legged women. He told me about when he was in the Army. In his last years I really did learn a lot about him. He would drink a beer with me too—even though he was kind of a teetotaler. He'd say, "Come on, boy, I'll drink a beer with ya." I'm pretty sure I expressed to him how important he was to me. I hope so.

He was eighty-two. He had led what he considered to be a good life, and he didn't stay sick a long time. He got sick on Monday and died on Thursday. He had cooked his own breakfast that Monday morning. This may not seem like much now, but Daddy had $200 or $300 in the house when he died, so he was not broke or hungry. He didn't have a house note. His taxes and utilities were paid. He lived about a block and a half from his church, so he could walk up there every Sunday. He was doing pretty good.

I took it hard when Daddy died. He was always there. He was the stable one in my life. I don't ever remember him being anything but straight down the line. Patient and calm. Always solid and forceful too. He didn't mind telling me to my face where he was coming from. When I was seventeen, Daddy didn't let me buy a car. He told me I couldn't have a car because I would have to work too much to pay for it. School was the priority, so a car was not an option.

After Cleola died was the only time we got crosswise. We clashed, but that was not his fault. He was supportive, but I was just so goddamn angry at the world that I didn't want his damn support. I didn't want to be managed. He was old school too, born in 1896, but he didn't always act old school. He never got in my way during the boycotts. He was never critical. He never advised me to stop. He only said, "Be careful, son, be careful."

Daddy died in September 1978, and he left a big space. There was nobody else in the world who I could count on whether I was doing good or not good, whether I was being crazy or not crazy. It didn't involve a lot of hugging. Men didn't hug that much. It was just clear. He was always going to be with me. When I did something stupid, everybody else in the world would say, "Get your stupid ass out of my way." Daddy would say, "Come on, boy, let's see how we can work through this." I just knew that he was always there. It was not with money, but he was solid in terms of—whatever you call that—psychology.

Ethelyn remembered: "Olly's Daddy died when we were separated. Olly had called me when his Daddy got sick and said, 'I don't know what to do.' I was living in Memphis then and I got in my car and drove down there to see his condition. We put him in the hospital in Marianna, and then we transferred him to Memphis. When he passed away, the hospital called me, and I had to tell Olly. At that point, it was kind of expected that he wasn't going to make it."

Henry Jones's Critical Visit

When Daddy died, I decided to quit law school. I just didn't feel like doing it anymore. I guess that I had some basis for being depressed, but it was my last semester. There have been some ups and downs in my life, and I have had times when I didn't function so well. This time an old boy named Henry Jones came to Marianna to talk to me. And I was surprised to see him. Henry Jones was younger than me, but he had been out of law school for about ten years, and somebody told him, "Olly ain't coming back to school." So he got in his car and drove to Marianna. I thought this was beyond the call of duty. I didn't know him very well, and I will never forget what he did for me.

Henry Jones was known to be brilliant. He was academically gifted and had passed the bar exam high up. He stayed in Arkansas and in the late 1980s he became a federal magistrate and served there until he retired in about 2010. Apparently, he had some other skills too because he didn't just come and slam me. We talked about my Daddy and all that stuff. He didn't know my Daddy at all, but, hell, we talked about him and I gained a degree of confidence and when he left about three hours later, I was going back to school. I'm glad I did.

Graduation and Passing the Bar

I graduated on January 6, 1979, but I didn't participate in my law school graduation ceremony. I did not walk across the stage. I told them to mail me my diploma. Ethelyn and I had gotten back together after Daddy died. She was still an adjunct professor in the University of Arkansas Medical School, and I had read that a university professor could be the one to place my hood during the graduation ceremony. So I made this request, but the dean's office said no. In their response, it sounded to me like they didn't think that an adjunct professor was good enough. That pissed me off and I felt like punishing the law school, so I refused to participate. Yes, I was acting like a child.

In January soon after I graduated, I bought a little building for my law office in Marianna on the corner of Poplar and Main. By then, J. B. Smith and I had gotten to be friends, and he put the deal together for me because his wife was a real estate agent. When he came to me saying, "Charlotte got a building for you right downtown," I told him, "Hell, J. B., I don't have that kind of money." And he said, "They don't want but $18,000. You come on over to the bank and I will make sure they give you a good loan." I was somebody who had not been much of a law student, and I bought a building before I passed the bar exam. A lot of people don't pass the bar the first time either. I had not thought it out, and I had no business buying that building. It was just plain dumb.

The bar exam was February 26, 27, and 28, 1979. Ethelyn and I did all the Christmas stuff that year, and on the first day of the new year, I left for Little Rock to study. I told her, "Don't call me. I'll call you when I can." I took a bar review course during those two months. I studied with Randy Rice, who was bright and a good student. We would spend twelve or fourteen hours a day studying. Jewel Brown, who had already passed the bar, was our guide. He did what he could to help us. He told us about the kind of stuff that would be on the test. He was a tough guide. I got into the books and put everything into it.

I also have to admit that I did something that I should not have done. I knew someone who was a pharmacist, and he gave me those pills to stay awake and alert. The bar exam took three days and on the last day when it was over, my eyes wouldn't close but I was done in. I was too tired to drive home to Marianna. After a big exam like that some folks will think "I wish

I had done this" or "I wish I had done that," but I didn't have any of those thoughts. I gave everything I knew to that test. I focused on my goal. I gave it my full attention. And I was impressed with myself for being able to concentrate enough to force all that stuff into my head

Ethelyn remembered: "We were living in Proctor then and I was the one who called to see if Olly had passed the bar exam. He was nervous all weekend because the scores were coming out. And I said, 'Well, why don't you call?' But he said no. So I asked, 'Could I call? Let me see if they will tell me.' And he said okay. When I called, they told me and I told him, 'You passed!'"

I don't remember exactly where I came out. I think it was in the middle somewhere. When the results were published in the *Arkansas Gazette*, the headline said, "Marianna Clinic Director Passes Bar Exam." Lower down in the second headline it gave the name of the person who had the top score. It wasn't me, but I got higher billing. The whole thing was amazing. And putting that I had passed the bar in the newspaper laid pressure on me. It seemed they were saying, "Now let's see what he can do!" Also, I was always somewhat paranoid, and that headline made me wonder if I could still be a target for somebody.

My Daddy Ollie Neal when he was eighty years old with my daughter Karama Neal and her Momma Janet Cobb.

The Neal brothers at our Daddy's eightieth birthday party in Marianna. From left to right are Agin Muhammad (Granville), Rowan, Willie, me, Donald, and Thad.

2010 Neal family reunion. From left to right are Donald, me, Donald's daughter Lisa, my sister Gloria, Rowan, and Agin Muhammad (Granville).

My sister Betty Neal Walker in her Marianna apartment in March 2017.

Me, my sister Gloria, and my brother Rowan in February 2015 at Gloria's granddaughter's wedding.

My sixth-grade Moton school picture taken in the spring of 1953.

Mrs. Mildred Stubblefield Grady, my high school English teacher, who caught me and helped me steal library books.

My Momma Willie B. Neal in 1965 pinning a corsage on Mrs. Anna P. Strong, longtime principal of Marianna's black Moton High School.

My LeMoyne College sophomore yearbook picture, spring 1960.

Harry Durham, a student Mrs. Strong took under her wing. This picture was taken October 5, 2018, at his home in Memphis when we were sharing our memories of Moton School.

STATE OF ARKANSAS

MARRIAGE LICENSE

COUNTY OF

LEE

To any person authorized by law to solemnize Marriage, Greeting:

You are hereby commanded to solemnize the rite and publish the banns of Matrimony between Mr. OLLY NEAL Jr.

of Chicago in the County of Cook and State of Ill. aged 21 years

and M CLEOLA DAVIS

of MARIANNA in the County of LEE and State of ARK. aged " 20 years

according to law; and do you officially sign and return this License to the parties herein named.

Witness my hand and official seal this 16th. day of JUNE 1962

D. W. Bullard
County Clerk

Deputy County Clerk.

CERTIFICATE OF MARRIAGE

State of Arkansas,
County of Lee

I, Rev E K Gaines do hereby certify that on the 17 day of June 1962 I did duly and according to law, as commanded in the foregoing License, solemnize the rite and publish the banns of Matrimony between the parties therein named.

Witness my hand this 17 day of June 1962

My Credentials are recorded in Recorder's Office.

Phillips County Ark.

Book E Page D

Rev E K Gaines

Olly Neal J. K

Cleola Davis

NOTE—This License with the Certificate duly executed and officially signed, must be returned to the office whence it is issued within sixty days from the date of License under penalty of forfeiture of the bond.

June 17, 1962, license when I married my high school sweetheart Cleola Davis.

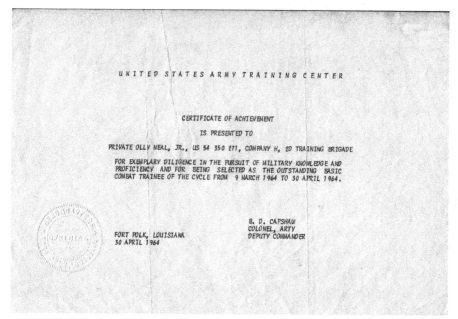

My April 30, 1964, U.S. Army commendation for becoming the most outstanding trainee in basic training.

T. F. Vaughn in his home office on April 24, 2017, when we were talking about old times.

JAN 1 5 1971

RECEIVED

JAN 6

MEDICAL DEAN'S OFFICE

UNITED STATES DEPARTMENT OF JUSTICE
FEDERAL BUREAU OF INVESTIGATION
WASHINGTON 25, D. C.

4-11-69 506 MKC

J. Edgar Hoover
Director.

The following FBI record, NUMBER 564 490 D is furnished FOR OFFICIAL USE ONLY.

CONTRIBUTOR OF FINGERPRINTS	NAME AND NUMBER	ARRESTED OR RECEIVED	CHARGE	DISPOSITION
PD, Memphis Tenn	Olly Rogers Neal Jr. #74601	3-19-60	DC loit thrt br of peace	
PD Memphis Tenn	Olly Rogers Neal Jr. #74601	8-23-60	dist peace loit DC consp to obstruct trade & commerce	loit - dism DC - fine $51 dist peace & consp obstruct trade & commerce dropped on recomm. of Atty Gen 8-24-60
PD Memphis Tenn	Olly Rogers Neal Jr. #74601	8-24-60	loit, DC	8-25-60 dism fine $51
PD Memphis Tenn	Olly Rogers Neal Jr. #74601	8-26-60	DC - loit - consp to interfere with trade & commerce - dist peace	8-27-60 fine $51 - dism - held to state - dism
PD Memphis Tenn	Olly Rogers Neal Jr. #74601	9-21-60	vio Sec 373 P vio Sec 39.101- DC - loit	9-22-60 dism - held to state- fine $51 - dism
CSC	Olly Neal, Jr. #762 5922	10-9-61		
PD Jackson Tenn	Olly Neal Jr. #6061	4-4-69	Inciting to riot College campus disturbance	

My FBI record showing my arrests in 1960 for loitering and disturbing the peace during the Memphis student sit-ins and my 1969 arrest for inciting to riot and college campus disturbance, which ended my student career at Lane College in Jackson, Tennessee.

The first Clinic building in an old house on Liberty Street donated by Lacey Kennedy. My office was where the upper story window is.

Poster of Dr. Dan Blumenthal; this was used to recruit doctors—especially Dr. Irwin Redlener.

Harry Conard (inside) and his helper building a new outhouse placed downhill from the hand-pump water well for the woman standing on the right.

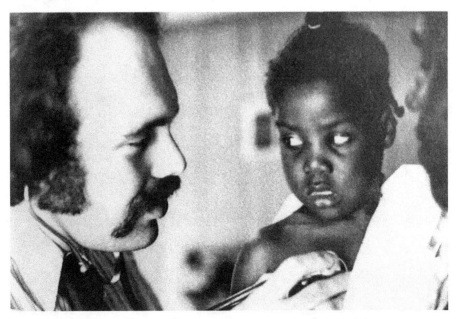

Dr. Irwin Redlener, Clinic pediatrician 1971–1973, and a suspicious young patient.

Dr. Irwin Redlener with Joan Baez, folk singer and activist, who gave a 1972 concert in Memphis to raise money for the Clinic's new building.

Ground-breaking ceremony for the new Clinic building on Atkins Street. I'm holding a shovel on the right.

Dr. Ethelyn Williams-Neal in her Memphis medical office on March 11, 2017.

Dr. Irwin Redlener (left of me in mustache) and me holding a staff meeting in our old Liberty Street building.

Thomas Ishmael's calling card when he was running for Lee County Judge in 1970.

VOTE FOR THOMAS ISHMUL

COUNTY JUDGE

A Man for All the People

Robert Morehead, who we hired to help us monitor the "stolen election" of November 1970. Photo taken in Pine Bluff on March 12, 2017.

Sterling King and me in 1973.

I'm shaking hands with Mr. Thomas Ishmael.

Sterling King, my high school classmate, my friend, and a most valuable member of the Concerned Citizens organization. Picture was taken in 2017.

My brother Prentiss in 1971 with one of the signs he carried during the Marianna economic boycott.

Andrea Hope Howard, whose father ran the black cotton gin and who was a junior at Lee High School in 1970–71, the first year of integration.

Clifton Collier in 2019. He was a Lee high School student during the first year of enforced integration, 1970–71, and he was CEO of the Clinic from 2010 through December 2016. His grandmother Willie Mae Collier helped me get hired as the Clinic's CEO.

Mrs. Sarah Sauls, the midwife on our board who spoke up and convinced Governor Bumpers we needed the Clinic.

New Clinic building soon after completion, with temporary sign.

Dr. Irwin Redlener, Ben Anthony Sr., and me probably taken in 1973 soon after the new building was completed.

The Clinic's very enthusiastic staff members at our 1973 annual meeting. From left to right: Francine Jenkins, medical administrative assistant; Doris Lewellen, accountant; Stella Crawford, LPN; Barbara Hooks, LPN; Pearlie Thomas, office assistant; and Joyce Savage, receptionist.

Part Three: Law Career

Judge Wendell Griffen, Judge Andree Roaf, and me in 2001 while on the Arkansas Appellate Court.

Chapter 12
Marianna Law Practice January 1979–October 1991

I learned that I passed the bar in April and started practicing law on May 1, 1979. Most law school graduates are in their mid-twenties, but I was thirty-eight. I carried an old, beat-up briefcase. I liked that briefcase. Soon after I started practicing, a young lawyer came up to me in the St. Francis County Courthouse and asked me some question. He thought that I had been practicing for years, but it was my first time there.

My very first client was a woman who had waited a whole year for me to get out of law school. Viola Robinson and her husband, Dertha, had been married about twenty-five years and had no children. Before they were married, her husband owned forty acres and after they got married, he bought another forty. When Dertha Robinson died, his brothers claimed the forty acres he owned before their marriage. She had hired Carrold Ray, a white attorney in Marianna, who told her that she was entitled to the forty acres acquired after they were married but that the forty from before they were married would have to be divided among her and his brothers.

She didn't think this was right, so she just delayed and delayed meeting with her attorney to sign any papers. When her lawyer wanted her to come in to sign, she would get sick or say she couldn't get a ride into town. She put him off for a whole year that way, waiting for me.

On the first day in my office, she came to see me and explained the situation. I looked at the statute and the law was clear that anyone married more than ten years inherits all the property of the spouse. But I didn't think that her lawyer would tell her a damn lie, so I called Jimmie Wilson, a black lawyer in Helena, and I asked him where I was wrong. He told me, "You damn fool, you ain't got it wrong. That's what these white folks do to niggers."

So I wrote a letter to her lawyer and told him that I had been retained to represent her and would appreciate him making her file available when I went over there the next morning. Our offices were right next door to each other.

The lawyer for her husband's brothers was in Marianna, and he also was white. I wrote another letter telling him that I had read and understood the statute and since Dertha Robinson had died without a will, my client was due all her husband's land. If he disagreed, he should go ahead and file a lawsuit. I never heard anything from him.

Capital Murder Case

During my first year of law practice, I got assigned to a capital murder case by Circuit Judge Henry Wilkerson. He was one of two judges who presided over felony cases in the First Judicial Circuit, which included the mid-Delta counties of Phillips, Lee, St. Francis, Monroe, Cross, and Woodruff. This was back in 1980. Wilkerson assigned me to represent Walter Lee Thompson, who had been accused of robbing and killing a white woman. Usually lawyers could get out of appointment to capital murder cases if they had not practiced criminal law. But I was taking everything that came through the door, and I accepted the case. Judge Wilkerson chose me because I was black. He didn't want to be seen as someone who was not fair to a black man accused of killing a white woman. This was his way of dealing with the racism problem.

The incident took place in Round Pond, a little town outside Forrest City, and the prosecutor was in trouble because all the evidence had been collected illegally. The sheriff was Sonny Hamilton. He had kicked the door down, stepped over the woman, and gone in the back room to get the pistol without having a search warrant. So I knew immediately that if I was strong enough in court I should win it, or if I lost I could win on appeal.

Sonny Hamilton was one of those sheriffs who expected everyone to shut up and listen whenever he spoke. When he said jump, he expected you to ask how high and start jumping. It was kind of like being in the cowboy days. Hamilton was tough, and he didn't take shit off anybody. Anyway, they hired me. I had never tried a case where the death penalty was called for.

It was obvious that in this black-on-white capital crime I really had a special situation, so I had to know the best way to select the jury. I called one of Arkansas's most respected black lawyers and asked for his notes on what to ask potential jurors. He was brilliant and experienced, but he wasn't helpful. He told me to call a court reporter and ask for the transcript of a trial he had just won, but I was too inexperienced to be able to find the name of the court reporter. I think that he was mad at me because of some woman. I called another black lawyer, Christopher Mercer, who sent me a whole box of stuff. He said, "Read this, and you will be able to figure out what to do."

My first motion was to suppress all the evidence the sheriff had collected illegally. None of it was admissible. I knew the law, but back then I didn't know enough about how the court operated. I wanted to get a hearing on my motion before the trial, and I filed that motion four times—month after month.

When I didn't get any response from the court, I thought that I was being played, and I was scared that I was going to fail this guy. I was so inexperienced and insecure that my greatest fear always was that I was doing something wrong. I eventually learned that about a week before a trial, the judge gathers all the motions to act on them at once. (I did it this way too when I was a judge.) The day before Thompson's trial was scheduled, the judge looked at everything and based on my motions, he dismissed the trial! I had only needed one motion at the right time.

It was Sonny Hamilton who ended up going to the penitentiary. I don't remember exactly what they got him on, but he was a bad dude. He didn't think nothing of black folks. He was known for just slapping a person in the face, and he would take people's stuff too. About that time, they were going after corruption in St. Francis County, and Sonny had been at the top of the list.

Excluded

I believe this happened in early 1981. The Office of Economic Opportunity (OEO) funded Legal Services, and this program had just come to Arkansas. I was one of the founding board members for Legal Services serving the fifteen counties in eastern Arkansas. The bar association in each county could elect one member to the board, and at our Lee County bar association meeting, I was trying to convince them to elect somebody who would represent the poor people needing help from Legal Services.

I started my spiel at the beginning of the meeting. After a bit, Jesse Daggett said, "Well, I don't know, Olly. We'll just have to see how it plays out." Then, David Cahoon said, "Okay, Olly, who do you want to see elected?" I can't remember who I wanted, but when I said who it was, he said, "I'm going to join you in that nomination." I made the motion and he seconded it. Then, somebody else nominated Dodd Daggett, who was Jesse's brother and was old school just like their father, Jimason. I knew that Dodd was a terrible choice. David and I were the only ones to vote for my candidate. Everybody else voted for Dodd. They knew how to shut me up and go around me to vote for who they had already decided on. They got me.

Exclusion happened to me a number of times. Gene Raff was the prosecuting attorney for our district. Raff was like most older white lawyers. He could not conceive of a black person operating equally with him. I had been practicing for about a year when Raff's deputy in Lee County, Jim VanDover, resigned. I had worked in the criminal court and developed some courtroom skills. While my cases were not the kind to be written about in the *New York Times*, I was successful in the courtroom. But I was still struggling hard to meet my expenses. I was desperate for work so I could pay my secretary, and I had talked myself into the idea that I might still serve the black community in the deputy prosecutor job.

When Gene Raff was getting ready to select a new deputy prosecutor, I talked to him. I said, "Gene, you know I can do the work. Now that you don't have anybody up here, why don't you make me your deputy in Lee County?" And this is what he told me, "Yes, Olly, but the white people in Lee County aren't going to accept a black deputy prosecutor." That is exactly what he said, and I wrote it down with the date and time. I still have that piece of paper somewhere. Gene appointed David Cahoon, and it wasn't long before I proved that could walk all over him. I may not have been the best lawyer, but I had a big personality and I could whip Cahoon in the courtroom.

I would go drinking with Gene Raff sometimes because even though all the other black folks would say that he was a low-down dog and I thought so too, I had to be around these folks to know what they were thinking. Every year, I would go down to his office Christmas party in Helena, and we would drink whiskey and sing carols. That is where I later told him, "I could have been on your side, Gene. You could have made me your deputy, but you didn't want that." And when we'd be drinking, he'd say, "Aw hell, Olly." I was a strange person to him, and he couldn't figure out what to do with me.

I would sometimes speak straight-out rough with Jesse Daggett, Bob Donovan, and some of the other white lawyers who were my age and younger. Part of what made me talk to them this way was how I felt about Gene Raff appointing David Cahoon instead of me. I would say to them, "I don't give a damn what any of you say about me. I don't care if I am not friends with you, but I intend to be treated like you treat each other." What I was telling them was that they had a system and I didn't like being excluded.

This is crude sounding, but all the white attorneys in Lee County had what I called their lawyer kitty. The lawyer kitty was regular work that brought in money to pay their office expenses. Bob Donovan was the municipal judge. Jesse Daggett was the school board's lawyer. Dodd Daggett handled all the child support enforcement cases. I told them, "From the way you divide up the work, you all have a check coming to your office so you can pay your secretary. I have nothing." I also told them what Gene Raff had said to me about not hiring me because Lee County was not ready for a black deputy prosecutor. I said, "So Lee County won't stand for nobody black to be in charge of a goddamn thing. Let me tell you this. If you let me in and share a piece of that work, I'm going to be grinning with ya. But if you keep me on the outside, and you don't share any of it, I'm going to be fighting you like hell because I don't have a goddamn thing to lose." That is the way I used to talk to those guys. And I think that Jesse and Bob understood. But many of those white lawyers didn't. My point is that they created this circumstance, and I did not get mad and just stay quiet. I told them what I thought. And I used to enjoy beating them and making them look bad in court too. I stayed excluded until 1988 when we defeated Gene Raff and Dan Dane became prosecutor.

Making the City Attorney, Police, and Judge Look Bad

In the 1970s and 1980s, when black folks used to come home from Chicago or Detroit, they would get pulled off the road for something small. Since they had "forgotten" how to be properly deferential to the police, they often got treated kind of rough and ended up in jail.

Soon after I started practicing law, Helena's two black attorneys, Jimmie Wilson and Kathleen Bell, and I formed a loose association that we called Wilson, Bell, and Neal, and we would cover for each other. We would represent black folks in the small-town municipal courts where there wasn't much respect for us. And when I was going to one of these towns, I would tell the others to be on standby to come and get me out in case I got put in jail for contempt.

My style was to appear tough. I would wear my cowboy boots. I drove a big F250 diesel truck, and it was loud. Sometimes I would park in the county judge's parking space. When I went in one of those little county courthouses and walked down the hall, people would peek out of their doors wondering, "Who IS he? What is HE doing here?" The idea was if they thought I was tough, they wouldn't know what to do with me. I only had one occasion where I had to call for help, but I managed to get out before my folks got there.

I would tell my clients, "I have enough of a reputation so the city attorney who is prosecuting your case knows me, and I can work out a pretty good deal with him. You won't get off perfectly clean, but it will be a good deal and you'll only have to pay the white folks a small amount of money.

Or I can put on the full show for you, and I'll make all the white people in charge look bad. But then I'll probably lose, and it will cost you." I told them, "If that's what you want, that's what you pay for, and that's what I will give you."

I had one client who told me that he wanted the full show and he didn't care what it would cost. He was convicted of three or four misdemeanors, and he ended up having to pay about $1,900 in fines. But he wanted to watch me make the city attorney, the police, and the judge look bad. We both enjoyed it.

Counting on Pat Lamar

Earnestein Broadway was my first legal assistant. She was a black woman who had been working for Sheriff May in the tax collection office. She handled the work really well, and she had a great personality. She left because she wanted to do something else, probably where she would make more money. This was after my first capital murder case and at about the time I got crosswise with Judge Henry Wilkerson over being appointed to represent someone I did not want to represent.

When I was appointed to represent someone by the court, I was paid a maximum of $300 for a felony case and $1,000 for a capital (death penalty) case. Money had nothing to do with this conflict, though. I just did not like the son of a bitch and refused to represent him. I told Judge Wilkerson that I had a strong personal dislike for this person and needed to be excused. But that judge felt that what he wanted could not be questioned—and our conflict might have had some racial overtones in it too. He might have thought a black lawyer had to do his bidding, but I would not. It really was a "war of wills." I was so mad about being run over that I quit doing criminal cases for a couple of months. For a while after that, I had less work and was without a secretary for a month or so.

My second office manager was Pat Lamar. And she stayed with me for most of my legal career. This is how Pat remembered our early years, in a 2017 interview:

> I had graduated from Phillips County Community College with an associate's degree in business management, and I was still living at home. My Daddy was a farmer and my parents had twelve kids. I could afford junior college, but I couldn't afford a full college education, so I needed to find a job.

I was volunteering at the Lee County Cooperative Clinic senior center and my sister worked there too. She saw Olly's ad in the newspaper and told me about it. I put in my application and did my interview. Then I started calling him asking if he had made a decision. He didn't have anybody, and he needed the help, so I called him every day for about a week. And he finally said, "You sure are persistent. If you are nothing else, you are persistent. Okay, I will give you a chance."

I told him, "You will not be sorry!" And he found out that he could count on me. Everything he needed, I was trying to do. When I was growing up, we couldn't go to the field and stand on the hoe. We had to be chopping cotton. My Daddy always said, "If a man pays you for a day's work, you give him a day's work." So I knew how to work. And I ended up working for Olly Neal twenty years: February 1982 to January 1993 when he was a practicing attorney in Marianna and January 1996 to the end of 2006 when he was on the Court of Appeals in Little Rock.

In the beginning, it was Wilson, Bell, and Neal. There were three attorneys, but Olly had his own office in Marianna and the others were in Helena. I got trained in Helena and then I came up to Marianna. I answered the phone. I typed. I did the bookkeeping. I interviewed clients. I did everything.

I had worked as a clerk in a bookstore and with my Daddy in the cotton fields, but I hadn't worked in the legal field. At first I didn't know what I was doing. I learned a lot working for Olly Neal. He was a great teacher. After I was working for him for about a year, I was at home talking to my Daddy and I was cursing. My Daddy was looking at me funny and he asked me, "Do you hear yourself?" And I said, "Oh stop, I'm sorry. I didn't mean anything." I picked up certain things from Olly that just rubbed off. That was a bad habit. I had to stop.

Most of it was fun learning, but at first I thought Olly was pretty impatient. I guess I was a little timid too. He told me later, "I wanted to fire you after two days." I had to learn to speak up. He expected me to figure out how to get things done, and I couldn't let the white people walk over me. When I went to file something at the courthouse in Marianna, it took forever because all the clerks ignored me. Olly told me that I had to get tough. He said, "You've got to go over there and say, 'Listen, I need to get this done!'" So I started being bossy. My Daddy had taught me about respect. He said, "You respect people, they will respect you." White people were supposed to respect me, but of course they probably didn't feel that way. I had to demand respect.

After Pat came back from her training in Jimmie Wilson's office, she still couldn't do some things very well. I remember saying to Jimmie's secretary Betty that I was going to have to let Pat go. But Betty told me to give her a little more time and I did. I paid Pat every Friday, and many weeks I waited to give her the check until after 4:30 p.m. when the bank in Marianna had closed, so she would have to go down to Helena to cash it. Then on the weekend, I'd try to scare up some work so I could cover her check. Pat says that I missed a few weeks. I don't remember that, but if she says so I don't doubt it.

I'd go to the club that Wilbur Peer and Ben Anthony Jr. had over on Liberty Street. They served whiskey by the drink, and Ben cooked up some great steaks on the weekends. He could make a cheap cut of meat taste really good. Ben was such a good cook that one time somebody who didn't know who was cooking said, "Bring the cook on out here, I'm going to marry her."

At the club I'd tell anybody who was complaining about a problem with the law, "I can turn that around." I wouldn't push myself or seem desperate. I'd just say, "I can help you take care of that." I charged $75 for a speeding ticket or a disorderly conduct and $150 for a DWI.

One of my cases was a guy who was ticketed for speeding in his truck that had new over-sized tires on it. I asked him if he had a receipt for those tires and he did. In court, I showed his receipt to the judge and argued that it was not his fault. Since the big tires made his speedometer inaccurate, he didn't know he was over the speed limit. I also had him go get the speedometer adjusted and showed that receipt to the judge too. And he said, "Okay, dismissed."

Another time I got hired by an old boy who had whipped his girlfriend. She didn't want to, but her Momma made her file charges. That old boy had a wife too. When I saw him at the club, he admitted that he had been in the wrong and told me that he didn't want his wife to know about it. In court, I asked the clerk to just say the case number and when they called it, I stood up and said that I represented the defendant. When they asked, "What's the plea?" I said, "Guilty and my client will pay the fine today." It was easy. I got $250 for that case.

Dan Felton was the Marianna municipal judge who heard the misdemeanor cases, and he liked me there because I helped him make his court run smooth. Those first few years were lean. I had to work this way for maybe two or three years until I got to making more money.

Lost Cases Taught Important Lessons

When I was getting started I lost a couple of cases by making procedural mistakes that I didn't make a second time. First, in late 1979, I had a property case down in Phillips County against a white attorney, Gene Scheiffler. He was known for not being too bright, but he had been practicing law for thirty years. He caught me missing a procedural deadline and won the case. I might have won if I had been better prepared. The second mistake also took place in Phillips County when Gene Raff was the prosecuting attorney. A black man had been killed by a white man inside the white man's house. The gossip was that the black man was involved in an ongoing sexual relationship with the white man's wife. The wife of the black man came to me and told me that her husband was going with this white woman, who had called him to come over there. And they had been caught by the white woman's husband.

I called Gene Raff. Gene thought highly of himself and usually wouldn't bother with anybody. But I was able to get through and talk to him probably because of my reputation in the Marianna economic boycott. He said, "Well, Olly, that boy was in the man's house and he was shot in self-defense. You are just wasting your time." I was inexperienced and I told him that I might still be interested. It really wasn't a case you could do much with because of where he had been killed, but I went ahead anyway and started gathering information. I looked at the law and what I could expect.

I was thinking like a community organizer, not like an experienced lawyer. I had access to the press, so I was thinking, "A black man inside a white woman's house because of their relationship is a scandal that the newspapers would like to publicize." I thought that with enough public interest, Gene Raff might be pressured into seeking a warrant for the white man's arrest. I filed a motion with the judge asking for Extraordinary Relief under the Circuit Judge's General Powers over Criminal Matters. I knew it was a stretch, but my community activist spirit overrode my newly acquired legal reasoning. The judge did not oblige.

To correct my ignorance, Raff decided to teach me a lesson and show his muscle. One day he called me and said that he was going to accommodate me and ask for a preliminary hearing. The way he said it was sort of condescending, but that didn't bother me. A preliminary hearing is where, instead of calling a grand jury, the prosecutor presents his case to the judge. And the judge decides if there is enough evidence to go forward with the charge.

I should never have agreed, but I did. I should have waived that probable-cause hearing because it is not set up to be for both sides. I was not allowed to question or present any witnesses. All I could do was object to something the prosecutor said that I considered irrelevant. Raff came in with a two-inch-thick notebook. And for about an hour and a half, he showed that the black man who had been killed was totally out of place and the husband was justified in shooting him. He was prancing and delivering. The judge found no probable cause to charge the white man with murder, and that was the end of it. Case dismissed. I couldn't do anything but sit there feeling sorry.

Gene Raff gave me my lesson in prosecutorial discretion, and he whupped me good. He embarrassed me. He made me look like I didn't know what I was doing. I didn't make that mistake again. If that woman had come to me five years later, I still would have considered what had happened to be wrong, but I would have told her, "I'm sorry but as a lawyer in this case there is nothing I can do to put it right."

Murder Got Me My Reputation

The murder case that made my reputation as a criminal lawyer in the black community came when David Cahoon was deputy prosecutor. A young black woman killed her husband. They lived in Marianna, and I knew a little bit about this woman and her husband. Her husband's brother and I were high school classmates, but she was from the Conway area. I knew that her husband was abusive and rough on her and that he had another woman.

On this particular Saturday, she saw her husband standing in downtown Marianna talking to his other woman. She went up to him and said that she wanted to talk to him, but he told her to go on home and that he would be there in a little while. So she went over to the Western Auto store and bought a five-shot .38 pistol and some ammunition.

I talked to her a bunch of times to figure out what happened. She went home, loaded that pistol, sat down in a chair facing the door, and never took off her coat. Later when he came in, they ignored each other at first and he must not have seen the pistol. He picked up his rifle and was cleaning it as a kind of threat to her. By doing that he was saying, "My gun will be ready if I need it." They got into a hot argument while his gun was still dismantled. And when they stood up, she shot him two or three times, but that wasn't all. She shot him one more time in the back of the head while he was lying on the floor. Shooting him in the back of the head sure as hell took her action out of the realm of self-defense.

I was in the joint on Liberty Street that night and after we heard about what had happened and I had had my three drinks, I started bragging and said, "If I represented her, I'd get her out and she wouldn't spend another day in jail." That was just whiskey-talk bragging. The woman's friend was sitting at the other end of the bar. She heard me and went right over to the jail and told the woman that Olly Neal had said he could get her out and get her off. So the woman sent for me. By now the whiskey was wearing off and I'm thinking, "Goddamn, what the hell have I gotten myself into?"

I went over there to talk to her, and she told me that her husband had a hole in the back of his head. She was telling me where she had shot him. I told her that I would represent her, but my fee was $10,000 and she had to pay $7,500 in advance. That was a lot of money, but she said okay. She called her sister in Chicago and the next afternoon her sister was in Marianna with my $7,500.

I convinced District Judge Wilkerson that she was not dangerous and wouldn't go anywhere because she had a job here and she had her two boys to take care of. I said that her defense was the so-called burning-bed argument. She was a member of the Atkins Street Church of Christ and I asked for a signature bond signed by her pastor L. C. Mitchell, who was also a dentist in Marianna. The judge said that he wasn't sure if Mitchell was worth $15,000, but I knew he had the money. I agreed to sit down to evaluate Mitchell's assets, and the judge let her out.

Then, I hired two psychiatrists. One was to treat her because she was having a rough time, and the other one was a super-star professor-psychiatrist from a university in Ohio. He had a reputation for being really good in the courtroom. I believed that he could convince the jury she had the burning-bed syndrome by testifying that the poor woman had just snapped and gone crazy after her husband treated her so badly. The rule in Arkansas criminal court is that a witness had to appear in court, and this was in 1981 before video depositions became common. I wanted the jury to see this psychiatrist, but I didn't want to pay for his travel. So I got special permission from the judge to present the psychiatrist's testimony in a video of his deposition taken in Ohio.

Deputy Prosecutor Cahoon was an absolute racist redneck. He was not an old guy, but racism was in him because that was what he had been taught. He was of the era when a white man did not lose to a black man, and I wanted him to be afraid of looking bad in the trial. I thought if I created enough fear, he would negotiate with me, and I could get the charge reduced to negligent homicide.

What happened had nothing to do with reality or logic. I wish you could have seen it. Cahoon lost his mind because he couldn't stand the possibility of a "nigger lawyer" beating him. In our pretrial hearing, I presented the videotaped expert testimony and put out so much stuff about the burning-bed defense that right before the trial, Cahoon moved to withdraw the charges. And the judge dismissed the case based on his motion! This was the dumbest shit I'd ever heard of, but I got my reputation by talking big and getting that woman off when she shot her husband in the back of the head.

In small towns, everybody knows everybody. There was a black deputy sheriff in Lee County at this time named Thomas C. Holmes, and in 1972 the Concerned Citizens had supported him when he ran for sheriff. After all this happened with Cahoon, Holmes told me that he had tried to convince Cahoon to prosecute the woman. After all, she had shot her husband after he was on the floor. But Cahoon just wailed, "That nigger is going to come and make me look bad!"

The woman had their two sons, and after this they moved to a suburb of Chicago. One of her sons is doing pretty good, but the other is not. Those boys really needed counseling to help them deal with what had happened, but they never got it. This is automatic now, but nobody understood that back then. I sure as hell didn't know about it, but I guess that I should have. The woman eventually remarried and is doing okay. I have kept up with her through her brother's wife, who got to be one of the first black court reporters in Arkansas. Black folks couldn't be court reporters back then either.

Practicing Law Was Less Stressful than Leading the Clinic

My work as a lawyer was intense but not nearly so much as when I was managing the Clinic. The Clinic was vital to my whole community, and that made me responsible to everybody. As director, I could never do anything that might not be good for the Clinic. I'm someone who thinks in terms of failure. If I failed the Clinic, I would be letting all my people down. As a lawyer, if I failed my client, I would be letting down only one or a few individuals. It just didn't have the same magnitude as failing everyone who depended on the Clinic. It put less stress on me and had a different feel.

Personally, I felt freer. I had a client named Robert Grubbs who was not satisfied with my work and told me that I wasn't as good as John Walker. I returned my fee and told him, "You don't like what I'm doing? Go get somebody you like." I was free to return his retainer. That was it. At the Clinic, if community members were saying that we ought to be doing something a certain way, I had to be accommodating. I had to tell them that I would at least consider their ideas. It was a different situation. Practicing law was me being who I preferred to be and doing what I preferred to do.

"Pat, You Need to Come in Here"
When I started, I had gone around to government surplus stores to buy some furniture, but I hadn't done anything else to fix up my office. After I had some more money, Pat helped me improve it a little more. We had the walls painted and put carpeting on the floor, and it looked pretty good when you got inside. The office was never great, but we made a living there. Pat was always solid, and she was involved with everything.

Here are some more of her thoughts about that time, as she told them in a 2018 interview:

> It was OUR office. It was always an "us" thing. Olly had ups and downs, but I think he had a really good career with a lot of influence over different situations. He probably did not make the money he felt like he should have made, but we didn't starve. We could always buy peanut butter. We didn't always have big criminal cases. We incorporated towns. We incorporated Lexa and Haynes when I was there. We did a lot of work with legal services. We did five or six divorces, and we knew we were going to get paid for those. We had a client once who was well-off and did not have any children. She and her husband had made very good investments. He died first and when she passed away, Olly was the administrator of her estate. She left all her money to charities like the Diabetes Association, the Cancer Foundation, and Meharry Medical School in Nashville. He took the $100,000 check over to Meharry, and we mailed the money to all the charitable organizations.

> Most of our clients were farmers, and the farmers were always needing some type of lease or warranty deed. We did a lot of Farmers Home Administration (FmHA) stuff. It's not called that anymore. We did a lot of work where people got loans from FmHA to build their houses, and we closed those loans. Every once in a while, we'd get a personal injury case where we'd make some money.

Olly had a rule to protect himself from gossip. When a woman was in his office, he'd say, "Pat, you need to come in here." So, it was sort of like with a male doctor. Get in here with the patient. It was with any woman. And he did that even after he came up to the court of appeals in Little Rock. You know how people are. He had to keep it on the "we are here for business" level.

When they came to Olly Neal, people knew they were going to get the unadulterated truth. They could count on him to say what he was thinking. He just told it like it was: "This is what is happening now. This is what is going to happen. These are the pitfalls and you've got to be able to maneuver around them."

Defamation of Character Case

In 1985, I got a new client, Walter White, who was a black man accused of having out-of-wedlock sex with a white woman. Walter White worked in the St. Francis County Natural Resources Conservation Service (NRCS) office. He was at a fairly high level in the agency, and the white woman was a secretary. He told me that two white boys, while at work, had written a letter to someone else in the agency accusing him of having sexual relations with this white secretary. He had seen the letter, but he didn't have a copy. I immediately said, "Get a copy of that damn letter! And don't tell anyone you have come to see me or are going to do anything. As soon as they find out you have me on this case, they are going to sanitize those files."

He knew the head of the secretarial pool. She found the letter, made a copy for him, and put the original back in place without telling anyone. I filed a defamation of character case against the white boys in state court. During discovery, I did not find the letter in their files, and those boys were denying the existence of any letter. But, of course, I had the copy that would prove my case.

Because it was defamation of character, I actually represented Walter White, his wife, the white secretary, and her husband. This type of case is normally tried in circuit court, but the defendant's lawyer had it moved. They said the case had to be tried in federal court because NRCS is a federal agency. Whatever their reason, I wasn't opposed to the move because I didn't trust the circuit court judges to be fair. Judge G. Thomas Eisele was the federal judge assigned to this case. He had a reputation as a decent guy who never said bad things about black people, but he was very, very conservative.

By 1985, I had been practicing for six years and I had some confidence in my trial abilities, plus I got good help. As soon as the case was moved to federal court, I asked Kathleen Bell to come work the case with me because she knew federal court procedures a lot better than I did.

We put on a show for Judge Eisele. When we got to trial, I put one of the white men who signed the letter on the witness stand. I don't remember his first name, but his last name was Harlow. I asked a few preliminary questions to let him relax and get confident, and then I took out the letter and asked if the signature on it was his. And he said yes. Everybody could see this was true because the guy had a distinctive signature. So, then I started reading the letter with all the incriminating words. I was grinnin' and prancin' and Harlow was finished.

This case was about racism pure and simple. That letter never would have been written if it had been a white guy having sex with a white secretary. Those people were just riled up because a black man was with a white woman. Secondly, they had lied to me when they said that the letter didn't exist. Those white boys had a U.S. government attorney for their lawyer, and he was over there with them complaining and whining. When Harlow broke down on the stand, I felt no sympathy for him. None whatsoever. Sometimes when I climbed on people like that, I did feel bad, but in this situation, which was clearly a case of outright racism, it was my job to help these ignorant people get past that old stuff. We were in trial only a few days, and I won the case.

Chapter 13
Gene Raff, the Tyrant Prosecutor

Gene Raff was a prosecuting attorney with way too much power. He thought he was king, and he acted overbearing in every way. Gene had his thumb on all the lawyers practicing in his district, and just about everyone was afraid of him. Every lawyer who had to try a case against him agreed that he was out of control. Jimmie Wilson and I were the only ones who dared stand up to him. I'm not sure about Jimmie, but I felt like I had nothing to lose. One time, Jesse Daggett asked me, "Why are you taking on Gene like you do? Don't you know that he is going to make life impossible for you?" I told him, "Jesse, Gene Raff has never done a damn thing for me, so why should I show any deference for him? I don't care what he thinks. I have nothing to lose." Maybe it was harder for the white lawyers to stand up.

In 1980, Jimmie Wilson and I tried to get someone to run against Gene. There had not been a black prosecutor in all of Arkansas since Reconstruction. And it still seemed impossible for a black lawyer to get elected. So, we talked to a white lawyer from Brinkley, Dan Kennett, who was interested. We thought we had convinced him to run, but Kennett never filed.

Governor Clinton Awarded Gene Raff Even More Power

I went with Jimmie Wilson, Leon Phillips, Wilbur Barnes, and my eight-year-old daughter Karama to see Governor Clinton after he lost his reelection in the fall of 1980. We went to tell him we could help him get reelected next time. We told him, "When you run two years from now, you won't have to worry about eastern Arkansas. We can deliver all the counties up and down the Delta."

We also used that conversation to talk about Gene Raff. The one thing we asked for had to do with controlling Raff. We said it out straight to Clinton, "Don't put Gene Raff on the police commission." Clinton told us that he wouldn't do it. That was easy for him to say because at the time there was a law preventing a prosecutor from being on the police commission. But as soon as Clinton was reelected, the legislature passed a new law allowing prosecutors to serve, and Clinton immediately appointed Raff to the goddamn commission.

After Gene got that appointment, he was even more powerful. He could inject himself into a police investigation. For example, when Henry Wilkerson, circuit judge in Gene's district, got a DWI up in Jonesboro, the charges disappeared with no explanation. Somebody had to have told the state police to make those charges go away. I have no proof, but I have always believed it was Gene. Henry Wilkerson was his circuit judge and as prosecutor Gene benefited from Wilkerson's favor when trying cases in his court.

Raff's Rangers

I bet you have never heard of anything quite like this either. Gene had his own special police force called Raff's Rangers! Raff's Rangers were made up of deputy sheriffs from the six counties in the First Judicial Circuit. Each deputy reported directly to Gene as well as to his county's sheriff. That meant Gene didn't have to go through a sheriff if he wanted to get something done. All he had to do was contact one of his Rangers. I suspect all this was possible because the sheriffs were afraid of him too. Gene was so strong that they felt like they had to do whatever he said.

Raff's Special Chair

Gene held criminal court in each county four times a year, and everyone saw him get extra-special treatment. Cross County was probably the most extreme. He was treated like a god up there. The guy who cooked for the Cross County jail was pretty good, and the jail prepared a special lunch for Gene whenever he was in town. Gene would sit down in his own chair that nobody else dared sit in, and he would have lunch with the sheriff, the circuit judge, and one or two other people. He had a chair like that in all the county courthouses.

When I was the circuit judge, I didn't have a special chair, but I did eat lunch over at the jail in Cross County two or three times because there was no restaurant close by. The few times I ate in like that, it was with my court recorder or maybe the bailiff. I never ate with the prosecutor or any of the others involved in a current case.

The Stolen Roundup Case

Gene Raff was a dishonest autocrat and I felt it directly sometimes. Jimmie Wilson farmed a couple thousand acres in Phillips County, and his cousin Willie Weaver was Jimmie's farm manager. In the mid-1980s when the farmers were just starting to use Roundup, it was expensive—about $500 per gallon—and everybody wanted the stuff. So, if you had farm workers, they were stealing it and selling it.

When Willie got caught in possession of several gallons of Roundup, I represented him. It was clear that the Roundup was stolen property, and Gene Raff charged him with "theft by possession of a farm chemical." So, I said to Gene like I did in every farm theft case like this, "Gene, can he make restitution, pay a reasonable fine, and get a suspended sentence?" For about a year, I kept pushing him, not getting a response and having to put the case off whenever it came up on the docket. One day down in Helena I said to Gene, "What the hell are you going to do with this?" I knew that Jimmie had made some enemies in Phillips County. And this is what Gene told me, "The people want me to send Jimmie to the pen. I can't get Jimmie on this one, but I'm going to give 'em his cousin. Willie got to do time." Gene did stuff like this, but I fought him on this one.

Raff's White Suits and Fancy Boots

Gene Raff also had style. If he knew he would win, he could put on a show like nobody else. I remember when he prosecuted an old-timer medical doctor in Searcy. The doctor was in his seventies and he had something going with his receptionist, who was in her twenties. The old doctor had killed his wife so he could be with this woman, and Gene prosecuted his ass. Every day he strutted into court carrying a Bible. He put on a show. Gene had his picture in the paper every day during that trial. In each picture he wore a different white suit and different pair of fancy boots.

Prosecutorial Misconduct

Then in 1986, a young black Lee County attorney, Bill Lewellen, got in serious trouble with Gene Raff, but it was Raff who lost in the end this time. Lewellen was defending Almore Banks, a black pastor accused of sexually assaulting a twelve- or thirteen-year-old girl who was a member of his church. Lewellen was giving his client solid and aggressive representation by interviewing all the potential witnesses, including the girl and her mother.

Lewellen had a belligerent style. He would talk tough and was not deferential at all. Lewellen would say to Gene things like, "You don't have enough to get this man. I am going to send you back to Helena." He packed the courtroom with unruly spectators from the black community, and Raff was no longer in control of the whole show. Raff started to worry that he could lose the case, and out of desperation he filed a criminal charge against Lewellen, accusing him of attempted witness tampering with the mother and daughter. Witness tampering is a felony—a serious crime— and if convicted Lewellen could lose his license to practice law.

When I became aware of the case, Lewellen had filed a counter suit against Gene in federal court, and he was asking the federal judge to enjoin (meaning to stop) the criminal charges against him in state court. Up until this point, Lewellen had acted as his own attorney, so at first he didn't have anyone representing him. He wanted John Walker but was having a hard time getting in touch with him. Lewellen and I had never been close, but he had my friend Wilbur Peer tell me that he was in trouble and needed my help. So, I called Lewellen and asked, "What do you need me to do, Bill?" He said, "I don't know if I want you to be my lawyer or to testify for me."

I agreed to do either one but told him that John Walker would be the best lawyer to represent him in federal court. Lewellen did get John Walker to take the case, and I went in as a witness. To win, Walker had to prove that the entire system in the First Judicial District was broken. He needed to show that they all were biased and corrupt: circuit judges, chief prosecutor, and deputy prosecutors.

I had been witness to this corruption and bias, and in part of my testimony I said that I had seen Raff and Judge Yates going to court in the same car. I testified, "If Gene [Raff] is not happy with you, you are not going to get a continuance, because of Raff's influence over the court. Gene uses that to bring you in line. It is clear to me that Judge Yates is controlled by Mr. Raff and that Judge Wilkerson is most responsive." Background to all this was that Harvey Yates had been a struggling lawyer until Raff recommended he be appointed circuit judge in 1983. Then, in 1984, Yates was elected unopposed because Gene made Dan Kennett, who was going to run against him, back down.

I also gave evidence about Raff's racist practices. I testified that the way Raff, Cahoon, and Circuit Judges Yates and Wilkerson treated black lawyers was different from how they treated white lawyers. And I told them about when Raff had said to my face that he would not hire me to be Lee County's deputy prosecutor because I was black.

Lewellen won. The federal court had never before enjoined a state prosecution in Arkansas. This was big. It was a profound incrimination of the First Judicial Circuit, Gene Raff, and all the men he controlled in the judiciary. Gene Raff was guilty of prosecutorial misconduct. The trial was in Little Rock, and the legal community paid close attention to it. Of course, the impact was greatest in east Arkansas, but Gene looked bad to every-body in the legal community statewide. Even today the Arkansas lawyers who are sixty and above remember it well.

Dan Dane against Gene Raff

Dan Dane was a highly ethical white lawyer in Forrest City, and the next step in Gene Raff's downfall came when Dane decided he had to take on Raff. In a letter describing how he came to his decision, Dane stated:

> In the spring of 1988, I got a group of lawyers together to discuss the problems in our district. The conversation turned to Gene Raff's personally. He had become totally arrogant and obnoxious. He bragged publicly that the sheriff in each county had been obliged to give him a pair of expensive cowboy boots. We put up the money to have a polit-ical consultant conduct a poll to see if Raff could be defeated. The poll showed that for an 18-year incumbent, very few voters recognized his name and 80% of those who did had a negative opinion of him. Essen-tially, we only had to get a candidate to run and let Raff run against him-self. But here was the rub. All the lawyers other than Olly or me were afraid to cross Raff. Yes, physically afraid of him. Olly had no chance of winning a district-wide race as a black man so that only left me.

I remember one day Dan Dane and I were standing in front of the St. Francis County Courthouse after a circuit court session during which Gene Raff had been obnoxious as usual. We saw a car go by carrying the circuit judge, prosecutor Raff, and the court reporter on their way back to Helena. Dane commented, "Any lawyer who has ever been anywhere knows how that completely destroys any appearance of impartiality." We all were mad, but it seemed like we couldn't do anything about it.

Then one day before he filed, Dan came up to me in the Forrest City courthouse and asked, "If I run, will you and Jimmie support me?" I told him, "Stand here just a minute." We didn't have cell phones then, so I went to the clerk's office and used their phone to call Jimmie. He said, "Hell, yes. Tell him to run." Jimmie and I were involved in Dan's campaign from that moment. From our civil rights work in the 1970s, we still had a good rap-port with the preachers. Dan's campaign didn't feel like it was just political. It was almost religious. We took him to all the black churches. He would speak a little, give a big wave and grin, and then we would get the hell out of there and go on the next church. Generally, it was two churches each

Sunday, but down in West Helena and Helena where the churches were closer together, we would do three. If Dane couldn't make it, me, me and Jimmie, or me and somebody else would speak for him, telling folks why they should vote for this white man. It was not a stealth campaign either. We did not slip around about what we were doing. We even had a big campaign fish fry at the Lee brothers' house just west of Marianna.

Gene and I Had Something in Common

Gene knew that we were absolutely opposed to everything about him in politics and the legal system. And when I would be in the middle of a serious fight with him, I thought he was a son-of-a-bitch. But that was all. My relationship with him did not include personal animosity. You may not believe this, but Gene and I actually had some things in common. And even in our most intense, contentious times, if we met at a function like a bar meeting, we would be drinking and bullshitting about the "scenery." Both me and Gene were stupid in that regard. We would be grinnin' and talkin' about the pretty women. They usually didn't hear what we were saying, but sometimes a woman got the word and she'd be grinnin' back and sometimes you could tell that she thought you were a damn fool.

Gene Raff Took It Pretty Well

Dan Dane won the 1988 election, and all of us were surprised at how bad he beat Raff. I expected Gene to carry the white vote because I didn't think the white community would vote for anybody black folks supported. But it turned out that not only did black folks want to get rid of Gene Raff, white people did too. Dan Dane won the black vote, and he also won in Gene's own majority-white precinct. Dane became prosecutor in January 1989.

When Raff got his ass whipped by Dane, he accepted it pretty well. He went back to being a regular lawyer, no longer the main event wherever he went, and he was mostly out of the news. At least with regard to me and Jimmie, he understood it wasn't about us hating him. He still came to some of the social functions. He still had a drink of whiskey and if you stood next to him, he would comment on which woman was the most attractive, which man had more than he deserved, that sort of thing. I know it's crude but that was how we talked. There didn't seem to be anything special about him anymore. He took the beating and settled down. He did all right and lived a good long time.

I never knew exactly what Dan Dane thought of Raff. He might have thought him to be the worst thing since Hitler, but I understood Gene to be part of the old system. Because we were black, he couldn't help wanting to keep me and Jimmie Wilson and Bill Lewellen in our place. I had dealt with his kind before. He was just another white boy who was in my way. Gene was more direct and tough, but I saw him as I had seen Lon Mann in the 1970s. Gene Raff was just a white boy I was up against, and I had to figure out how to beat the son of a bitch.

Chapter 14
Arkansas's First Black Prosecutor 1991–1992

I didn't understand it at the time, but many circumstances were leading up to me becoming the first black prosecutor in Arkansas. Gene Raff had been replaced. Dan Dane, the lawyer who replaced him, was not well suited to the job. These were two big factors. Then, there I was with plenty of trial experience. And when the offer came, I had to accept. But I must say, I never wanted the job and for good reason. Being prosecutor was by far the greatest challenge to my personal integrity I ever faced. It was hard, and I was not prepared.

Becoming a Deputy Prosecutor

Most of the prosecutor's work in the First Judicial Circuit is criminal cases, but Dan Dane's experience was in business law. Since he had very little criminal experience, soon after he was elected, Dan asked me to be his deputy prosecutor in Lee County. In Lee, St. Francis, and Phillips Counties, 80% of the defendants were black, and it was just a little bit less than that in Monroe, Cross, and Woodruff Counties. I was more comfortable financially now, and I told him, "Hell, Dan, I really don't want to be prosecuting black folks." But he said, "I want somebody who can do the job and somebody I can trust." So, I went to talk it over with my old friend Pitson Brady, and Brady said, "We would rather you not prosecute black folks. But it could be good for the black community to see you representing the law." I agreed with Brady and accepted the job.

I was Dane's deputy prosecutor from 1989 through most of 1991. During that time, I prosecuted mostly drug, theft, and burglary cases, and the judges responded pretty well to me and my courtroom style. We started the policy of requiring anyone who received probation and did not have a high school diploma to get a GED (General Educational Development diploma) as a probation requirement. Since Dane was the prosecutor, I had to clear the idea with him, but he had no problem with it.

Appointed Out of the Blue

Dan Dane was reelected in the November 1990 election, but Dan was not cut out to be a prosecutor in eastern Arkansas. He was from New Mexico, and I think he had a limited understanding of the regular order of how things worked in the Delta. Dan was a good lawyer. He had high moral standards. He got involved in the fight against Gene Raff because he saw him as a threat to the rule of law, but not having experience in criminal law and not being raised in the Delta meant that he was not prepared for the what came after the election.

Somewhere in the middle of 1991, Dan became completely frustrated with what he saw as the insufferable efforts by the sheriff deputies and former deputy prosecutors to undermine what he was trying to do. He even made a trip to Washington DC to talk with Senator Dale Bumpers about it. Dan said of the situation, "I tried to contact Gov. Bill Clinton. He was out of the state running for president. I knew that he was loyal to Raff. I would not resign if he was going to appoint one of Raff's deputies as the PA. I would only resign if Olly were appointed in my place. I had known Lt. Gov. Jim Guy Tucker since law school. I met with him to tell him the same thing. He agreed. He called Clinton on the telephone while I was there and Clinton agreed. By September, I had a job with the FDIC in Atlanta and submitted my resignation to Jim Guy. He appointed Olly."

About three or four days before he resigned, Dan called all of his deputies together and told us about his decision to leave. Jim Guy Tucker was the acting governor. There still were no black prosecutors in Arkansas. I told Dane that he should ask Tucker to appoint Ashley Higgins, the white deputy prosecutor in Phillips County. Ashley had been my classmate in law school, and I had always thought well of him.

The call from Jim Guy Tucker came in the evening, and I was caught off guard. I thought that Dane and Ashley might have conspired. I didn't know what to say, so I told him that I needed twelve hours to talk to my folks and think about it. I talked to Jimmie Wilson and the other black lawyers I was working with. Most of them thought that if we were going to raise hell about what the prosecutor was doing, we had to assume responsibility given the chance. But Jimmie disagreed, and he was the only one who was forceful. He said, "You ought to get the hell out of there completely." However, by that time, Jimmie had figured out that he couldn't muscle me to where he wanted me to be. He just gave me his opinion and then let it alone.

Helping Me Decide

I had to go back to my friend Pitson Brady again. Brady was an uneducated old-timer who knew how things worked. He had big bug eyes. Hell, we used to call him Bug Eye and make fun of him. But Brady always gave me thoughtful advice. He said something like, "Well, you probably ought to do it because this thing has got to be turned around, and I believe you can show them how it ought to be done." I don't know how Brady understood like he did. He was not raised up in the church. He was a fixture in the church when he died, of course, but he started out as a gambler and a hustler. Brady didn't have to twist my arm. What he said was consistent with my beliefs. I just needed to know I had support in my community. I felt if Brady was with me, I didn't need anybody else. We weren't like running partners or anything. I just needed to know he was behind me. This is the kind of influence he had on me.

Jim Guy Tucker Took a Chance on Me

So that's how I got to be prosecuting attorney in the First Judicial Circuit of eastern Arkansas. Jim Guy Tucker called me on October 8, 1991, and I was officially sworn in on October 9 by Arkansas Supreme Court chief justice Jack Holt. It was in the presence of acting governor Jim Guy Tucker, who gave me my certificate of appointment registered with the Arkansas secretary of state. The next week, Bill Clinton came home and signed another certificate so he could be on record as making my appointment. I was active in the political circles of eastern Arkansas, so maybe he wanted to make certain of his political standing in the Delta. But I thought then and still believe he would not have appointed me on his own. Bill Clinton is a brilliant politician, and he was careful. I have the impression that he always saw me as too unpredictable. I think he wanted me to be close but didn't trust me, because I was outspoken and he thought that I might say something that would embarrass him.

Appointing me was risky. Some people still saw me as the bogeyman of Lee County, and when thinking about why he had decided to appoint me, I considered one thing that might have worked in my favor: I never tried to use other folks to enhance my own situation. If it looked like something would benefit me and hurt the other person, I would say, "Don't do it. It might be good for me, but don't do it." I would put it just that way. So, I thought that Dan Dane and Jim Guy Tucker might have picked up on this, and maybe this is why they were willing to take a chance on me.

Later, in a 2018 interview, Calvin King, who is founder/director of Arkansas Land and Farm Development and someone I have worked with since the 1980s, had this to say about me and why I might be considered trustworthy: "Olly is not an ego-driven person. He always has your back and that means a lot. He looks out for others who might not have experienced as much as he has. When I was a naïve kid and later too, he would warn me to be careful when there was someone undercutting my efforts. And he can bring out the best in everybody. He works from the perspective of—don't only think of yourself; think of the greater good. He will say, 'Let's choose the option that will help everybody, and we'll all grow together.'"

Finally, in spring of 2019 when we were having cocktails after a meeting on implicit bias, I asked Jim Guy Tucker himself why he had had enough confidence in me to appoint me to be a prosecutor. He told me something like this: "I knew you had a reputation for being pushy. But I also had heard you say more than once that you always make damn certain to assure the same rights to others that you demand for yourself." And he was right. I have always said that to both white folks and black folks.

New Order

By the time I became prosecutor, the old order of how blacks and whites interacted had changed, but most of the white people I dealt with were still ignorant. They had not caught up with the times, and I had it pretty rough. Once, in the courtroom up in Wynne, a lawyer saw the pistol I kept in my briefcase and told the judge, but the judge already knew I carried a pistol. What I was announcing to people quite simply was, "Please let me get along with you, but if you gotta have a fight, you will get one."

As prosecutor I needed the cooperation and support of law enforcement, and this was the first time law enforcement had to deal with a black man as an official who was over them. They had to be receptive to me and do what I wanted. I told them how I thought it ought to be and how we ought to function. Fortunately, because I had been appointed, I did not owe my position to those sons of bitches. And because I had been appointed a state statute prevented me from running in the next election for the prosecutor job in the same district, so I wasn't afraid of them working against me.

Sometimes I had to get tough. Dave Parkman was the St. Francis County sheriff, and his office was in Forrest City. He was a little guy known for hitting black people in the face. One day soon after I was elected, I was in his office talking to him, and I had to put my briefcase on his desk with my hand in there on my 9mm. I was prepared to shoot him if I had to.

Here's what happened. I had too much work. I was busy as hell and always pressed for time. A court proceeding to review the current criminal cases was coming up on Tuesday. I had sent word to Sheriff Parkman and the Forrest City chief of police that I needed to meet with all of their investigators about their active cases. I had to talk to them so I would know which cases to prepare and present in court on the following Monday. But when I got to Parkman's office, none of his investigators were there—and I was pissed.

As I came up to him at his desk, Parkman started raising up from his seat, and I told him right up in his face, "Just wait a motherfucking minute. What I will do is dismiss all your goddamn cases. I don't need your motherfucking ass." I was cussing at him like that. I had my hand on my pistol because if he grabbed me by the collar and hit me with his fist, I was going to shoot him. He sat back down and told me, "We'll get somebody for you. We'll get somebody for you." I was so mad that I said to him, "You don't have to get no-goddamn-body," and I turned around and walked out to my car. I knew he was going to look real bad and be embarrassed when none of his cases came to trial. His chief deputy Glenn Ramsey ran after me and said, "The sheriff just messed up. Will you come back tomorrow? We'll have it all ready for you then."

Dealing with Rednecks

It was never easy, and I don't regret acting ignorant and crude. I don't think that those boys would have understood the sophistication of, "Well now, boys, can't we work on this together?" I don't think there was any other way to deal with them. They had to know that I was somebody who could be just as ignorant as they were. Of course, I had never been your regular nice guy who was used to being pushed around, either.

And I have to say something more about a redneck who thinks that black folks are lesser and need to be controlled. If you give him a lot of room, he will push you, but if you push him back on his heels a little bit, he acts better and is like everybody else. And once a redneck gets to know you and decides you are all right, he is going to get along with you and treat you right. This has been my experience.

Prosecutor Power and Fear of Failure

Being the district prosecutor felt nothing like when I was a deputy prosecutor. As a deputy, I had coverage. As a deputy, if somebody didn't like what I was doing, they would call Dan Dane. When I was the district prosecutor, there was nobody they could call besides me. If somebody didn't like what I was doing, I was the one they called to complain. If somebody didn't like what one of my deputies was doing, I was the one they called for that complaint too.

For me personally, the magnitude of being the district prosecutor came in two parts—the power of the position and my fear of failure. The title gave me the responsibility and the power to do what I wanted within the confines of the law. It meant that as prosecutor of the entire district, I could stand up strong for myself and what I thought was right because I WAS IN CHARGE. Fear of failure was always with me too because I had to keep my own prejudice under control. I also had a lot of pressure from my folks to give special treatment to the black community. When I was making decisions, I had to get my prejudice and the pressure from my community out of my head.

Memorable Cases

They were not newspaper-coverage big, but some cases were memorable for me. One involved a white boy in Phillips County who had done something immature and stupid having to do with drugs. I can't remember exactly what it was, but he had not put the world at risk. He had not injured anybody seriously. This young boy was the son of a prominent white family, and there were black folks down there who wanted me to go after him and get even. They wanted me to use the boy to send the white community a message. David Solomon, a well-known lawyer, represented this boy, and he thought that I was going to put something heavy on him too. But I couldn't do it. I had a nephew who was in and out of shit all the time. I thought about him and decided that I was going to treat this white boy the same way I would treat my nephew. We didn't have much community service going on back then, so he got a $400 or $500 fine and a suspended sentence.

Another hard case for me personally was also in Phillips County. A white cop in Helena slapped a fifteen- or sixteen-year-old black boy. It happened at a high school dance that the cop was chaperoning. The boy and the cop's daughter were dancing, and their dancing got to be close in a way that the cop considered unacceptable. He couldn't stand it, so he slapped the boy with the flat of his hand. It was third-degree battery because the boy was not bruised or marked in any way. (Second-degree battery requires some injury; first-degree battery requires serious injury that affects the person's health.)

So, I had this racist white cop and I wanted to punish him. I felt like charging the son of a bitch with second-degree battery and forcing the issue. If it had been a black cop who slapped a white boy for dancing too close to his daughter, I was sure that a white prosecutor would have charged him with second-degree battery. Hell, yes! The black folks in Helena were saying, "You've got him! You've got him! Hurt him while you've got him." But I couldn't do it. I charged him with third-degree battery, and as happens in most of these cases he was charged a fine and the court costs. That's all. It didn't feel like enough. I knew the cop too. He certainly was not a likable person, but I could not charge him just to pay him back for being white. I did not like him, and my folks in Helena were MAD AS HELL—at ME. I was part of the black community, but I had to act like I was part of the white community. So that was a tough one for me. Was I happy? Hell, no.

Speeches about Being Fair

Back when I was a community organizer in Lee County, I met with people all the time. This habit continued after I became a lawyer and a prosecutor. I would go to meetings whenever they asked me. I would talk to big church groups and small groups. If they called, I went. Now, folks in Phillips County were talking about me bad. Gossip in the black community was that the goddamn cop had beaten that poor black boy half to death. And I had let him off! They saw me as a Tom. The way I got past all of this was by talking to my people about what I did and why, and by telling them how difficult it was for me. And I think that many folks understood me. I really do.

I had a regular talk I gave a lot. I would speak to folks from the standpoint of practicality and the standpoint of fairness. And I would emphasize the practicality. I'd tell them, "I will not be prosecutor very long. You can tell me to get them bastards while we got 'em. But that may create a circumstance where they will get you worse when I go out of office." And then I would talk about the fairness of it. I'd tell them, "It is important to the overall community if we can move ourselves up a level." This was a philosophical thing that I had to deal with in my own head anyway.

Educating Myself Along the Way

As I was going along, I was getting an education. If you had asked me about all this before I became prosecutor, I would have been wondering what the hell you were talking about. I had not run for the job, so I never had to campaign, and I had never formulated a theory of how I should treat white people when I became the prosecutor. On the job, I was talking to myself while I was talking to my folks. I was thinking out loud too.

I remember one particular church session in Helena, where this guy was beating around the bush for a while, and then he said, "I will make it plain to you. What we want you to do is put all the white boys in jail and let all the black boys go." He was overstating it, but his point was that, as payback, I should be lenient toward blacks and aggressive toward whites. Since I felt some of that myself, I understood his point of view. But this way of getting even did not make any logical sense to me. Not that I was a brilliant, good person. I wasn't John Lewis saying it is good to love everybody or anything like that.

I looked at it this way, and I told him, "First, I am the only black prosecuting attorney in Arkansas, and there probably won't be another one for a long time. And second, even if I try to go easy on blacks and hard on the white boys, I could not pull it off, because there are forces in the legal system to bring my conduct in line. So, it just isn't practical. In my opinion, the way to get even is to get in the middle of it and do your best to make the system run like it is supposed to. I'd like to see more black folks who are dedicated to being strong and fair in the courthouse." I realized this then and still believe it today. We need black people in leadership roles like sheriff, circuit judge, district prosecutor, county judge, mayor, and more. And at every point in my life, I have tried to create circumstances where black folks can be involved.

Keeping My Reputation with Black Folks

I definitely don't want to come off as sounding like I was rational all the time. My reaction was not always out of intelligence. Before I got to be prosecutor, I would sometimes go shoot craps in a place down on The Line in Phillips County. This joint was a rough place where somebody was killed at least three or four times a year. We called it "The Line" because it was where black folks drew a line and said, "This is ours. White folks, don't come here!"

After I became prosecutor and we had had the January 1992 term of court in Phillips County, two people told me at separate times that some old boys in that joint were saying, "He better not bring his ass down here anymore." And when I heard what they were saying, I got hot and had to go down there. I thought, "You want a part of me? I'm coming!" It was something that a sensible human being would not react to. But that was not my style. My style was, "Wait a minute, motherfucker. I can do what I want, and I can go where I want." I have no proof of this, but I might add that I have always believed Jimmie Wilson was behind those boys telling me what was being said about me. He probably just wanted to see what I would do. Jimmie had his ways.

I put on my sport jacket. Stuck the 9mm in the small of my back. Put my .38 in my boot, and I had a 12-gauge shotgun on the rack in my truck. My Lee County deputy prosecutor Don Trimble was a black guy from Little Rock, and his office was in my building. He saw me and said, "What you doing, Olly?" I told him, "You stay out of it. This is my goddamn east Arkansas nigger shit." He said, "I'm going with you." He didn't have a gun, so I had to give him my .38 pistol and my 30.06 rifle. And we went down there.

I probably should have, but as district prosecutor I had never thought of stopping the gambling. When Trimble and I walked in, I put my $2 on the goddamn craps table. They looked up at me and it got real quiet. That's all. Then, they started the next craps shoot. Later, when I got ready to leave and was at the door, I turned around and said, "See you boys later." They were my boys. I wasn't insulting them. That is the way you talk to your close folk. I felt like whoever had been talking about me would get the message.

At the time, I was not thinking everything out. I was not. I was not a brilliant, thoughtful person who planned. But looking back, I can say that going there probably did make a difference to those folks. That community was made of individuals on the criminal edge. They had absolutely no respect for the law. Their attitude was that the law was the power the state had to use and abuse them. And there is some truth to that.

They expected me to stay away from anywhere I would be in physical danger because they saw the prosecutor as their enemy. They thought that I would to do just like white prosecutors did—hide behind the law and not do anything without the police out in front. I think it was useful for black folks to see that I was the same man after I took on the title of district prosecutor. I would still go wherever they were, see what they were doing, and participate in their conversation. It helped them accept the notion that Olly Neal may be a son of a bitch who prosecutes black people but he is still one of us.

When I represented the law, I wanted my people to make decisions and do things that were consistent with the law. I also wanted to keep their respect and not rile up their resistance. If I was going to be effective, they had to see me to be the same as they were and understand that I was dedicated to making the law protect them too. Reputation for me is how I am seen in the black community. And this is how I was able to survive four years working in prosecutorial activities, including fifteen months as the district prosecutor, and still keep my reputation. I could put some of my folk in jail, but they could still say, "Olly Neal is all right."

They Were My Boys

I was the prosecuting attorney, and I was in charge. Sometimes I went straight at them. Like when a Chinese grocery store owner was having trouble. He was in an old building near some black joints in Forrest City. The Blue Flame was right around the corner. The black boys used to go in the grocery store and take what they wanted. They would just run over him. One day he saw me at the courthouse and told me about what was going on. I asked, "You got some names?" He said, "No, no, no names. Don't know names." It was clear that he didn't want to get crosswise with anybody by saying names. So, one day when I saw some boys in there, I came in his store. He sort of signaled to me that they were the ones.

I went up and told them straight out, "Don't fuck with this man. He's all right. He's Chinese. He ain't white. He's more like us blacks. Don't be fucking with him." That was my way. After that they let him alone. They were all my boys and they listened to me. I don't think I knew any of them, but, hell, they knew who I was. Also, my older brother Willie (one of Daddy's sons who never lived with us) had about nine children at home and he had another eight or nine more out on the street too. Some of them could have been in Forrest City. Any of those boys could have been my nephew. Our lives were not pristine.

Ollie Brantley Also Gave Folks Confidence in the Law

When Ollie Brantley was deputy sheriff in Lee County, he was able to help black folks come to respect and obey the law, but he was a nicer guy than I was. He was easier for folks to like. I'll give you an example. I would hear people say, "Oh, hell, I've got to slow down. Brantley may not arrest me, but I don't want to speed." Brantley was out there patrolling same as the white cops, but black folks never felt the same way about the white cops. Through liking and respecting Brantley, they gained some confidence in the law. They got to thinking, "The law is for me too."

Murder Case in Helena

I had a big murder case in Helena when I was the prosecutor. A black man was accused of killing two white people. Here's what happened. A white man, his girlfriend, and their friend were traveling down the Mississippi River in their boat. They were on their way to someplace in the Caribbean. The man was from Eads, Tennessee, and his boat had a big diesel engine. The engine broke down just north of Helena, so they docked at Helena to have it repaired. The dock is about a mile from town.

They were young, white liberals and while they were ashore, they were being friendly and talking to blacks. The girlfriend was a pretty woman of about twenty-seven or twenty-eight. Their friend was a big, muscled guy, and he helped run the boat. The woman liked to shoot pool and thought she could get along with everybody. She was put together in pretty good order too, and she would have gotten your attention even if you were a Baptist preacher because she was wearing a little bikini outfit. When I heard about her, she seemed to be like my girlfriend Karen, who is now my wife. Karen is someone who says things like, "I don't need you to help me do that. You don't need to go with me. I can take care of myself."

Back in 1991, black folks and white folks didn't associate much with each other in Helena. But the white woman and the white muscle man were in a black pool hall. I call it a black pool hall because black folks were the only people in there besides the two from out of town. A black boy, Calvin Marshall, took up with the woman, and he was behaving appropriately. He didn't push too hard, and she invited him and his friend to the boat for a spaghetti dinner.

Marshall really knew the territory very well. But after dinner when they were getting ready to leave, he said that he wasn't sure of how to get back to town. And the woman told him that she could show them the way. Her boyfriend said that maybe he should go with her, but she told him no, that she could take care of it herself. The man got their big buddy to go with his girlfriend anyway. And the big guy took his dog too.

The friend Marshall had with him was a young boy who was kind of slow or a little bit retarded. Anyway, they started back and when they got in a remote area, Marshall made his move. He grabbed the big guy and cut his throat. When the big guy's dog jumped at him, he caught the dog in the air and stabbed him right in the heart. By this time, the woman was running. Marshall ran her down and caught her, cut off her bikini, raped her, and killed her. I don't remember exactly what Marshall's friend's involvement was, but he clearly was just going along. We convicted him; he took a plea and served some time.

Todd Murray was my deputy prosecutor in Phillips County, and he really wanted to prosecute this case himself. He insisted, and since I was busy with other cases, I let him do it. I reviewed what he was preparing and saw that he had it laid out right, so I said okay and went back to my work in Marianna. But it turned out that Todd didn't know how to present the evidence very well. He tried the case and got a hung jury.

The hung jury could have happened in part because by this time Phillips County juries were almost always majority black and had been educated. Black participation was high because Jimmie Wilson had worked hard convincing black folks that to be treated fairly, they had to register to vote and serve on a jury when they were called. He had taught them that in civil cases they had to treat black and white folks the same and not follow the lead of the white jurors, who gave black folks just a pittance when they won. Jimmie had taught them that in criminal cases they had to stand up to the white jurors voting to convict a black defendant unless they were sure the defendant was guilty beyond a reasonable doubt.

The day after the hung jury was announced, I got a call from the Arkansas attorney general Winston Bryant telling me that he was going to come over and retry that case for me. It hit me right in the face. I knew what he was saying. He was implying that because I am black, I didn't know what I was doing, and he was going to have to take charge of my ass.

But I WAS IN CHARGE. I was filled with wanting to get back at him. I thought, "Damn you," but I tried to be calm! And I did pretty good not to resort to cussin' at him. I said, "I don't think so, Mr. Attorney General. I'M the prosecutor here, and if I need your help, I will call you." I used the power of my position and after our conversation, that man never spoke to me again for the rest of his life. Not one word.

This is not true in all states, but in Arkansas, the attorney general does not have supervisory control over district prosecutors. Here, the district prosecutor has discretion and is completely independent. The prosecuting attorney holds an elected position, and as was shown when Gene Raff was voted out of office, the voters have ultimate control. They can vote a prosecutor considered unsuitable out of office in the next election.

Prosecutors have a lot of power. In my opinion, they have the most powerful position in our state's judicial system. They are more powerful than circuit judges and supreme court justices. This is so because the prosecutor decides:

1. whether to charge you,
2. what the charge will be,
3. whether or not to negotiate, and
4. how aggressively to prosecute your case.

And all these decisions are colored by the prosecutor's personal experience.

It is different for a judge, who cannot tell the prosecutor to do or not do something based on personal preference. Judges are bound by the laws made by the legislature, and if a law allows something, the judge cannot change it. The judge can only use the law to decide whether or not the prosecutor is going too far.

Since Calvin Marshall's trial ended in a hung jury, I could try him a second time, and I did. We selected a jury of about nine blacks and three whites, and I won his conviction. When I argued the case, I told the jury, "Calvin Marshall is dangerous, and we cannot tolerate that kind of conduct no matter who does it." I told them, "If you are convinced that he killed these people, then he could kill anybody. If you acquit him, he and others like him will become bold and more dangerous to everybody, both black and white." Calvin Marshall got life without parole, which I thought was a good outcome even though the death penalty was on the table. I did not expect a black jury in Helena to give the death penalty to a black man. The editor of a statewide Arkansas newspaper commented on it too—and published his opinion that the verdict was satisfactory.

Calvin Marshall was a terrible, brutal guy. About seven or eight years later, I got a call notifying me that he had escaped from the penitentiary. He had threatened me because I was the one who had sent him to prison and the authorities were concerned for my safety. But Marshall never got to me before they caught him and locked him back inside.

Prosecutorial Discretion

Another important case for me was one where I chose to exercise prosecutorial discretion. I don't think race played a role in my decision because I would have decided the same way if the races had been reversed. This case involved a black kid who graduated from Lee County High School with honors and won an academic scholarship to the University of Arkansas (UA) in Fayetteville. I think he had a 3.7 grade point average. This was 1991, and UA Fayetteville was not noted for its hospitality to black academic students. However, they were very hospitable to black athletes who could bring their talent to the school's football, basketball, or track teams.

This young college student was out of a rural part of Lee County, where he had grown up with several hotshot kids who were nothing more than small-time thugs. When he was home from college at Christmas, he borrowed his Momma's car and picked up those boys to go for a ride. He was doing what I would have done when I was a kid, taking his no-count friends out to show that he was still a homey.

At this time in Marianna, there was a guy we called Bullett, who was maybe forty-five years old. He was known for his low mental capacity, but he was always good-natured. Marianna is a small town, and everybody knew Bullett. He had a hump back and he walked kind of bad. He used to come up to me and say in his deep voice, "Mr. Neal, gimme a couple of dollars." And I would tell him that I didn't have it, and he would say, "Mr. Neal, you're a lawyer and you don't have two dollars?" When I told him no, he would say, "Well, I thank you anyway." And he would go on. That was his style.

The boys were riding around in Marianna, and there was a baseball bat on the floor of the backseat. When the car went by Bullett, one of them in the backseat said, "Stop the car for a minute," and he jumped out with the bat and busted Bullett in the head. After that, Bullett never could function well at all. He had to wear a diaper and have a full-time caregiver. It was serious first-degree battery, and all four of the boys in the car could be charged with a felony that would justify sending them to the penitentiary.

I charged the boy who used the bat with first-degree battery and sent him to the pen for a good while. I can't remember the exact charge for the other two kids, but they got lesser time. I decided that the driver had just acted stupid when he agreed to stop the car and that I would not charge him with a felony crime for acting stupid. He was charged with a misdemeanor and got probation.

Every year at the Lee County NAACP banquet, I see that boy's Momma. She is always there because her husband is active in the NAACP. She tells me that her son has a good job and is doing well. She is proud of him, and I am proud of him too.

You can see that a prosecutor in Arkansas has a lot of authority. As a matter of fact, I think Arkansas prosecutors have too much authority. What we usually see in the newspaper about the legal system is news of a judge signing something or the appellate court deciding that something is all right or is not all right. Everybody should pay closer attention to the prosecutor because it's the prosecutor who decides how most of the legal system runs. That's my view.

Did I enjoy being the prosecutor?

My office manager Pat Lamar did not like seeing me send black kids to jail. But she stuck with it. This is what she had to say about my prosecutor years in a 2017 interview:

> I was there when Olly was deputy prosecutor and when he was prosecutor. It was hard for him, and it was hard for me too. We were prosecuting people and of course we were bringing legal action against African Americans—and most of them were male African Americans. Sometimes it was the bad ones that got off because the police didn't do what they were supposed to do, and the good ones…maybe a kid had made a mistake…would have to go to jail. Unless the kid had a good support system, we'd ruin his life forever when we sent him to jail. It might be just one mistake and when he got out, he couldn't get a job because of his record. Most of them don't have a support system at home or anyplace else. So, prosecutor was a difficult job. I wish we had not taken it. But that was Olly's decision. It was something he felt he had to do.

If you ask me, "Did you ever enjoy your time as prosecutor?" My answer is, "No, no, no, no, no, no, I didn't. No, I didn't." I had all this authority and power and I had to be FAIR. Being fair required too much conscious effort because I couldn't do what was right automatically. And all the effort I had to put into being fair made the job very difficult for me.

Another part of what made being prosecutor hard was that I was criticized in my own community. I was prosecuting so many black men. No one liked me anymore. Nobody. And my people turned hateful. They knew I was not someone they could push around, so nobody ever came after me, but sometimes when I'd go out to a club, I could feel the coolness and it was clear that they wanted me to get my ass out of there.

The feeling in court was different too. I was under a lot of pressure. My asthma got much worse, and I had to use my inhaler all the time. Thinking about this now, it is a little amusing, but one day as I walked into court, some old boy said loud enough so I could hear, "Here comes that son of a bitch with his can."

And even my friends would criticize what I was doing wherever they saw me. They would tell me what they thought when they saw me in church on Sunday or when I was walking down the street. One time, Odell Davis, who was on the Lake View City Council, told me, "Olly, I don't know why you took that goddamn job fucking with our people." I had nowhere to retreat. I couldn't go to the white community because they were not my people. I never got angry about it, but my position and what I was doing were hard to explain.

Miss Mamie Nelson Fought Me at First

Even Mamie Nelson jumped on me. Before this I never realized the influence she had on me. She had started the NAACP chapter in Lee County way back in 1957. This may not seem like much now, but it was just a year after Mississippi governor James Coleman created the super-secret Mississippi Sovereignty Commission, which collected information on who attended NAACP meetings. Members could lose their jobs or worse. Lee County is right across the river from Mississippi, and people were scared. Sometime later, I learned that the Arkansas Sovereignty Commission had actually collected information in Lee County. They had recorded my Daddy's 1958 Chevrolet going to Forrest City each week and suspected it was going to an NAACP meeting. My Momma was a member, but since she was afraid of losing her job, she kept it a secret. She actually was going up to Forrest City for a class she needed to get her teaching credential.

Anyway, Miss Mamie saw that even after I became prosecutor, there were still too many black kids in the court system. She believed her job as a community activist was to stop unfair prosecution of black folks, so she pushed me hard to do what she thought was right. She wanted me to drop charges and let a black boy out of jail. I don't remember his name or the exact charge, but he was a teenager who had gotten out of line and was doing bad stuff. I think it was selling drugs, and it could have been crack cocaine because that was how those kids could make quick, easy money. One day she talked to me in a back room of the courthouse, and it was tense. I had seen the evidence and had to tell her that I couldn't help that boy. I couldn't in good conscience get the charges dropped just because his Momma was doing good work. When Miss Mamie and I walked out of there, it was cold and I felt bad. I remember thinking, "Our friendship is finished. I'm losing everything I consider important in my community." But fortunately, I was wrong. Miss Mamie was with me when I was sworn in as circuit judge in January 1993. I remember hugging her, and it meant the world to me.

My Own Personal Growth

The positive part of being a prosecutor was my own growth and development as a person. When I had become a lawyer, I was mostly still focused on changing unfair policies that affected black people. This is what I thought about in my law practice. To keep working I had only to worry about looking good to my client and my client community. My clients included very few white people.

Everybody depends on our legal system for justice. So, when I became district prosecutor, my responsibility expanded. I felt a critical need to treat white folks the same way I treated black folks. That is how I saw my job, and this was a different stance for me. I was pushed into becoming a more complete citizen, if you will. And the greater responsibility of being a prosecutor affected me for the rest of my life.

Chapter 15
Arkansas Voting Rights: Redistricting Lawsuits, 1986–1990

A rkansas played a major role in gaining voting rights for blacks. The impact was felt all across the country. I was one of many black lawyers involved, and it was an exciting time for all of us. By filing lawsuits in the federal courts, we forced legislative and judicial redistricting that gave black voters the opportunity to elect candidates of our choice. Progress came step by step, case by case. With each step toward a level political playing field, I witnessed change in the attitudes of both blacks and whites who had been stuck in traditional and oppressive racist thinking.

In the 1970s and '80s, we were certain that if we could participate fully in the political process, black people's status and the confidence in our ability to govern would improve. We had to use litigation to implement the 1965 Voting Rights Act, which outlawed racial discrimination in elections. Section 2 of the Voting Rights Act specifically prohibited voting practices or procedures that resulted in discrimination (either purposefully or unintentionally) on the basis of race.

In Arkansas, we used Section 2, commonly called the "results test," to force redistricting of both legislative and judicial state offices. Legislative redistricting came first and involved three lawsuits. The first case was *Smith v. Clinton*, the second was *Whitfield v. Clinton*, and the third was *M. C. Jeffers v. Clinton*. The *Jeffers* case was by far the biggest because it was statewide.

Our state constitution requires redistricting to be done by an apportionment committee that has the governor as its official chairman. So in each case, Bill Clinton was listed as the defendant because he was governor of Arkansas when the cases were filed. As in other states, legislative redistricting happens every ten years, after the census. Arkansas is divided into 100 legislative districts. At that time, we had 100 state senators but there were not 100 single-member districts. Most were single-member districts drawn to have about 24,000 eligible voters, but a few districts were larger multi-member districts represented by two or three legislators elected at-large.

Legislative Redistricting Cases
Smith v. Clinton, July 1988

Winning this redistricting case gave us a burst of confidence. The lawsuit was instigated by Ben McGee, a black businessman in Crittenden County. He recruited Elbert Smith, president of the local branch of the NAACP, to be the lead plaintiff. Crittenden County was a large district with two representatives elected at large, and both were white. We argued that it should be divided into two districts: one with about 65% black voters and the other with about 84% white voters. Each would have a population of about 23,000. We won the case and gained a new black-majority legislative district. As a result, McGee was elected to the Arkansas legislature in the September 1988 special election. And he served from 1988 to 2000.

Whitfield v. Clinton, December 1989

Kathleen Bell and I worked on this case. Jimmie Wilson had pushed Sam Whitfield, a black attorney in Helena, to run for county judge. There were three candidates, and Sam got the largest number of votes in the primary, but he didn't win because he didn't get the 50% plus one necessary when there are three candidates. Consequently, there was a two-candidate second primary and the winner was the white candidate who came in second the first time. But this result didn't seem fair because Whitfield had gotten more votes in the first primary than ALL the votes cast in the second primary.

Jimmie came to me and said, "It's happened before and this time we are going to sue them over this runoff. But because of my reputation, I need to stay out of it, and I want you to take the lead." I told Jimmie that I was interested but I didn't know voter rights law very well, and he put me in touch with the NAACP's Legal Defense Fund (LDF). They had plenty of experience and brought in top-level expertise on civil rights law. They had the best experts to testify for our case, and they contributed the money to pay for an expensive lawsuit.

I think that LDF assigned Lani Guinier and possibly Pamela Karlan to take the lead. Kathleen and I were the local lawyers. We all worked well together as a team. Kathleen and I participated in discussions of the legal issues involved and identified witnesses from different areas. We were prodding and pushing. We talked to Jimmie all the time too. He was urging and encouraging, and he had his opinions about how the case should be laid out and how we should proceed.

We were challenging a statutory provision for the election of county officials, so the case was heard in federal court before one judge, G. Thomas Eisele. We argued that the total number of voters won by Whitfield in the first primary should have some meaning. Eisele ruled against us, but it was clear that he had a tough time deciding, so we appealed to the 8th Circuit Court of Appeals. Normally, a three-judge panel would decide this type of case in the Appellate Court, but they looked at our case and sent it to their full twelve-judge panel. It was a tie vote—6 to 6. With a tie vote, the initial opinion is confirmed, and we lost. We didn't win, but it was very close and with the ruling so tight we knew we had a strong argument.

M. C. Jeffers v. Clinton, February–March 1990

This was the big one. Winning *Smith v. Clinton* and almost winning *Whitfield v. Clinton* gave us the confidence and impetus to go forward with this lawsuit that had the potential of affecting many districts in Arkansas.

The *Jeffers* redistricting case also is based on Section 2, or the "results test," of the 1965 Voting Rights Act. *Jeffers* challenged the Arkansas district apportionment plan again, but this time it was statewide. We challenged how the districts were drawn for the Arkansas Legislature and the Arkansas Senate all over the state where there were large black populations.

To win a redistricting case, the first thing you have to do is show that the black community is a **cohesive voting population**. In a cohesive voting population, almost all of the voters vote the same way (in this case blacks vote for a black candidate). To prove this, we used expert witnesses who knew the racial makeup of the districts and the results of previous elections. The voter statistics for the districts in question clearly showed that a black candidate won in all the black precincts.

We argued against the three kinds of voter suppression—**cracking, packing, and multi-member**—used by the legislature in different parts of the state. **Cracking** is splitting up a large group of black voters into two single-member districts, so neither has a black majority. **Packing** prevents a black voter majority in two single-member districts by drawing lines to load one district with a huge (something like 90%) majority of black voters, so the other district has a white voter majority. **Multi-member** (at-large) districts like in Crittenden County were drawn so that black voters were put with a much larger white voter population, resulting in the election of two white candidates, and no blacks. Arkansas had two or three of these multi-member districts. Each one could be divided into two single districts, with one district having a black voter majority.

Different lawyers were chosen to examine certain witnesses based on their knowledge of the witness. I was assigned to cross-examine state witness Ernest Cunningham, who was in the legislature. I knew him personally and knew of discrepancies between previous testimony and what he had just stated in his deposition for this case. He couldn't dodge me.

Cunningham lived in Helena and represented Phillips County in the Arkansas House of Representatives from 1969 to 1998. When he was first elected, there were two legislative districts in Phillips County. Cunningham represented one, and Jim Linder represented the other. During redistricting after the 1970 census, Cunningham had wanted to protect both his and Linder's districts, and he had testified that both districts should be maintained. This is what they did. When Jim Linder died before redistricting after the 1980 census, they put West Helena and Helena together into a single district. Cunningham represented this district.

In the *Jeffers* case, when we were negotiating redistricting, we wanted the 1980 plan set aside and a return to two separate districts, so we could create one district with a black voter majority.

In his pretrial deposition, Cunningham testified against splitting his district. He said something to the effect that, to attract industry, they needed a single district that included both West Helena and Helena. I knew we had him on record in the past giving the opposite opinion. So, I was able to expose his inconsistency when I questioned him on the stand, and that weakened his position. I was grinning. He put his head down, and I did one of my prances that I do when I've got the son of a bitch.

I have to add that after that case, Ernest and I became friends and worked together in an attempt to attract a big agricultural research center to Helena. This was while I was practicing law, Ernest was in the legislature, and Clinton was president. Wilbur Peer developed the project proposal, and we needed Clinton's support. But he got tangled up in the Monica Lewinsky scandal and his impeachment took over. Then Senator Trent Lott of Mississippi (who was heavily involved in Clinton's Senate trial following the impeachment) pointed the project to Alcorn State University, a historically black institution in his state. So, we lost the project, but we couldn't really be mad because those folks over there were our friends. Anyway, Cunningham worked hard on this center that would have been good for the whole area.

We Won

Because we were challenging a constitutional provision and not just a statutory rule, the *Jeffers* case was heard in federal court by a three-judge panel. Richard S. Arnold authored the panel's opinion (with a dissenting opinion from Judge Eisele.) In the majority opinion, Arnold considered demographic statistics, economic statistics, and political practices including racial discrimination. Using the requirements of the "results test" in the Voting Rights Act, the majority found that past practices were relevant, and the *result* was that Arkansas's "black citizens had less opportunity than other members of the electorate to elect representatives of their choice."

Redistricting Negotiation

Once the court agreed that redistricting was required, we negotiated how the new district lines were to be redrawn. Everyone agreed that, normally, a 50:50 white-to-black population ratio would be fair. But we argued for what is called a "super majority" based on three causes of voter suppression. The African American population tends to

1. be younger than the white population,
2. have a pattern of lower registration, and
3. have a low voter turnout

Data presented by our experts successfully proved these three causes, and the court ruled in our favor on all three.

Here are some of Judge Richard S. Arnold's eloquent words in his *Jeffers* opinion explaining his reasoning for ordering districts redrawn with more than a 50% black voting population:

> On a strictly numerical and quantitative view of equality, any district with a BVAP [black voting age population] of 50% or higher would be per se lawful. We think the Voting Rights Act means something more than this. Suppose two people are in a race, and one of them has had to run the first three laps with a 100-pound weight on his back. Suddenly it occurs to the referee that this is unfair. Something must be done to correct the injustice. Is it corrected just by removing the weight from the disadvantaged runner for the last lap? Of course not. If no more than this is done, equality of opportunity is nothing but an empty promise, a form of words better left unsaid by honest people. Past injustice, especially centuries of it, cannot be ignored.

As a result of the evidence we presented, **we increased the number of black Arkansas state legislators from three to fifteen and the number of**

black state senators from one to three. Because the *Jeffers* case affected so many districts in Arkansas, it set a solid legal precedent. Dr. John Kirk, Distinguished Professor of History at the University of Arkansas at Little Rock and an expert on the civil rights movement, said in a February 4, 2015, article on voting rights in the *Arkansas Times*, "The ruling had the largest impact on black political representation since Reconstruction."

U.S. Supreme Court Refused the Appeal

The State of Arkansas appealed the *M. C. Jeffers v. Clinton* ruling to the U.S. Supreme Court, and the highest court declined to review it. This meant that a majority of the Supreme Court justices agreed with the Arkansas opinion. **WE GOT IT RIGHT.** And as soon as the Supreme Court declined to review it, the *Jeffers* case was considered to have set a precedent. And people followed our lead by filing similar and successful lawsuits in other states such as Texas and West Virginia.

Making Our Victories Count

The NAACP Legal Defense Fund considered redistricting cases worth the effort and expense, if they actually resulted in more-equitable representation. So they wanted to make sure their valuable time and their money were spent on cases which would produce real change on the community level. This was critical. In fact, none of us wanted to win a redistricting case and end up with no black candidates ready to run for office. So, we had to find good candidates to compete for the new legislature seats in the new majority-black districts.

We also had to have voters prepared to vote for black candidates. Throughout the legislative redistricting effort, we made certain that the black communities in question were "walking with us." And this was my job because I had so many contacts from my work with the water projects. I kept folks in the black communities aware of what we were doing, so they would be ready to support black candidates when new legislative districts were formed. I traveled all across the state looking for potential candidates.

In the southern Delta from Phillips County down to Chicot and Desha Counties, Jimmie Wilson and Kathleen Bell probably knew most about possible black candidates. One time I asked Jimmie who he knew down in Chicot County, which is in the extreme southeastern part of Arkansas. He told me that he had represented a man there who owned a garage. From time to time the city hired him, and the man seemed like he could be a good candidate for the legislature.

Often, I'd just call around, and somebody would know somebody. I'd call that person and go visit. Sometimes we would have a community meeting and sometimes I would visit with just two or three people. I did this all up and down the Arkansas Delta and in the southern two-thirds of the state, where the black voting population was a majority or close to a majority. In some places, when I went out looking for candidates, people would be eager to talk to me because they knew me. In others, because of my reputation, they were willing to learn about what we were doing and make suggestions for potential candidates even though they had never met me.

There weren't any superstars who I went up to and said, "You have to run." I never chose a particular person to be a candidate. My experience as a community organizer had taught me to find and work with someone who was already respected as a local leader in some role. Outside of Lee, St. Francis, Phillips, and Mississippi Counties, where I had worked and practiced law, I didn't know any of these people personally. But they were out there.

Jefferson County (Pine Bluff area) was different than the others. Because of the university in Pine Bluff, the folks living there had more experience deciding things for themselves. In Jefferson County, the people I talked to immediately liked the concept of what we were doing and had a good idea of who should run. In LaFayette County in far southwestern Arkansas, I had to do more education and guidance because they needed some help with the whole idea of selecting a candidate who would have a chance of being elected and who would do well representing them in the legislature.

Judicial Redistricting

After winning the *Jeffers* legislative redistricting case, Arkansas was on a voting rights roll, and we all knew that judicial redistricting had to be next. Actually, two black lawyers were in a race to file the judicial case. John Walker was the most experienced and well-known black lawyer in Arkansas, but a Pine Bluff attorney named Eugene Hunt came first. He had Lisa Kelly, a bright young lawyer in his office, file a lawsuit on his behalf. Hunt and his people were in such a rush, however, that they made some mistakes and had to amend their documents after filing. They also had not taken time to get LDF behind him, but Hunt was confident that LDF would support his case, and he was right. Hunt was lead plaintiff, and five or six others joined him and also were listed as plaintiffs in his case. I was one of them.

Most judicial districts in Arkansas have more than one judge, and they were drawn in such a way that a black judge had never been elected. Thus, the state had created a circumstance in which African Americans, a class of citizens protected by "the results test" of the 1965 Voting Rights Act, were purposely split up and therefore couldn't elect candidates of our choice.

Teamwork in the Judicial Case

The judicial districting case was easier than legislative redistricting. We found our experts and took their depositions. Before the trial even started, we got a consent decree (compromise satisfactory to both parties) that broke the multi-districts into two sub-districts with one of the sub-districts having a black voter majority. Thus, many more black voters gained a realistic chance of electing the candidate of their choice. A total of ten new black judicial sub-districts were created that still exist today. This was a huge advance for the black community, and we are proud of what we accomplished.

Unfulfilled Ideal

Those of us who were idealists thought that after ten or fifteen years, voters would no longer have to be concerned about race. And we still look forward to a time when white candidates truly represent both whites and blacks, and black candidates truly represent both blacks and whites. But in most places, this hasn't happened yet and probably won't for quite a while. Black voters continue to be cohesive and distinct from white voters all across the South and in northern urban areas such as the southside of Chicago, where there are high concentrations of low-middle- to low-income black folks. In Arkansas, we still have distinctive, identifiable differences in how black and white populations vote. Black majorities still elect black candidates, and white majorities still elect white candidates.

Loss of Voting Rights Progress in Pine Bluff, Arkansas

Voting rights for blacks were hard won, and we must remain vigilant and not give up what has been accomplished. The positive climate for our cause has changed, and what we gained through the early 1990s is being undermined. In 2001, powerful figures in Arkansas's political structure, primarily the governor, attorney general, and secretary of state, figured out how to change the legislative districts in a way that had a negative impact on black voting rights. But they had help from Henry Wilkins IV, a black state senator who was from a family political dynasty and had also served in the state House of Representatives.

Wilkins pushed to change his district by "packing." He got his district in the Pine Bluff area redrawn to have 85% black voters. As we have said before, we really only need 55–65% black voters to win a district. "Packing" brings in extra black voters creating an adjacent district with fewer black voters and an excessive number of white voters. And the result is that black voters in the adjacent district can no longer elect a candidate of their choice. This happened here because Henry Wilkins wanted his son to be able to win his district when he retired and he was afraid that his son couldn't win without a "packed" district. (By the way, the son never was elected, and as of May 2020, Henry Wilkins was awaiting sentencing for taking a kickback to influence discretionary legislative financing.)

Loss of Voting Rights Progress in the Arkansas Delta

The district in Pine Bluff was one example of how voting rights were eroded. Another is in a Senate district in the Delta where officials did something different during the 2010 redistricting. This Senate district includes a federal and a state prison, and the prison population is majority (maybe 80%) black. The incarcerated are citizens, but none of them can vote. During redistricting, officials added a mostly white precinct around the city of Marion in Crittenden County to the area including these two prisons, so the new district now has a majority of black citizens but does not have a majority of black voters. The new district then elected a white state senator Keith Ingram, who lives in the Marion precinct. It's all about politics and power.

Trend toward Conservative Judges Unsympathetic to Voting Rights

After the 1980s, another major change began happening to dampen blacks' struggle for voting rights. The people appointed to judgeships on the federal circuit courts became more and more conservative, so the courts gradually became a place where voters could no longer go to further their voting rights. By 2010, the federal circuit courts had become so conservative that if an area didn't have equal voting rights for blacks already, those voters were out of luck. This is now true in all of Arkansas and pretty much throughout the country.

Chapter 16
Circuit Judge 1993–1996

Following the 1989 judicial redistricting, a new career opened up for black attorneys in Arkansas. For the first time, we had an excellent chance of becoming a circuit judge in the new black-majority districts. And there were plenty of strong contenders eager for the new opportunity and challenge. Coming from community activism, for me it was a chance to say to the black community, we are part of the legal system, and we now have full participation. Black judges presiding over their own courtrooms could be part of the appearance and the reality of our legal system moving toward treating black folks equally.

Dispute Over Who Would Run in the First District

In most of the new black-majority judicial districts, lawyers worked out who would run with no apparent conflict. In my area, however, the First Judicial District lines were drawn to include six counties where there were quite a few black lawyers, and we had a little dispute. The conflict over who would run was between me and Jimmie Wilson. I thought that I could win in my home judicial district area, but Jimmie had his ideas about what was best for everybody. He wanted Kathleen Bell to be the circuit judge (handling criminal and civil cases), and he wanted me to run for the chancellery judge (mostly family law cases). When I told him that I was going to run for circuit judge, he tried to get another black lawyer, Sam Whitfield, to run against me. Sam was a protégé of his, and Jimmie looked out for him. Sam was loyal and went along with what Jimmie wanted. I had stood up to Jimmie, and maybe he wanted to teach me a lesson and put me in my place. I don't know.

Support from Some of Jimmie Wilson's People

Many of Jimmie's followers were people I had worked with in the past, and they supported me. One of them was Leon Phillips Jr. He was the same person who spoke up for me at the East Arkansas Planning and Development District meeting. He had been the mayor of Lake View in Phillips County, and he had been superintendent of schools in Lake View when Jimmie had his huge Lake View school funding lawsuit. Lake View has some special history too. In the 1930s following the Depression, the Resettlement Administration was part of Franklin Roosevelt's New Deal. It set aside federally owned land for poor farm families. Most of the resettle-ment communities in Arkansas were for white families, but Lake View was for blacks. Consequently, even today Lake View is more than 90% black. Families received forty acres, a barn, and a pair of mules, and the Wilson, Phillips, Fitzhugh, and Davis families were some of the first in Lake View. In the 1930s, the land was subject to bad floods, but it had very rich soil—partly because of those floods. After the Mississippi River levees were built to control flooding, this area became much more valuable.

Anyway, with Jimmie, it was his way or no way. And if you didn't do what he wanted, he would punish you. Leon Phillips believed in what Jimmie was doing, but he didn't always agree with Jimmie's style. Also, when he was the mayor of Lake View, I had been their city attorney, and I helped him accomplish some things, including Lake View getting its own sewer system. So, Leon knew me, and I had a good reputation with him. He knew that I wasn't just a stumble bum. One day, he pulled me aside and said, "Olly, I am going to vote for you. I sure am."

I also had Willie Weaver with me. He was Jimmie's cousin and farm man-ager, who I had represented in the Roundup theft case. I had managed to put some pressure on Gene Raff that forced a settlement offer. It was a higher-than-usual fine of $3,000 and a three-year suspended sentence, but I had kept Willie out of jail when Gene Raff was intent on making him do some time. So, Willie knew how I operated and where I stood. He said that he wasn't going to take on Jimmie at any public meeting. Nobody would, but he told me, "We are going to take care of you, Olly." There were several other people, like Odell Davis, who also had the same intention. He was a respected farmer in the Lake View community. These folks were part of Jimmie's team, but they were going to support me.

Once I knew that Jimmie was pushing Sam Whitfield, I went to the New Hope Baptist Church, where his Daddy was a deacon. I talked to Sam's Daddy and asked him to support me. He wouldn't go face to face with Jim-mie either, but he told me that he would support me. I also went to the First Baptist, where the preacher was T. K. Scott Jr. He said he would support me, and he brought along some other preachers too. They knew I was solid, and they were happy to speak up for me in their churches.

One thing about older people back then was when they told you some-thing, they stuck by their word. I think it was in March during the week of the filing deadline that Sam Whitfield came to me and said, "When I went to my Daddy, he told me that he had already promised to support you, so I have decided not to run." Sam wasn't mad about it. There never were hard feelings between us. He just had been under pressure to do what Jimmie wanted.

In the 1992 election, I was elected circuit court judge and Kathleen Bell was elected chancellery judge. We both ran with no opposition. Kathleen and I took office January 1, 1993. I served for three years, and Kathleen served for twenty-four.

Clarification of the Courts: Circuit Court, Chancellery Court, Municipal Court, District Court

At this time in Arkansas, the first court of record could be either the circuit court (also called the court of law) or the chancellery court (also called the court of equity). And there was a strict division of the type of cases each one could hear. The circuit court handled criminal cases from misdemeanors to capital murder and civil cases including personal injury and contract disputes. The chancellery court handled matters of equity like probate, guardianships, and domestic relations. So the chancellery court mostly dealt with matters of the family.

Kathleen Bell confirmed that this was the best fit for both of us in a 2017 interview:

> When Jimmie Wilson and I were partners, my work was mostly domestic relations, probate and some civil. I stopped doing criminal work years before I went on the bench. I ran as a chancellery judge. Arkansas was one of the last states to abolish this system. I don't ever remember the year we merged our courts because I hated it. I didn't want to do criminal cases. I only presided over maybe three criminal cases that went to a jury and two others where I dismissed the charges before they went to the jury.
>
> It was my firm decision that I was never going to death-qualify a jury. L. T. Simes II, who was a judge at the time, had presided over a capital murder case, and the jury came back with the death penalty. When it came time to pronounce the sentencing and set the date for the execution, he had to be out of town, so he asked me if I would do it for him. I said, "Sure, fine, no problem." When I got off the phone, I said to myself, "What the hell did you just agree to do?" I couldn't do it. I couldn't. So, I called somebody else who had been a prosecutor. I guess whatever it is you have to do to be able to do a death penalty case, he had done and made peace within himself, so he said that he would come down. Just

the idea that I would have my name on the order that said on a certain date somebody was going to die... I couldn't do it. I couldn't do that part. But anyway, I never had to. Thank the Lord.

The best cases are uncontested adoptions. Those are good days. Those are wonderful days. Everybody comes in smiling. In Arkansas, most of the time adoptions are closed proceedings, so we go back into chambers with the adoptive parents and the children. The children are happy and are holding on to their parents. And when I ask, "Who is that?" They say, "Daddy!" Sometimes they want to take pictures. Sometimes they want to hug the judge. The worst cases were contested adoptions.

When I was appointed to the appellate court, my position was filled by another black lawyer, L. T. Simes II. When Kathleen retired in 2018, Jimmie Wilson's son Dion Wilson was elected to replace her.

Most circuit court judges, like me, don't know every bit of the law. They are just trying to do the best they can to keep up and not make errors. Once a case record is made in the circuit court, if one of the parties in the lawsuit doesn't like the decision, he or she can go to the Arkansas Court of Appeals and try to convince them that the circuit judge made a mistake. In a criminal case, it might be that the judge didn't give the right instructions, and in a civil case, the judge might have given the wrong information about a principle of law.

It is almost impossible to change a circuit judge's findings of fact. For example, there might be a case where one person says that someone was in Marianna on a particular morning and another person says he was in Forrest City. When the circuit judge decides that the witness who said he was in Forrest City is more credible, that is a finding of fact, and the appellate court will not take that case. The only exception is when there is overwhelming evidence showing the circuit judge is absolutely wrong. To make sure they are not reversed in a fact-based case, circuit judges simply have to cite the facts they are relying on when they make a decision.

There is another set of courts in Arkansas that were once called municipal and are now called district courts. They are not courts of record. That means if you get a judgment in district court and you don't like the judgment, you can appeal your case to the circuit court. But nothing of what was said in district court is brought forward to the circuit court. You start all over again with a brand-new case, whereas anything said in circuit court is part of the official record and will follow all the way through as a case is appealed up the line to the appellate and supreme courts.

Riding the Circuit Court

When I was a judge in the First Judicial Circuit, my house was in Marianna and my circuit included six counties. Each county has a courthouse, so I rode the circuit through these counties. St. Francis and Phillips Counties have the biggest populations, so if I spent a week in the others, I'd spend two weeks in these two. In each courthouse there was a place where I could hang my robe, but some courthouses were much nicer than others. In St. Francis, Phillips, and Cross Counties I had an office called my chambers, but in Lee and Woodruff Counties I had a closet. They were the poorest counties.

Everybody in my counties pretty much knew me because I had lived and worked there for a long time. There were some white folks in each county who didn't like me. I didn't find much difference in the black folks, except in Phillips County. Black people down there were strong and aggressive about serving on juries.

A Tough Situation

In January 1993 right after I was on the bench, I had another difficult situation in St. Francis County with Sheriff Dave Parkman, who I had to get tough with when I was starting out as prosecutor. A black bail bondsman from West Memphis had filed a petition saying Parkman was not following the law and was denying all bondsmen equal opportunity to participate in making bonds in the St. Francis County court.

Bondsmen are licensed by the state, and when they get their full license and all their credentials, they present them to the sheriff, and the sheriff is supposed to put them on the list that all criminal detainees have a right to see, so the detainees can figure out who they want. Sheriff Parkman never put this black guy's name on the list, so he had never been able to make any bonds.

When I got the complaint, I looked at the law and read the statute, and I could see that if the sheriff did not agree to include this black bondsman, I was going to have to find him in contempt. That meant someone would have to arrest him and put him in jail. Who? Parkman's deputy wasn't going to put him in jail, and the coroner is next in line. I knew the coroner. He was a white boy and he sure as hell was not going to help arrest the sheriff. I couldn't believe the coroner would do it, because this thing was going to be all over the papers. I expected the sheriff to just not be found, and I didn't know what the hell I was going to do.

The lawyers for both Sheriff Parkman and the bondsman were at the hearing. The sheriff's lawyer was the district prosecutor, Fletcher Long, and he was a trifling son of a bitch. I thought that he and all of them knew I couldn't make anybody do a goddamn thing and they had me. But as soon as I convened the hearing, Fletcher Long stood up and announced that the sheriff was going to comply. Without it being seen, I let out a huge sigh of relief. I want you to know that among all the nerve-wracking experiences I have had, this was a big one.

So, you might want to ask, "What could have happened to make the sheriff comply?" I don't know. I really don't know. But this is my guess. You have to act strong. When these low-down white people push you, if you show yourself with no fear in all kinds of ways, they see that and they will come around. That is what I think happened with the sheriff and Fletcher Long. But Long was so petty that I never asked him to explain what happened, and he never did tell me. It just felt like the Lord had looked down and decided he had kicked my ass enough and was going to give me a break this time.

Useful to Be Tolerant

I'm not sure how I arrived at my philosophy of tolerance, but it was with me in my thirties, which is fairly early in life. Maybe it came from the influence Pitson Brady on me. I don't know. Anyway, I did not and still do not believe it is right to go after all the folks, black or white, who differ with you. Sometimes there are people who have physical attributes like you have and who have had certain types of experiences that you have had but who have internalized an attitude that makes them think different from you and at least appear to be an enemy of what you are trying to do. It is almost always best to be tolerant of these people. You don't have to shut them down because one day you may find that you can come together on some points, and when you do that, you will be stronger. So that's where I am on that.

The things that happened between me and Connor Grady in 1970 and 1971 are a good example. A lot of white folks, such as Lon Mann and his colleagues, liked Connor Grady and put him on the Lee County school board. He was present at the public meeting the school board held before forced integration started in the fall of 1970. This was when Lon Mann called Mrs. Davis by her first name and I jumped up and made a big fuss. When this happened, I had the distinct impression that Grady was very uncomfortable with my style and the point I was making.

Later, I think it was in the winter of 1971, Connor Grady came by my house one night at about 8:00 p.m. He had been at a school board meeting, and he looked distressed. It seemed like he just had to tell me what he had heard about a certain young black girl at the board meeting. Lillie Perry was an outspoken student leader at Futrell Junior High School. Apparently, the principal, Ronnie Austin, thought she was a hot-head and a problem they needed to get rid of. At the school board meeting, Austin had talked about Lillie and they had decided he should go ahead and push her, so she would talk back. Then, they would have a reason to put her out of school. Hearing about what they were going to do to this little girl really got to Grady, and he came to us about it. I knew Grady wasn't with us on everything, but he understood that we could protect Lillie in a way that he could not do himself.

As soon as he left, I got in my little Volkswagen and picked up I. V. McKenzie, and we drove straight out to the Perrys' house. They lived in the country down a muddy road. I thought we were going to get stuck. I just gunned it and didn't slow down both going in and coming out of there. We told Lillie and her mother what was being planned and that when the principal spoke to her, Lillie was to say nothing but "yes, sir" and "no, sir." Lillie followed our advice and did not get put out of school, and her Momma thought we were just wonderful for doing that for her daughter. You see, we were all better off thanks to Connor Grady, and nobody knew he was involved except me and I. V. McKenzie, who kept quiet.

Herman Young

During my first year on the trial bench, I overheard a few words that I have never forgotten. I was trying a civil case down in Helena involving timber poaching. A timber company was cutting trees and went over onto someone else's land and took those trees too. Herman Young owned the timber company, and he was a white racist son of a gun from St. Francis County. He was a little man, but everybody knew him because his land holdings were big. If you lived out near him and you were poor, you damn near had to go through his property.

The guy whose timber had been cut was a white person too. Arkansas law provided for triple damages if a land owner could prove somebody cut his timber and should have known it was on his land. It seems that this was almost always the case, because loggers should know where they are before they start cutting. Young's lawyer was a Jewish guy named Harold Sharp.

He was a decent white man who I could talk to back when I had my law practice in Marianna.

What I remember about the case happened after the trial. I was walking out, and I overheard Young say to his lawyer, "Goddamn, Harold, that nigger is the best damn judge we got over here." Young spoke those words even though he had gotten beat and had to pay triple damages. Herman Young did not mean to be kind when he said this. Part of it probably was just that I speak up and he could hear what I was saying, whereas some judges mumble. But his words were memorable because I had broken through something in him and made him receptive to a new idea.

A Civil Case

I had a good grasp of criminal law because of my experience in private practice and as a prosecutor. Consequently, if my ruling went a little bit beyond what had been established in previous criminal cases and it was challenged, I could expect the court of appeals to support my decision.

I was not that confident in civil cases, because I had less experience with them and didn't know as much civil law. I do remember one civil case where I knew my ruling was going to be appealed, but I still was confident in what I had decided and in how I had made my decision, and I fully expected the appellate court to uphold my judgment. This case involved a voting rights issue and an election challenge in Phillips County.

A white guy had been elected to a Phillips County justice of the peace position over a black man and the white man's election was challenged in a case in which the facts were in conflict. One of the defense witnesses for the election results was a black man, Delaney Alexander, who worked for the USDA. Alexander was well respected by the white community but not highly thought of in the black community. During the trial, Alexander reported on what he had observed during the election. However, some things he had seen and talked about actually supported the challenger's argument.

I ruled in favor of the challenge, and since this case was fact contingent, I wrote that I credited Alexander's testimony. I cited him and quoted him extensively, and the case went all the way to the Arkansas Supreme Court. They said that the facts, which I relied on, were not reversible and therefore they affirmed this part of the case. I should have stopped there and just stated that a new election was required. But I included a new election date in my ruling. A circuit judge does not have the authority to do that, so this part of my decision was reversed.

Governor Jim Guy Tucker set the date for a new election.

Decision Overturned in Difficult Civil Case

I had another civil case where I failed to get it right. My decision went to the Arkansas Supreme Court and was overturned. The defendant was a major corporation. During pretrial discovery, the corporation had declined to make certain subpoenaed information available. Subsequently, they filed a motion to quash that information because it was proprietary, but they didn't follow a procedural rule that said their motion had to be made within thirty days. So I ruled that because their motion was late, they would have to divulge the information even though it might have been proprietary. On appeal, the Arkansas Supreme Court pointed out that the procedural rule was more nuanced than I realized. If I had been thinking a little more clearly, I would have understood that and would not have decided that they had to divulge the business information.

Judicial Neutrality on a Pornography Case

An interesting criminal case I heard as a circuit court judge involved pornography in St. Francis County, where there are a lot of church people. The prosecutor, Fletcher Long, brought a criminal charge of promoting and distributing hard-core pornographic material against the corporation that owned a local pornography store. He had been trying to shut that store down for some time. I didn't know it when I was presiding over the case, but four or five years earlier, Fletcher had won a case and the store had been given a large fine, but it had been allowed to stay in business. This time the owners decided that they weren't going to pay another fine, and they wanted a trial. At the outset, I was pretty sure that the prosecutor would win his case.

The jury selection process went well. The jury was composed of five blacks and seven whites, and it included a church leader plus two police officers (one black and one white). The defense attorneys' argument was that what is done in the privacy of your home is your own business and that the pornographic videos were not sold in a provocative way. When a customer left the store, he took the purchase home in a brown bag. This was their reasoning in support of allowing the store to stay open. The jury found in favor of the defense, and the store was allowed to remain open.

I felt good about how I handled this case. Two separate jurors came up to me after the trial and asked me how I had wanted it to come out. They

238 OUTSPOKEN: The Olly Neal Story

said that I didn't show anything, and they could never tell what I wanted. I clearly had not told the jury what to think. I had dressed down the lawyers a couple of times and still the jurors thought that I was completely neutral. When they asked me after the trial, I told them that I didn't have a particular view.

The jurors did not tell me this, but I think that in accepting the defendant's theory they thought, "This is the kind of stuff I do not want my children to see and do not want in my house. These folks who buy it don't believe what I believe, but they are adults. They have a right to believe what they want to believe, and they have the right to buy pornography if it is not against the law." That's the impression I got from various people who have mentioned it to me through the years.

In my mind, that is exactly how a trial judge ought to be—impartial—so the jury can make its decision based on the evidence presented. The worst criticism is to say a judge is biased, and the highest form of praise is to say that a judge is impartial.

Judge Kathleen Bell said this about impartiality in a 2017 interview:

> Sometimes it is difficult for a lawyer to make the transition from being on one side as an advocate for the client to becoming a neutral judge who is the referee or the gatekeeper of the cases in court. I have been told stories of where judges who are former prosecutors never get past that prosecutorial bent. In a criminal case they almost want to take the case from the prosecutor and try it themselves. And you can't do that.
>
> A judge is not a prosecutor and a judge cannot take sides. After I was on the bench I never did go into anybody else's courtroom. So, I don't know personally how they were. But from what I have been told about Olly by other attorneys, which is how I would get that kind of information, is that they enjoyed practicing in front of him. They thought that they would get a fair shake. They might not get what they wanted but they would walk out of there knowing that he let them try their case.

Jimmie Wilson

By far the most controversial case I ever had as a circuit court judge was Jimmie Wilson's disbarment. But first I have to tell you some more about Jimmie Wilson. I've been trying to make it clear since the beginning that I don't fool around with Jimmie. He can be a mean son of a bitch, and we have not always gotten along too well. But Jimmie is the best lawyer I have ever known. And Jimmie followed the dictum of Dr. Charles Hamilton

Houston, dean of Howard Law School, when he said, "A lawyer's either a social engineer or…a parasite on society."

Jimmie has been highly effective at using the law to shape society and expand the rights of black folks. I tried to follow Dr. Houston's teaching too, but I was never as skillful as Jimmie. A good example is Jimmie's Lake View school funding case. The fifteen-year-long court case *Lake View School District No. 25 v. Huckabee* examined the structure for the funding of Arkansas's schools, and when he first discussed it with me, I thought, "You can't beat the state of Arkansas on that." But Jimmie took this situation that I couldn't figure out and molded it into something that made sense. The *Lake View* case went all the way to the state Supreme Court, and the outcome was profound. That case ultimately changed the way Arkansas funds public schools and led to the rule that a certain amount of money had to be allocated for each student. The *Lake View* case is still the bellwether for school funding in some other states as well.

When Jimmie was getting ready to try the *Lake View* case in 1992, I had just been elected circuit judge. And when I was attending a six-week course at the Judicial College in Reno, Nevada, I met up with then Chancery Court Judge Annabelle Imber (now Annabelle Tuck and retired from the Arkansas Supreme Court). Annabelle told me, "I can only stay here a week because I have a trial starting. It's that *Lake View* school funding case. I know it isn't going to amount to much because the lawyers over there don't get prepared." And I said, "Annabelle, that is Jimmie Wilson's case. He talked to me when he was getting started. I don't know exactly what he has now because I haven't kept up, but I do know he is going to bring you something. You had better do your reading." Then, when I saw her again two or three months later, she said, "You sure told me right about Jimmie Wilson. When he was presenting his case, I had to be reading every night to keep up with him."

Here is another thing to show you that Jimmie is a brilliant lawyer. I argued before the Arkansas Supreme Court a couple of times, and I always had my notes and would carefully follow them to make certain I hit every point. Jimmie would have a notepad in his hand, not looking at it. He would just stand there covering his points. If a judge interrupted him with a question, he would answer the question in detail and keep going strong right where he left off. Those judges' questions often were hostile too, and he never let that get to him. I mean he was good. When I was an appellate court judge and Jimmie was arguing before the Supreme Court, I used to tell my clerks, "Take a break and go listen to Jimmie Wilson argue his case. He is the best."

Jimmie's Plea Bargain

Jimmie was a successful lawyer, and he had been farming since he got out of law school in 1972 or 1973. He had inherited 140 acres in Lake View from his grandfather. By the time he got in trouble with the USDA, he was working nearly 2,000 acres. As was common practice, Jimmie borrowed money from the USDA to buy seed and equipment, but he was not a good farmer and got into a situation where he could not pay back his loans. So, in 1983, the USDA foreclosed on him. It was a civil case tried in federal court because a federal agency was prosecuting him.

In 1985, Jimmie was tried again in the same federal court for misuse of one of his USDA loans. Misuse of a federal loan is considered fraud, so this time it was a criminal charge. To some extent the same information was involved in both cases, but there were two separate trials, appeals, and negotiations.

When Jimmie had been found liable for not paying his USDA loans in the civil case, the USDA took his 140 acres, because his land had been his guarantee for payment. In the criminal case, when he was convicted of fraud for misusing a federal loan, the court automatically suspended his license to practice law in federal court.

Jimmie appealed and by 1990 he had worked out a deal in the criminal case. He ended up pleading guilty to five misdemeanors, and he only had to serve six or eight months in the federal prison in Texarkana, but his license was not reinstated.

Kathleen Bell had this to say in 2017 about Jimmie's fight with the federal government:

> The federal indictments had to do with Jimmie's farm loans. It had nothing to do with his law office. So, in federal court they took his license immediately. State court did not do anything until after. I remember this. There was an article in the newspaper that said, "Jimmie Wilson and the Federal Government have decided to not fight each other anymore." I thought that was the funniest thing in the world. But, anyway, he pled guilty and it went from serious felony to lesser misdemeanor charges. And he accepted some time in a federal pen. It must have been less than a year because it was for misdemeanors.

Jimmie's Disbarment in State Circuit Court

I believe it was sometime in 1991 that they started proceedings to suspend Jimmie's license to practice in the *state* courts. Up to this point Jimmie's problems were in *federal court*, but the powers that be in Arkansas disliked Jimmie. He was a supremely confident and effective lawyer, and his style was disrespectful and aggressive. He would not only beat those white lawyers in trial but would go up to them after and say, "Beat your ass, didn't I?" Another time, I heard him say to one of those tall-building lawyers, "I don't know why you bother bringing your ass over here, since I am going to send you back to Little Rock with your tail between your goddamn legs." Jimmie talked rough, and he was not joking. Plenty of white lawyers could not stand his animosity, so his trouble over farm loans was their chance to get Jimmie.

The Arkansas Supreme Court had recently created a Professional Conduct Committee for lawyers (and a Judicial Discipline and Disability Committee for judges). Even though Jimmie had only been convicted of misdemeanors, his misdemeanors involved dishonesty and theft, so the Professional Conduct Committee charged him with an ethics violation and threatened to remove his state law license. Judge Henry Wilkerson was the circuit judge who normally would have heard this case, but he and all four of the other judges in the First Judicial Circuit recused themselves.

Why would they all recuse?

It was pretty clear to me and everyone else that those judges wouldn't try Jimmie's disbarment case because they were afraid. Circuit judges have to be elected every six years, and Jimmie was very well-connected with the Phillips County black electorate. Plus, he was unpredictable and could be vindictive. He could hold a grudge and he had a long memory. Although I cannot know exactly what those judges were thinking, it is my opinion that they recused themselves because they all knew Jimmie's disbarment would be taken hard by black voters and it would affect their chances for reelection.

After the First Judicial Circuit recusals, a judge from Lonoke County, Lance Henshaw, was appointed. He tried the case and arrived at a judgment that Jimmie should receive a suspension and not be disbarred. Judge Henshaw was not a great friend of black folks, but that is what he decided based on the evidence.

In the eyes of the Professional Conduct Committee members, however,

Jimmie was so troublesome and disreputable that they appealed Henshaw's ruling to the Arkansas Supreme Court, which reversed Henshaw's opinion and sent the case back to him for further consideration. Judge Henshaw basically told the Supreme Court, "You are crazy as hell. I have decided this case like it ought to be decided and the only option left for me is to recuse myself." (These are not his actual words, because judges almost always use respectful language.)

This happened in May or June 1992. The Supreme Court did not make a new appointment before January 1, 1993, when I began serving as circuit judge in the same division of the First Judicial Circuit Court as Judge Wilkerson. Jimmie's case was waiting, and I had to decide whether I would take it or not. I understood that Jimmie was a controversial person, but I considered presiding over cases like this to be part of the job, so I did not recuse and tried the case.

Lee County attorney Bob Donovan had been asked to represent the Professional Conduct Committee in the case in 1990, I believe, when it was before Judge Henshaw. Donovan was still with the case when it came to my court. This is what he said about his involvement in a 2017 interview:

> Jimmie Wilson got in trouble and a lot of lawyers wanted him disbarred. People from Little Rock came and asked me to handle his disbarment, and I said no. A month or two later they came back and asked me again. And this time, I said that I would do it on one condition: they had to keep their noses out of it. I didn't want anybody coming in and telling me what to do. I couldn't help but like Jimmie, and I had no grudge against him. I had respect for Jimmie, and I wanted to see that he got a fair shake. It was a mismanagement of money and I didn't want to make it a racial issue. To me it was just a case that needed to be tried and we went at it for six or seven years. I think they finally gave him a suspension. They did not disbar him.
>
> I really don't know why they came to me. They wanted somebody from over here in eastern Arkansas to do it for some reason. But the first judge who heard it was from somewhere else. I just wanted to stick to the facts. And I didn't do anything else.
>
> Jimmie Wilson is a character and a good lawyer. His son Dion is a great lawyer, and now he will make an excellent circuit judge. I've told Dion myself that I am proud of him. He was a kid when I was starting out. I'm proud to see him grow up and practice law successfully and get a judgeship.

Courtroom Atmosphere during Disbarment Trial

Trying Jimmie's case definitely was memorable. We were in Phillips County's small courtroom and the audience was full, with fifteen to twenty lawyers watching every day. They all wanted to see what the hell was going to happen. Some of them were from Wynne, which is more than an hour's drive away. Jerry Malone represented Jimmie and was quite well prepared. Bob Donovan represented Jim Neal, who was chairman of the Conduct Committee, and Bob was well prepared too. He pushed me to recuse myself based on something I considered insufficient. I wasn't going to let him push me, and Jimmie and I were not talking at that time.

Taking the case was not an easy decision for me, but once I had it straight in my mind, I did not feel any discomfort. I thought that Jimmie should be treated just like anyone else. I was not feeling charitable to him. If he deserved to be disbarred, he should be disbarred. I had read a lot of cases about disbarment, and I compared his conduct to those who had been disbarred up to six, eight, or ten years ago. I read the briefs and heard the arguments, and I concluded that what he had done did not rise to that level, so I decided against disbarment. I ended up giving Jimmie just about the same verdict as Judge Henshaw had. I think it was a six-month suspension and a fine to cover the cost of the Professional Conduct Committee's investigation.

The Professional Conduct Committee appealed my decision and asked the Arkansas Supreme Court to give the case to some other judge. The Supreme Court then vacated (meaning, set aside) my opinion based on the fact that the court hadn't appointed me and claimed that no other judge was eligible to take the case, so I had no jurisdiction. Consequently, the court appointed Judge Johnny Lineberger from northwestern Arkansas to hear the case. He found in favor of disbarment and Jimmie was disbarred. Jimmie challenged his state court disbarment, however, and got his license back sometime between 1996 and 2001. I was on the court of appeals then, and I don't know the details, but I do know that he did not have to retake the bar exam.

Jimmie was eligible for presidential pardon for his federal court disbarment, and according to the U.S. Department of Justice, on January 20, 2001, he was pardoned by President Bill Clinton for "converting property mortgaged or pledged to a farm credit agency, and converting public money to personal use." Jimmie's pardon meant that he was absolved of guilt as if the act had never occurred.

I believe Jimmie never would have been convicted in the first place if he had only kept the proper records. He merely was guilty of failing to make a lending paper trail showing how much money he had loaned to his farm account from his personal money and how he paid himself back with money from his USDA loan. When he was tried, he had nothing to show to prove that he had not stolen USDA money and had done nothing wrong.

All of Jimmie's legal dramas received a huge amount of publicity, and at least some of the controversy in his state disbarment case was over whether or not I should have recused myself. My position was that I had been elected to do this job and no one had to appoint me. Since I had never recused myself nor been removed from the case, they had absolutely no legal grounds to give the case to somebody else. It was pretty clear to me that the Arkansas Supreme Court simply wanted me off Jimmie's trial and wanted to appoint somebody who would disbar him.

My position concerning recusal was vindicated in 2015, when the Arkansas Supreme Court took another case concerning what they call "presumptive recusal," and this time they found that the judge had a right to stay on the case. In their ruling, they also set aside the previous court's decision for Jimmie's disbarment because "as duly elected, Judge Olly Neal's disqualification should not have been presumed." This kind of thing is very important to a judge, and I was gratified.

Important Impacts of Having Black Judges

It is true that black judges are not all perfect. I'm not claiming that for myself or anyone else. But the presence of black judges builds essential trust in our legal system. Because of historic and current inequities, black plaintiffs feel particularly insecure and at a disadvantage in the courtroom. Black plaintiffs often feel more comfortable or safer facing a person who looks the same as they do. They perceive that they have a better shot at being treated fairly, and this builds their confidence in the legal system.

The influence of black judges on their white peers has an even greater impact on the legal system and how it serves the black community. By the time I was a circuit judge, it had become easier for me to make sure that the legal system was fair to everyone, but I still lived with the struggle to be fair. I had to put out a conscious effort every day to control my personal prejudice. And when I was on the bench, I had the opportunity to talk to other judges about confronting their prejudice. Many had a tendency to say something like, "I don't see color." But that is not true. WE ALL SEE

COLOR. To be as fair as we possibly can be, judges have to recognize their own prejudice and work to counter it in their judgments.

I worked with four other circuit judges (one black and three white) in the First Judicial Circuit, and our job required regular meetings where we talked about how to efficiently handle the cases on our docket. I didn't lecture. I would just make comments at our meetings about trying to do certain things. And some of the things that I recommended were adopted by my colleagues. Of course, this doesn't mean things became perfect. But it does mean that those white judges became conscious of a different approach.

One thing I promoted was requiring those who were convicted but given suspended sentences to get their GED as part of their probation if they didn't have a high school diploma. Also, there is a video I did on what is expected of jurors in a jury trial. Even though it was made years before, that video was still used to train jurors. One day I was in the Crittenden County Courthouse and when I looked in the courtroom, the sheriff saw me and said, "You come on in. You are our movie star!" And another time when I was over there, someone I didn't know came up to me and said that when he was on a jury, he had seen me on the screen talking about what they were supposed to do. So, yes, I made some difference, but it does not make me the godfather.

At the annual 2017 state bar meeting in Hot Springs, a group of us made a presentation on implicit bias. One of the things we were trying to get judges to think about was how our thinking is shaped by our life experiences. After that presentation Judge Richard Proctor, who was still a circuit judge in the First Judicial Circuit, came up to me and said, "We are still trying to follow some of the things you told us." And it also was in 2017 when we got the Arkansas Supreme Court to include something on dealing with implicit bias in the instructions a judge is required to give every jury. It is something, but we could be doing more.

Chapter 17
Appellate Court

Until the offer came in November 1995, I had never thought of being an appellate court judge. Up until then, I expected to continue as a circuit judge in eastern Arkansas and retire after twenty or twenty-five years. But when the legislature expanded the Arkansas Court of Appeals from six judges to twelve, Governor Jim Guy Tucker had to appoint three new judges to start in January 1996. He appointed two black lawyers, me and Wendell Griffen, and one white lawyer, John Stroud. And he appointed three more to start the next year. They were black lawyer Andree Layton Roaf and two white lawyers, Terry Crabtree and Margaret Meads.

My Reservations about the Position

When Governor Tucker called me to offer the court of appeals job, I had strong misgivings. I asked him for twenty-four hours to think about it. I talked to my son Nic, my old friend Pitson Brady, and my wife Karen Buchanan. My hesitation was both emotional and practical. I was attached to my home in Lee County, and my emotional ties to the Delta affected everything for me. Even when Bill Clinton was elected president and all of us (me, Wilbur Peer, Carol Willis, and Bob Nash) who had helped him were encouraged to apply for jobs in Washington, I couldn't do it. They left to go work in Washington DC, but I didn't. I had it figured out that I was going to spend my entire career in the Delta. If I took the court of appeals job, I would represent the First Appellate District of Eastern Arkansas, but I would work in Little Rock full time and could no longer live in my home in Marianna.

On the practical side, as a circuit court judge, my reelection was every six years. I knew everyone in all the counties of my district and felt confident of reelection. Although the appellate judges are elected for an eight-year term, the legislature set it up so that all six of us appointed in 1996 and 1997 would have to be up for our first election in 2000. And I wasn't at all confident of being reelected. The First Appellate District has twelve counties, so as an appellate court judge, I'd have to campaign in twice as many counties. The worst part was that two counties, Clay and Greene, are almost all white and I didn't know anybody up there. There were all of thirty-five black folks in Clay County and about 150 in Greene County. Getting reelected was a big reservation.

My son Nic was living with me in 1995 and he didn't want to move to Little Rock, but Pitson Brady and my wife Karen encouraged me to accept the appointment. Karen worked in Little Rock, and she was the one who really sold me on the job and the move. So, Nic and I moved in December, and I was sworn in with the other new judges on January 1, 1996. I have to give credit to both Karen and Jim Guy Tucker for giving me this new life. It has been a good one.

The Appellate Court Job

The Arkansas Appellate Court chambers are marble. Marble floors. Marble walls. Marble everywhere. All that marble was a long way from Delta poverty. But I didn't react to anything that made it an upper-crust place. There were two or three things, however, I knew I had to do right away. First, I had to put more black faces in the court offices. I couldn't go over there and do just like the white judges—select an all-white staff to run my shop. So, before I arrived, I notified them who I was going to hire. I never heard the full details, but I do know that Rita Cunningham, the lawyer who was the court's chief administrator, had to have a full staff meeting about me to tell everyone that I was hiring an all-black staff: two black clerks and one black administrative assistant.

They were concerned that what I was doing was racist. That was the way they saw it. They were talking about this new guy Olly Neal coming in from Marianna, who was "going to make it real dark down there." One of them made a snide comment like that. Arkansas Court of Appeals chief judge John Jennings must have discussed this "problem" with the Arkansas Supreme Court chief justice because another justice on the supreme court asked for a diversity report on both courts. When the diversity report came back, it showed that out of a total of twenty-six clerks on both courts, there was only one African American, and out of thirteen administrative assistants, there was not a single African American. They also had one black assistant librarian and one black janitor. That was it. So, the supreme court's response was that I was improving court diversity and that was a good thing.

To make their work more efficient, appellate court judges and supreme court justices hire clerks to help write their opinions. The second thing I had to do was hire the very best clerks I could find because I was not confident of my writing ability and I knew that I would have to write decent opinions. Most often, our clerks were young lawyers who stayed at the job for about two years. I knew my clerks had to be able to think like I did and would have to write much better than I did. Looking back, I believe that I nearly always had two of the best clerks on the court of appeals. In my last year up there, I was going to hire my first white clerk, who was from Batesville. She had clerked before and was damn good, but she took another job instead of coming to work for me.

How the Appellate Court Operated

At the Arkansas Court of Appeals, we heard appeals from circuit courts all across the state. We heard on-the-job injury appeals from the Worker's Compensation Commission, and once or twice a year we heard a case from the Public Service Commission, which sets rates and fees mainly for the big power companies. Cases that get to the state supreme court are considered by all seven judges, but the appellate court divides its twelve judges up into four three-judge panels, so normally only three judges hear each case. This is how it can deal with so many cases from such a broad jurisdiction.

Every four weeks, a random computer drawing reassigns appellate judges to a different panel (a group of three judges). I don't question the randomness of the system. While I was there, we never had an all-black panel, but on one occasion we did have a panel of all women. Our cases were assigned weekly also by random computer drawing. They were delivered to us every Wednesday afternoon. We had a full week to review our cases and prepare our opinions, and one judge was assigned to write the panel's opinion for each case. If everything went smoothly, we would release an opinion in three weeks.

My practice was this. I divided my cases and sent them to my two clerks early every Thursday morning. Each clerk then sent an opinion memorandum back to me by Friday evening. On Monday I would meet with them to tell them what changes I wanted made. If all three of the judges on a panel agreed, that would be the decision of the court and our opinions were released on Friday. If all three panel judges didn't agree, then the case would go to a six-judge panel. In this panel, if the vote was 4-2 it passed, but if it was 3-3, the case went to a nine-judge panel.

My Performance

I was driven to do my best. I come from the old school, which says when we are one of the first to take on a job, we represent our race and the whole world is watching. If I don't do a good job, the next ones in line will never get a goddamn chance. I think that we now are moving away from this in the whole country. But in my time, when you took a job and you didn't do it well, there were whites out there watching. And if you messed up, you would have confirmed their expectations. They would be free to say that all blacks are incompetent just like you.

As an appellate court judge, I think that I was definitely above average but not superior. When we conferenced about our cases, I didn't talk all the time, but I did speak up sometimes. Judge Roaf used to say, "When Judge Neal talks, everybody listens." That was because when I saw the judges veer off course, I would remind them of what the law said. I could justify my opinions, and sometimes I convinced them to agree with me.

In one of my worker's compensation cases, the question was whether this guy who claimed an on-the-job injury should continue to receive his compensation checks even though there was some evidence that he was substantially recovered. The worker's comp act has a provision that says for a certain kind of injury, such as loss of a limb or a back injury, you will be assigned an exact benefit, and there is no rule saying if people feel better, they should go back to work. The guy had a back injury, which qualified him for a specific number of weeks of compensation. But before he was fully recovered, someone got a video of him lifting a lawnmower onto a trailer. That mower was a big son of a bitch, so the other two judges saw that he was all right and thought he should not receive any more benefits. Remember, a judge must follow the law whether or not he or she agrees with it, so my position was that the law gave the injured guy a specific benefit amount regardless of whether he felt better or not, so we couldn't take away his benefit even if he was able to life a heavy mower.

In the three-judge panel, without unanimous agreement, the case would have to be sent on to a six-judge panel. My clerk Tonya Alexander said to me, "Judge, I don't think that we can win this one." And I said, "Tonya, I don't give a damn. I want you to write your very best in support of my position." She went back and got to work, and she did a damn good job. When the two judges who disagreed with me read what she wrote, they backed off and went along with me. Our three-judge panel decided the case.

Overall Impact of Black Appellate Judges

In our first year on the court, many of our colleagues did not believe that blacks had the innate ability to do their kind of thoughtful work. I'm pretty sure that we disabused them of that notion rather quickly. Judge Wendell

Griffen and I soon became known for our abilities. The white judges came to see us as colleagues who read, prepared, and had opinions worth hearing, and our performance influenced them to have a more realistic view of our people's intellectual ability.

Circuit court judge Wendell Griffen in a 2018 interview remembered that we impressed because we were prepared:

> It is probably true that some of our colleagues might have wondered if we were up to speed. They never made this known to me directly, but I think that they may have been surprised when Olly and I showed that when it came time to be prepared for case conferences, we didn't take a back seat to anybody. We were going to be prepared! No one was going to be able to say that we hadn't read the cases, read the briefs, analyzed the arguments, or anticipated how the case conference would go.
>
> He and I both had come out of the same kind of background, the people we came up from. He in the east Arkansas Delta around Lee County and me in the southwest plains in Pope County. We knew that...we were expected to represent our families, to represent our people and put our best mind forward.

Andree Roaf came on the court my second year, and she was an appellate judge most of the time I was there. We were friends, but we had very different styles and there was a substantial difference in how we were perceived by the white judges. I was loud and profane. I was a country boy who cussed half the time. I had done all that civil rights stuff that they thought to be real bad. Judge Roaf was mild mannered and cultured and maybe even a little bit nerdy. She was committed to black folks, but the white judges saw her as different, more refined than most black people, certainly more refined than me. She fit into the white world, and they saw her as exceptional.

Josephine Hart, from Mountain Home, Arkansas, was elected to the Arkansas Court of Appeals and started on January 1, 1999. (She moved on to the Arkansas Supreme Court in 2012.) Judge Hart is a strong, outspoken white woman, and we worked pretty well together. This is what she remembered about our time on the appellate court, in a 2018 interview:

> When I came on the court of appeals, those judges weren't accustomed to a woman talking back, and I think that I was a total surprise to them. But it appeared that Judge Neal saw my outspoken style as welcome en-

tertainment. Judge Neal has a sixth sense of right and wrong. And we had one important thing in common: both of us always tried to do what was right whether it was popular or not. I believe that commitment to doing what was right even when it was unpopular was a big part of the reason we could get along. But that does not mean that Judge Neal and I always agreed. We could get really mean with each other when we didn't agree, so we worked hard not to rile each other up.

I'll tell you about a case when Olly stood up and we worked together. Each published opinion from the court of appeals is a collective decision. When I served with Olly, we sat in panels of three, six, or nine judges. In my first year, I had a worker's comp case. It was about a woman who worked on the line in a chicken-processing plant. The facts were that the workers had continued on the job through their break time because they were doing what they called "working through the run." When the woman told her supervisor, "I need a restroom break and I can't wait," he said, "I will work your station. You run on." She took off running, slipped and fell, and broke her leg. The law provided that a worker had to be advancing the employer's interest in order to get benefits. So, because she was not working on the line when she was hurt, it was determined that she didn't get worker's comp.

When I looked at the case I thought, I cannot go along with this. So, I read, and I studied. Olly's chambers were right next to mine, so I went over and told him that as far as I was concerned, when you hire human beings, a certain level of creature comfort including lunch and break time does help the employer. Not only that, under our Arkansas labor law, this woman was entitled to a paid fifteen-minute break. And if the time when she was injured was paid time, then her injury should be covered by worker's comp. Period.

Judge Neal looked at me and said, "You know that the 'stare decisis' cases are against you." And I said, "Perhaps we need to reread them." And right away he said, "Okay, I'll help you." We went to reading and working. Ultimately, we got five out of a nine-judge panel to say that the woman was advancing the employer's interest and therefore she was entitled to worker's comp. When the Supreme Court reviewed it, they agreed with us. This is now the law in Arkansas. I was so relieved.

Another impression I had of Judge Neal was that he has a full understanding of why we have two ears and one mouth. He knows that we are supposed to spend twice as much time listening as we do speaking. And Judge Neal had the ability to listen to a presentation to the very end without interruption, even if his mind was busy drafting a response. He really could listen twice as much as he spoke. Judge Neal had that down.

It might have been that his time on the trial bench had helped him.

Judge Neal was a fine ambassador for race relations. He has a special ability to create a working relationship even in a hostile or adversarial environment. When speaking he could create a common environment with his audience, and this gave him the ability to get his point across without being offensive to other people's sensibilities. It's an art. This is a special talent. Some people have it and some people don't.

Reelected in 2000

After I was on the appellate court, I used to go up to those very white counties in my district once a year. I took Karen one time and she said that I looked like I was having a good time working the room. The "room" was a picnic ground where they had a big fish fry given by some lawyers who had gone deep sea fishing. They brought back their fish and cooked it up for all the lawyers and judges.

One year at the fish fry, this white woman lawyer was pregnant, and we took a picture together. The next year she brought her baby and we took another picture of her and me holding the baby. So, they thought that I was a pretty good politician, but I still didn't think that the white folks up there would vote for me if I was running against a white candidate. I could have been wrong though. White folks all across the country voted for Obama, and I didn't think that would happen either.

When I had to run for re-election in 2000, I borrowed $50,000 and put it in a campaign account in a Marianna bank where I knew the bankers would tell everybody how much money I had. They're not supposed to do that, but I knew they would. It was a nice chunk of money to start a campaign.

A couple of old boys said that they might run against me, but D. "Price" Marshall up in Jonesboro was the only one who was serious. He was white and he was a practicing attorney who had an excellent reputation for his appellate briefs. He would be a good candidate, and I was worried that he could beat me.

One day he called me on the phone to tell me that he was entertaining the idea of running for my position. I answered that he certainly had a right to do that. I was going to be in Jonesboro that weekend, and I told him that maybe we ought to sit down and talk, so I could hear what he had in mind. We met and I said to him, "You know I have to do what I can to win. You may beat me, but I am going to give you a fit because I am going to run hard. I know folks all over this district and I'm going to spend all the damn money I can get my hands on." I was smiling and talking tough. That was a Sunday. Price Marshall was a courteous guy, and on Tuesday he called to tell me that he had decided not to run. Once I got past the filing deadline with no one running against me, it was a beautiful day. I spent less than $2,000 on my campaign, so I celebrated and took $35,000 of the $50,000 I had borrowed and bought me a brand-new over-sized, diesel F250 pickup.

Reaching Out to the Community

On the appellate court, I was still an organizer at least to some extent. It was my practice to stay connected with my community. Even in the last two years, when my health was starting to go down, I found time to visit with folks. There were some organizations that invited me year after year.

Also, every year, I would ask my colleagues if they were amenable to me bringing in a group of high school students. The students were usually seniors with a chaperone and were never disruptive. If we had an oral argument, they would sit in the audience and watch the proceedings. I was the only one who brought in students, but the other judges always agreed. For about five years, I brought one or two classes over every year. High school groups came from Marianna, Holly Grove, Marvell, Lake View, and Forrest City. Their school administrators could justify the trip, so the schools usually paid for the transportation.

Judge Griffen liked these encounters and opening the appellate court to outsiders, and he had this to say about it in 2018:

> I was proud he did it. One of the things that happened when Olly and I came on the court of appeals is that all of a sudden black folks might come to the justice building. They were people who had never been there. I mean students and visitors who would just come and look. Because you have to understand the appellate judge is not like if you are a trial judge. When you are a trial judge, people are coming in all the time for their business. They have various kinds of trials. They have juries that come in. There are people coming into the courthouse to get marriage licenses. Coming in to file deeds. For adoptions and divorces. So, the circuit court and the county courthouses really are places that are accessible for almost pedestrian kind of work.
>
> The appellate court hears appeals from trials, and first of all, not every case is appealed, and secondly, unless you are a criminal defendant who has an appointed lawyer, an appeal costs money. Therefore, you are not

going to have very many. But more importantly, most people just never go to the appellate court to see anything. There was a former chief judge, William H. Arnold, who was also on the state supreme court and he had been a circuit judge before he was elected to the supreme court. He used to tell people, "Being on the supreme court was like living in a nursing home. I had a phone, but nobody called. And I had an address, but nobody wrote me. And when people came, they were scared and wanted to leave as soon as they could."

A couple years before I left the appellate court, Chief Appellate Judge Stroud and Chief Justice Arnold of the Arkansas Supreme Court decided that we should hear an oral argument proceeding somewhere outside of Little Rock once or twice a year. We went to Fayetteville one year and to West Memphis another time, and I think we went to Texarkana too. We were taking the court to the people. I liked this because it made the court more accessible, so citizens could get a better idea of how our part of the justice system worked. From a skeptical point of view, however, their intention could have been more political than anything else. Getting the appellate judges out into their districts made it so the voting public could see them doing their work. And this might help them win reelection.

Back on First Judicial Circuit Again

During my last two years on the appellate court, my health wasn't what it used to be, and I retired at the end of 2006. Then, in 2009, First Judicial Circuit Judge L. T. Simes II got crossways with the Judicial Discipline Committee and the Supreme Court suspended him for all of 2010, which was the last year of his term. Governor Mike Beebe appointed Harvey Yates to fill in while Simes was out. Then, in only one month, Harvey created so much confusion that he decided to quit, and Beebe was looking hard to find somebody to replace him.

Mike Easley, a prominent white attorney in St. Francis County, told me that when asked by the governor to look for someone to fill in again, he talked to black and white lawyers in all six counties of the First Judicial Circuit. They all wanted me to be appointed and agreed to put my name forward because I had done a good job when I was over there before. So, I went back to eastern Arkansas and served for ten months, March through December. Simes got reelected for the 2011–2017 term.

Beebe would never have appointed me on his own. Beebe was a Democrat like me and we knew each other, but we were not close. Easley caught me by surprise, and I was kind of amazed by the support. I knew Easley, but I didn't think that we had any kind of a special, warm relationship. I'd grin and go to the functions. That was pretty much it.

I still thought back to the 1970s when I had been the "bogeyman" civil rights activist in those counties. That was forty years ago and now if all those people thought I had served well as a prosecutor and a judge, I could see that the whole area had moved forward. This was an eye opener for me and gratifying. The biggest part of this appointment, which made me feel good, was that I was supported by both black and white lawyers in all the counties. I wasn't a friend of any of those lawyers, but still they all spoke up to say that I had been a good judge. This made me proud.

In court, lawyers want the judge to be fair, prompt, and efficient, and I think that I met all three of those requirements. Being fair meant that I was not influenced by political power or by my friends. And I did my best to follow the law, including times when the law wasn't what I would like it to be. For me, prompt was pretty easy because I like being on time. If court was to start at nine o'clock, I was on the bench at nine o'clock. And I was efficient with courtroom time too by keeping the proceedings moving along as quickly as possible. In fact, during those ten months, I reduced Phillips County's criminal docket by more than half.

Trial Judge of the Year

Another thing happened to me in 2010. The Arkansas Trial Lawyers Association gave me an award. That came to pass because my brother-in-law Eric Buchanan was a very active member and he is pushy as hell. You either like Eric or you don't like the son of a bitch at all. I like him because he is brazen. But I just have to be honest about it and say that I don't think I would have gotten that award without him. Most of the time I can think that maybe Eric pushed them to do right. That's fair. But I do have this self-doubt thing, and sometimes I just know that my friends are looking out for me. They gave me the award at their annual meeting in Eureka Springs, and Karen and I drove up. So, my résumé now says, Trial Judge of the Year, Arkansas Trial Lawyers Association 2010.

Chapter 18
Health Problems

Mental Exhaustion

I ended my career at the Arkansas Court of Appeals because I was exhausted. I had been exhausted once before, right after I got out of law school. At that time, I was still doing some work for the National Demonstration Water Project and when I had to write an ordinary research report, I couldn't do it. I was just too tired and had to get someone else to write it for me. That time I recovered in three or four months and was able to open my practice in April 1979.

The exhaustion at the tail end of my service on the appellate court was different. It felt like mental exhaustion, and I just couldn't recover. I couldn't explain why I was on a downward spiral, but I had a little system where I would rejuvenate myself by going over to Marianna early each Wednesday evening to walk with my cows. They would run to me to be fed. I had an old tractor and I might start it up and bring in their hay. Then, I'd come back to work on Thursday morning. Going home to Marianna did sort of sustain me for a while, but I continued to feel out of it mentally. Throughout 2005 and 2006 I was struggling internally, and this was how I knew that I had to stop working.

Examples of My Unbalanced Thinking

When I retired, they assured me I would get a retirement check deposited in my bank on the last day of each month, but I did not trust the state. I knew I had a car payment, credit cards, our house note, and some other things Karen was doing that had to be paid, so I put $5,000 away in my safe. I figured my check was bound to be late sometime and I was scared I wouldn't get my money when all my bills were due. I don't think Karen even knew I had that $5,000. Normal thinking would have told me that the state's payments are all done by computer and were never late. I kept the money in my safe for a while in case stuff went bad, and finally when I realized my mistake I spent it down a little at a time.

Worrying that my stuff might go bad is an old fear for me. Going to law school, on at least three occasions, I rode to class in Little Rock with someone going over there, so I would have to hitchhike back to Marianna in the dark. Of course, catching a ride at night was hard, and the harder it was, the more I knew I had to do it. One time it took all night to get home.

But I had to do it to prove that I was still tough enough. I had to reassure myself that if I lost everything, I could still survive. That knowledge gave me security. That is stupid, I know, and probably a little insane, but that is what I was thinking.

Then, when I had my law practice, I always thought that I needed some kind of backup in case things went bad. If I ever lost my license and couldn't continue working as a lawyer, how would I survive? My security then was that I could always raise some chickens and grow vegetables on my twenty acres outside of Marianna. Later, when I started to think about signing that land over to one of my children, I wondered if I ought to convey and retain a life estate. I was aware that it could have been some kind of paranoia, but I always thought about making certain I still had a place to go in case things went wrong.

After I retired, Bob Donovan called me one day about putting up a plaque in my honor in the Lee County Courthouse. As soon as I got off the phone I called my friend Wilbur Peer. I told him, "Stop what you are doing and think about this hard. What could these sons of bitches be setting me up for?" I even got nervous about going to Marianna. I'm not making this up. I'm serious. I got real careful. I used to have two drinks when I'd go out and I started drinking only one because I was thinking that something was getting ready to happen. Hell, they weren't setting me up for nothin'! I know, I was probably insane.

Source of My Troubled Mind

I've come to believe that the stress of unrecognized fear could have been the source of my unbalanced thinking. First of all, I think that growing up black in the Arkansas Delta during the 1940s and 1950s gave all of us some kind of basic insecurity. It was unconscious. No one talked about it. And none of us realized how our "normal" fear of breaking cultural taboos might affect us later in life. Disrespect from a poor white boy and a mean white bus driver made me angry, and I got a warning to be careful from my Momma. I was a hot-headed teenager and got riled up but had to just turn my back and walk away from the white store clerk who acted disdainful toward me. In 1955, while white kids went to school without question, we had to move off the tenant farm and Daddy lost a source of income to keep his sons in school. In the same year, Emmett Till—who lived only sixty miles from Lee County—was tortured and murdered by a gang of white men! Our parents scared us even more with their warnings meant to protect us from danger. As black kids, we came up knowing you got to be scared.

In the 1960 Memphis sit-ins we were told that it was too dangerous to go anywhere by ourselves after dark, but I walked three miles to get home at night many times. I was tense and alert for trouble. When working at the Clinic and during the Marianna boycotts in the early 1970s, there were years when I had to act fearless. Yes, I stood strong in the face of night riders, angry white mobs, and the hitman, but I was operating scared of everything.

A Strong Man

My Daddy didn't get any farther than the third grade, and he had done alright. His Daddy had been born a slave and he had figured out a way to survive. They were tough enough, so surely, surely I could handle my own shit now. And I really did think that I was tough. I had survived Cleola dying and if I could get through that, I could get through anything. And when I was at the Clinic and had survived the hit those guys had on me, that made me bona fide tough.

If I was now facing a mental problem, I knew I had to be a man. And my way of looking at any mental health issue was, "you have to get past this bullshit by using your brain power because that is what a man does." I really thought that I could work my way through anything by thinking through it logically. But at this point, I was helpless. I felt great anxiety. I was afraid of every damn thing that came along. I would get stuff in the mail and think, "Oh no, this son of a bitch is getting ready to destroy me. This is going to be the end."

I definitely could have benefited from psychological counseling, but that was not something I would do. I never had any inclination to talk about how I felt. When I was a judge, I can tell you that there was no way in hell I could let anybody know I was going for some goddamn counseling. There was never a thought in my mind about getting help. I knew I couldn't be elected as a crazy person. You know folks snitch. Plus, I couldn't share my problems with some son of a bitch who didn't even know any of my life experiences. And I didn't go to my friends either. Remember, we all were of the notion that if you were a strong man, a man who could make things happen, you ought to be able to plow through any kind of mental difficulty. This is how we were raised.

The Mental and Physical Connection

For me the decline (and recovery) of my mental health and my physical health were connected. First, I was down mentally and then the pain and physical disability of arthritis pushed me down even farther, and it finally pushed me over the edge. At the end of 2010, as I was finishing my extra assignment in the First Judicial Circuit, my ankles were so swollen up that I couldn't wear my cowboy boots to the last case I heard. It wasn't just my ankles either. One day I got over to the courthouse in St. Francis County and my left wrist was so big I couldn't get it through the arm of my robe. I had to cut the sleeve in order to get it on. I cut it on the inside so you couldn't see. My hands were swollen too, and I couldn't write with a pen because my fingers wouldn't come together. One of Karen's friends who worked with school children having disabilities gave me a big round thing to put over my pen. That's what I used to sign my name in that last case.

I was in so much pain that Karen finally got me to go to a doctor. Then, because of all my swollen joints, I was referred to a rheumatologist. Karen was there when he examined my joints. I had swelling and pain in my ankles, hands, wrists, and elbows, but she hadn't seen the new swollen knot as big as a tennis ball on my right elbow and I know it scared her. In January or February 2011, the rheumatologist diagnosed me with rheumatoid arthritis. And he also told me that it was going to be at least six months before I got better. But the doctor was low key about it, and I got the impression it was going to take that long to *cure* me.

After about four months, I still couldn't get up and walk without serious pain. This is when my mental health gave way completely. I couldn't figure out how to do anything. I felt hopeless. I was defeated, but I didn't give up entirely. I went to the VA to see if they might be able to help me. And Dr. Hugo Jasin, my VA arthritis doctor, said the same damn thing as the rheumatologist Dr. Columbus Brown IV and my regular physician Dr. Gary Nunn. They were absolutely consistent.

After about six or seven months I still felt kind of rough but better, and in November I was able to fly to Denver to see my dying brother Donnie and attend his funeral. I stayed three or four days and I was in the room with him when he died. I came back home and nursed myself along for a year or so. But I continued to feel miserable mentally and had a hard time thinking clearly or doing just about anything.

Karen witnessed my struggle and she remembers some of it like this:

My sister's baby girl Trinity Hudson would come over here every day to check on Olly. One day she caught me in our backroom and told me that she was afraid for Uncle Olly. I asked her why and she said because of his eyes. Olly had lost so much weight (over thirty pounds) that his eyes were bulging. He had lost muscle tone and he looked real bad. I told my Mom how worried I was about him and what Trinity had said. My Mom came down to see Olly and told me she thought he was dying.

Olly did nothing but sit, so I had asked the doctor if he could go to the gym for some exercise and the doctor thought that Olly was in too much pain and should wait until it was less. But I thought that he need-ed to get off the couch and stop watching TV all day. So I asked my athletic trainer Curtis White if he would talk to Olly. He told him, "I can't take away the arthritis and I can't stop the pain. You will just have to work through it. But I can help you improve your energy level, and I can help you get your muscle tone back." What the trainer said made sense to Olly, so he decided to give it a try. On the first day, the trainer did an assessment to see where Olly was, and he was so weak that he could do NOTHING!

But Olly is reasonable. If you can get to him with something that makes sense to him, he will change his ways. And that is what he did. He started coming to the gym on a regular basis. I think the exercise helped him feel better and accept the arthritis for what it was. Olly is not the sort of person to talk about how he feels, but I noticed that he was getting better and better, stronger and stronger. He even started to take on some paying jobs. And when he moved up to bigger jobs, I knew something was happening.

On the advice of his arthritis doctor, Olly also started going to a coun-selor that he ended up really liking, and he takes a small amount of antidepressant. He will tell people that he goes to the counselor too, so he is proud of the progress he has made, and he accepts that he may not be the Superman he once was. Since 2015 his health seems to be better and fairly stable.

Hitting Rock Bottom and Recovery

For most of my life I didn't consider going for mental health counseling because I knew myself to be tough. I had to get there in a roundabout way. When I was at the VA being treated for the rheumatoid, I also had a VA primary care physician, and based on some of the stuff I was saying, he suggested that I go talk to a therapist. I was not the same Olly Neal I had been and I was willing to try anything.

Hitting rock bottom was my chance to get better. The therapist helped me realize that whatever my mental difficulty was, I could not get better by willpower or by the force of my mind. I had always relied on my brain, but a mental problem turned out to be like a physical problem. Sometimes you need assistance—counseling and medication too. When I have trouble with my shoulder, I go to the arthritis doctor and he tells me to keep it moving and take the medicine he prescribes. With mental stuff, I can talk with the therapist and take the medication he prescribes. This was a big breakthrough.

Exercise for Physical and Mental Health

As the rheumatoid medicine started to kick in, I finally felt less pain. This regular exercise makes sense and appeals to the "tough guy" in me. At the gym, I do an hour of resistance exercise primarily for my shoulders on Mondays and Thursdays. And on Wednesdays and Saturdays I walk at least three miles on a track with my daughter Karama. The doctor tells me that the exercise is why he has been able to reduce my rheumatoid medicine. The only time I have to take anything special for pain is when I am doing something extra and I have to make it through a long, hard twelve- or thirteen-hour day.

Even though I don't particularly like it, exercise has become something I almost won't give up. I have Karen and Karama getting after me too. When I say, "Hell, I'm not going to that damn track tomorrow morning," Karen says, "Well, Olly, you got to go because Karama will be looking for you." So, I go walk the track at 5:30 a.m. and Karama is out there waiting for me. And I eat better too. When my health went down Karen pushed me to eat right because she eats like that too. She doesn't keep any of the food I might want, like steak and Hostess cupcakes, in the house, and I've gotten so I don't need it. Most of the time, I don't even need to eat ice cream anymore either.

So, the exercise does keep my body going. I don't think that I am in great shape. I'm not going to tell you that. But I am up to doing things again and that feels good. My mental health is at an acceptable level. I have my head on right, so I am not always fixed on getting only what I think is best. The downs don't come too often or go too low. I am mentally stronger, and I am reasonably content.

My Mental Health Advice

I'm not sure exactly what to teach our children about mental health, but they should not be like me when I was having my own trouble. I really didn't know how to deal with this kind of problem. I didn't know that many people find it difficult to manage everything by themselves. I didn't think that it was all right to get help.

One thing that we ought to say to whoever looks up to us, is that the mind is influenced by many critical things like hormones, illness, or something bad that happened to you, and the mind can get off track. So just like going to a doctor to get your body back to good health there's nothing wrong with going to a doctor when your mind gets off track. You have to figure out a way to deal with reality and you cannot just fight it on your own. Just like the particular medicine used to control arthritis, there are medicines that can help the mind go in a different direction and get back in balance too. This is where you want to be.

Depression and the Judges and Lawyers Assistance Program (JLAP)

Judge Dion Wilson, in the First Judicial Circuit where I served, had this to add about lawyers and depression, and he gives some good advice on how we can get help when it is needed:

> Depression is real. Everybody gets depressed to a certain extent, and a lot of times lawyers don't have good coping mechanisms. They never have a chance to slow down and deal with it, so they end up trying to "put a band-aid on a tumor." And like many others, they often feed the "tumor" with drugs and alcohol or whatever they can use to temporarily dampen the pain.
>
> We have to reeducate society about attorneys being human. People see the attorney as someone who can help solve their problems. But an attorney may be suffering from serious mental health issues. Life doesn't stop because you are a lawyer. We all need to understand that it is okay and normal for lawyers to get help for themselves. I also have to add that exercise and diet have been keys to my own health.
>
> I was at a judges' seminar in Rogers, Arkansas, and the last topic was JLAP (Judges and Lawyers Assistance Program). This is a nonprofit organization that helps judges, attorneys, and law students deal with mental health and drug addiction problems in a way that protects their privacy. The JLAP office is in Little Rock and they schedule appointments

so that no one ever sees you in there.

One of the issues they were talking about at this seminar was depression and how lawyers are in a profession with the highest depression diagnosis. That being said, after listening to them and before I left Rogers, I made up my mind to be a volunteer and get trained to go out and speak on behalf of JLAP, to tell law students, lawyers, and judges about the mental health issues that affect us, about the JLAP program, and how to get help when it's needed.

Henry Jones, retired federal magistrate and the person who talked me into going back to law school in 1978 after Daddy died.

Pat Lamar, my longtime office manager and friend.

Political activist Joan First, who was a member of the Arkansas Humanities Council, and me during my fall 1973 Arkansas Senate campaign.

Portrait taken in about 1980 for my law practice in Marianna.

Walter White, the USDA agent for whom I won a 1986 defamation of character case.

I'm standing with Arkansas governor Jim Guy Tucker on October 9, 1991, the day I was sworn in as the first black prosecutor in Arkansas since Reconstruction.

Pitson Brady and me when I had my law practice in Marianna. Brady is my friend who helped me decide to accept the prosecutor job.

Olly Neal, 2017.

Judge Richard Arnold, who wrote the majority opinion for the landmark voting rights legislative redistricting case M. C. Jeffers v. Clinton in 1990.

Ernest Cunningham, Arkansas state representative, who I deposed during Jeffers v. Clinton. *We later became friends and worked together. This picture was taken in Helena-West Helena on March 10, 2019.*

My wife Karen and my daughter Karama helping me get ready for the January 1, 1993, circuit court judge swearing-in by Federal Judge George Howard, who is on the right. He was the first black federal judge in Arkansas.

My friends Calvin King and Harvey Williams (in the middle and partially hidden) with me after I was sworn in as circuit court judge in 1993.

Willie Douglas (big guy in the middle), who eventually started a Boys and Girls Club in Phillips County, brought some young boys to witness and get inspired by my 1993 circuit court judge swearing-in ceremony.

When I was a circuit court judge, my wife Karen and I were invited (with about 100 of Bill Clinton's friends and supporters) to a 1994 Christmas party at the White House.

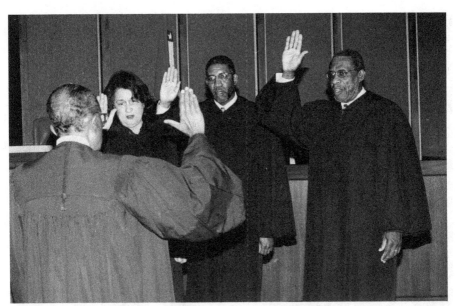

Judge Andree Roaf, Judge Wendell Griffen, and me being sworn in to the Arkansas Appellate Court by Judge George Howard, January 2001.

My 2004 staff on the Arkansas Appellate Court from left to right: Rosalyn Middleton, clerk for three years; Pat Lamar, office manager; me; and Gwendolyn Rucker, clerk for two years.

Justice Josephine Hart, a strong, outspoken, and smart woman I worked with on the appellate court. We didn't always agree, but we worked well together.

Me and one of my longhorns in November 2002 on my land outside Marianna.

The portrait Bob Donovan arranged to have placed on the Lee County Courthouse wall in 2012 when I was suffering from depression and paranoia.

Jan Wrede, 2015.

*Working out at the Real
Fitness gym in Little Rock,
September 2019.*

Because of arthritic weakness in my right shoulder, Lisa Walker, staff trainer, is spotting me as I lift the twenty-five-pound weights. Lisa was a college track star at the University of Arkansas in Fayetteville.

My son Nic Neal and his children from left to right: Miraj, TreShuane, and Nakia, September 2019.

Anisha Phillips and her children Ava M. Phillips and Alton C. Phillips Jr., November 2019.

Nyerere Billups and his family, from left to right: Napier Billups, Deuce McFadden, Nyerere's wife Kerri Billups, Nyah Billups, Nyerere Billups Sr. (with K on sweater), and Diesel McFadden in June 2019.

From left to right are my daughter Karama's mother-in-law Akosua Mercy Obiri, her daughter Ayoka, Karama, and her husband Kwadjo Boaitey at the 2014 induction of Judge Olly Neal into the Arkansas Black Hall of Fame.

From left to right: Dr. Dorris Gardner, graduate school dean at Jackson State University; my son-in-law Kwadjo; me; and my daughter Karama at my retirement party on December 30, 2006.

Karen and me at the governor's mansion in 2014 when I was inducted into the Arkansas Black Hall of Fame

Karen and me at the 1995 Moton School Reunion.

Lee County Sheriff Ocie Banks in his office on March 7, 2017.

My friend Calvin King in 2018. He and I were unsuccessful in getting the heir property law changed. Then my daughter Karama came along and made it happen in 2016.

Karama Neal and her daughter Ayoka Boaitey on the Belk family heirs' property in southwest Arkansas.

At the fiftieth anniversary gala celebration are LCCC Board Chairman Lazaro English; LCCC board members Charlet Jones, Evonda Williams, Desi Sims, Christine Smith, Earnestine Jackson, Jessie Gist, and Saundra Blocker; and LCCC CEO Dr. Kellee Farris. I am between Desi Sims and Christine Smith.

Olly and Dr. Kellee Farris at the fiftieth anniversary gala celebration in Marianna.

Part Four: Family

Karen and me in Washington DC for President Barack Obama's first inauguration in January 2009. The picture was taken at a party given by an organization called the Arkansas Connection.

Chapter 19
Nic Neal

My son Nic was born December 27, 1978, and my biggest regret is failing to be a better father to him. To me it is my greatest infraction on doing what was right. I think that Nic could have done better if he had been raised up in a household with two steady parents. I couldn't stay with his Momma, but if you are going to risk making a baby, you should make damn sure you can live with the Momma. It is pretty simple to state, but you are a damn fool when drinking that whiskey.

I used to tell my son, "I've got two children including you and I have never been married to either one of their mothers. Don't do that. If you can figure out how to make a baby, you can figure out how to pick out a woman to be your wife full time. I'm not necessarily promoting the Christian principle of marriage, but you ought to be living together so you can see your children every day." Or at least you need to be in their life.

Nic has fathered two babies with two different mothers and has never been married to either one, so he followed in his Daddy's footsteps. My daughter is older, and my son is younger. His daughter is older, and his son is younger, so we are two damn fools together. That's it.

Nic's Early Days in Marianna

Nic was a surprise. Back in the spring of 1978, my last year of law school, I was taking classes on Monday, Wednesday, and Friday nights. One Friday evening, I started over to Little Rock but before I got very far I had the thought, "Hell, why am I doing this? I ain't going." So I pulled over at Brinkley, went into a liquor store, and bought a pint of gin and a jug of orange juice. I drove back to Son O'Donnell's joint in Marianna and met up with Willie Mae Broussard, a woman I knew. And that was that. The next week I got my head back on straight and did what I was supposed to do getting over to my night classes.

I knew the man who was regularly with Willie Mae, and when Nic was born I didn't have any notion in the world that he was my son. In 1983 when Nic was four, Willie Mae started pushing that I was his Daddy. Nic had asthma and nappy hair like me so maybe that was what she was going on. Anyway, I thought it was bullshit, so we had a blood test and it proved he was my son. After that, I would go pick up Nic maybe once or twice a week and take him with me. We would ride around in my truck on whatever I was doing. I paid child support of a specific amount on a certain day each month. I think that his mother was pleased to have my child, but she never pressed me for anything. And we didn't say bad things about each other in front of Nic. Never.

When Nic started school I saw more of him. Because it was only four blocks from my office, he could walk over after school. One day when he was only six or seven years old, I told him, "Why don't you work for me and you can make some money." He agreed that this made some sense, so he would come over to my office and drag out the big paper bags of trash. It was pretty funny because as a child Nic was very small and those bags were bigger than he was. Pat was kind of Nic's supervisor and Nic liked her. They got along real well, but Nic could have an attitude when he was crossed. When he was about eight, Pat wanted him to do something that he didn't want to do. So he came to me and said, "When I get to be big, I am going to fire Pat!"

Move to Minneapolis

Nic was nine or ten when Willie Mae moved to Minneapolis looking for better opportunities, and she took Nic with her. After that Nic would come back to Arkansas in the summer to visit. He helped me on the farm, and I think that he had a lot of fun down in Marianna during those summers.

One day I got a call from Willie Mae. Nic had left school and come home telling her that the teacher had lied on him and accused him of throwing a spitball. He insisted that he had not thrown a spitball. Willie Mae called me because she wanted me to help her get him back in school. I called Nic on the phone and discussed all this with him. Then, I called the school principal. She was very helpful and right away put me through to the teacher. The teacher told me that Nic had not thrown a spitball, but he had thrown a piece of chalk.

After talking to his teacher I called Nic back and told him that I had all the information now. "You threw a piece of chalk, didn't you?" He got quiet and said, "Yes, sir." I had checked with Pat to make sure that there was enough money in my bank account to pay for a ticket to Minneapolis, and I told him, "You are going to school. And here is what we are going to do. You have a dime to ride the bus to school, right? You take that dime and go back to school. And if you don't do that, I am going to get on a plane and come up there and it won't be to just visit with you." He said, "Yes, sir, Daddy." And he went back to school.

Minneapolis is a big city where nobody knew his Momma or Daddy, and Nic tended to be rambunctious. He might have been in the eighth grade when he got into some serious juvenile misconduct. Apparently, he had been with some boys who set a big fire that burned down a building. That's when Willie Mae called and told me that they were going to put Nic in the juvenile detention center, and she asked if he could come down to live with me in Marianna. Willie Mae always thought that I was too strict, and I knew that she would be calling and bothering me. So I didn't agree to take him until she promised not to interfere with my parental guidance.

Moves to Marianna, Little Rock, and Back to Minneapolis

I don't think that Nic really wanted to come back, but he didn't have any choice. He went to Marianna's Lee High School from ninth through the first half of eleventh grade. Nic lived with me, and the two of us needed a better place, so that's when I moved out of the apartment above my office and into a little house I had built on my Crowley's Ridge property. I've had it since 1986 and still own it.

When I became a judge on the Arkansas Court of Appeals in January 1996, Nic did not want to move to Little Rock either. He had gotten used to going to school in Marianna and had made friends he didn't want to leave. Plus, Karen and I had married by then, and Nic and Karen didn't get along too well. So in his senior year Nic ended up moving back to Minneapolis and has lived there ever since. He finished high school up there and graduated with a very good grade point average. He always was a bright boy. I think that he did some college classes too.

Prison Time

After high school Nic was involved in selling drugs, and he got caught and ended up in prison. He was in federal prison for six years. Nic got out in January 2017 and seems to be doing all right now. I've concluded that he has figured out some things for himself and is on a path that makes sense for him. I've stopped expecting him to do what I think is the appropriate thing, and this is a trial for any parent. There is stuff you can give advice about and some stuff that your children have to learn on their own.

This is what Nic has to say for himself:

I am not living in the life I had before I went to prison. My old life is the last thing on my mind. I am doing really well now. I am practicing a trade, concrete masonry, that I learned in prison. I have a good job and I'm getting $25 an hour. I'm doing amazingly well for somebody who just came out of prison. My kids want for nothing. I don't get as much money as I did when I was going wrong, but I don't have to be looking over my shoulder all the time.

You should know this too. I missed six years and I am still trying to play catchup. I have a fifteen-year-old daughter, a six-year-old son, and a four-year-old daughter. I watched my son grow up in visiting rooms and photographs. I missed all my older daughter's time coming up to being a teenager. The four-year-old was not mine, but she is my baby now. She is my daughter's little sister, and her father got killed before she was born. Me and this guy didn't get along at all. I was in prison and he was dating the woman I had a child by, and I didn't like him for that. Basically, you could say that I have sort of adopted my little girl. She needed a Daddy and I've never been one to leave any babies out. I wouldn't feel right going to get my big daughter and not picking her up too. It is an important part of my character. My children are the best thing that's happened to me.

When I went in, I had a big house with four bedrooms and a yard and all that sort of stupid stuff. Now, I'm in a little-bitty studio apartment. But it is way bigger than the prison cell, so living in a small apartment doesn't bother me. It is my house. It is mine. I don't have to worry about anybody telling me what to do.

Now, I am just happy to be free. I know that it's not a great thing that I went to prison, but it opened my eyes to a lot of things I didn't pay attention to before. I appreciate small things way more. A mattress with cushioning. Carpeted rooms. Being able to talk on the phone for thirty minutes. I'm just happy to be free, man. To be able to be with these babies on a regular basis. I wouldn't trade that for nothing.

I love my kids.
If I could,
I'd give them the world
on a silver platter,
and keep only
the scraps for myself.

Glad to Be Nic's Daddy

When I went to Minneapolis about a year and a half after Nic got out of prison, it was a very good visit. I talked with Nic's oldest child Nakia. She seems so mature. She had to deal with the fact that her Daddy spent that six years away from her. We talked about all kinds of things. She pulled me aside and thanked me for being a grandfather to her baby sister Miraj Denise Haynes, who is her Momma's but not Nic's child. She explained to me that Miraj's Daddy had been killed and both of the grandfathers are deceased, so Miraj didn't have a Grandpa either. Of course, the little girl was crawling all over me, and she called me Grandpa.

When Nic says he was "living in the life," it means he was doing his drug business out there on the street. I used to prosecute those boys who were selling drugs on the street in east Arkansas. They recognize that they are living a separate life from other people who don't have to watch out for the law. They have a different set of rules to survive, and I don't think all of it is bad. They believe that when you are "living in the life," it is critical when you say you are going to do something that you do it. It makes you a man of your word. Not a bad thing.

Nic and I have talked some, and I do believe he is past his other life. But I don't believe he has forgotten. He knows what the risks are and how to handle it. He realizes that he can't go out there and then back away from it. They have all this language to talk about trying to make quick money and then get back. Do a deal, one and done, hit a lick. I think he understands that a one and done is probably not going to hold. Very few people can do that. I don't think he is just following my directions either. He has figured out everything for himself, and this is much better than if he were trying to follow directions from me or somebody else.

Nic Is Like Me

Nic and I discussed that, in my judgment, I was not much of a father. He does not seem to judge me as harshly as I do, and I don't think he is angry at his Momma Willie Mae either. Nic and I agree that he is strong-willed like me. The difference was that when I came along, I had a Momma and Daddy who were together on how to raise me. But me and Willie Mae didn't agree. She would countermand and undermine my instructions. Nic knows that you have to have a situation where the parents work together. He knows that because his parents weren't working together, he could do some things that were not proper.

I think Nic and I have a fairly healthy relationship now. Sometimes we talk about how you need to figure out what you need to do. And sometimes we just bullshit about women like I used to do with Gene Raff. Who looks good and stuff like that. I know in the proper world this is not the way to talk, but we don't always talk proper. I think our relationship is healthy because our style doesn't differ too much. He speaks his mind straight out like I do. That can get you into trouble, but we don't mean any harm. It's just the way we are. So I'm pretty sure he would tell me straight out (or maybe just go silent) if I was way off on something important to him.

Good Relationships

Naturally, Nic wants to spend time with his children. Part of it is he really wants to make sure his children grow up close to him. From our conversations, from our emails and his Facebook comments, I can see that Nic gets along excellently with both of his Baby Mommas. And they get along with each other too. But then I don't know what will happen when he gets to the point where he has to deal with teenagers. Nakia is already a teenager and she is related to me, so she has to have some damn fool in her. I don't know how they will work that out. But in terms of getting on a bad path because the Momma and Daddy can't come together, Nic is trying to make damn sure that his children don't have the same fate he had.

Nic will be under federal supervision until July 2020. Supervision requires you to stay employed, and he has had a steady job as a mason since he got out. If he is good enough at this kind of work, he probably can make more when he is free to go look for better-paying jobs. But he knows it is a big hill to overcome when you have to tell somebody that you were an inmate. If someone has a big support system when he comes out, that is a big advantage. Nic did not have a big support system. I can't claim to have done anything positive for him, and his Momma didn't have any way to help him either. So, he was on his own.

Nic may have a good relationship with his Baby Mommas, but things don't always go the way he would like. In 2018, when they both decided to take their children away from Minneapolis for the Thanksgiving holiday, Nic was hurt and pissed and going a little bit insane. He called me and was talking about being ready to snap. Nic seemed close to doing something that would fuck up his life again long-term. I believe that he called me because he was trying to find a way to keep control of himself. He wanted to talk to me about his frustration and what he ought to do and what he ought not to do. Until now, I don't think that he would have bothered to go to any-damn-body with something like this. But he came to me like I used to go to my Daddy.

When Nic called me, it really made me feel like his father. I said to him, "Nic, these things are difficult sometimes. And life is almost never fair. As humans we are conditioned to have a relationship with our children. And our children are conditioned to have a relationship with their parents. When the relationship gets stretched, it is hard on us. Sometimes it makes the children be less than they ought to be. Sometimes it makes the parents be less than they ought to be. My relationship with you has not been nearly what it could have been, in part because your mother and I could not raise you in a two-parent household. And you have created a similar situation. I'm not blaming you for what you have done, but you have to take it the way it is and accept the things that come with your situation." Nic didn't snap. Finally, he said, "Yah, that's right."

He is back to laughing with his children, and I can tell you it was good to feel like his Daddy.

Chapter 20
Anisha Phillips

I met Anisha for the first time when she was in the sixth grade. She and another girl came to my office at the Arkansas Court of Appeals to interview me. Anisha stood out because she was so tall and so skinny, and her clothes didn't fit. She was wearing a sweat suit type thing that was way too big. No matter what she was wearing, though, Anisha's intellect was the most impressive I had ever seen in a twelve-year-old child. The other little girl asked her own questions first, and they were what you would expect, mostly about my personal life. Do you have a daughter? How old is she? Do you have a son? How old is he? Where you a lawyer before you got to be a judge?

When it was Anisha's turn, she pulled out a little piece of paper and started off with a preliminary. She said, "So, you had to be a lawyer before you became a judge. When you were a lawyer, did you represent people?" And I said, "Yes." And then she went to the question, "How do you decide that you can defend someone who you know is guilty?" It was profound. I used to speak to students in a prelaw program preparing them for law school. This was the kind of question I would discuss with them. And I knew a boy once who didn't make it through law school because he couldn't get past that question. I explained to her about the constitutional requirement that you are presumed innocent of a criminal charge until proven guilty, and you are not proven guilty unless your guilt is beyond a reasonable doubt. This reasoning appeared to make some sense to her. She was an impressive twelve-year-old.

Rough Beginning

Anisha was born December 4, 1984, and she had a rough beginning. Her mother was a drug addict and her father was a pastor who didn't acknowledge her publicly until she was a successful college student. She and her mother moved from place to place, and Anisha was on her own a lot.

Anisha attended Booker T. Washington Elementary School where my wife Karen was principal, and from the beginning she recognized Anisha as a child who was not well cared for. When Anisha was in the sixth grade, she fell in with the wrong group of kids and got in trouble for stealing. Anisha had to go to court, and the judge ordered both Anisha and her mother to be drug tested. Anisha was clean and her mother was not. After that, they moved to North Little Rock and Anisha says that her mother did better because the court was watching. During her seventh- and eighth-grade years they stayed in one house the whole time. But they lived with her mother's boyfriend and evidently there were some serious fights in Anisha's presence. Anisha said that when she told the boyfriend to leave her mother alone, he threatened to kill her. And apparently, as soon as the court-ordered surveillance period was up, her mother returned to the drugs.

Anisha and her mother moved back to Little Rock for Anisha's ninth-grade year, and that summer they moved in with an elderly friend. After his daughter came and took the old man with her (perhaps just so she could get his checks), Anisha went on to spend the rest of the summer with a friend. Around this same time, she was raped by a family member of the friend she was living with. Shortly after the rape and not too long before school started, Anisha moved in with an aunt, who was not always in the best situation, but she made room for her. The good thing about this move was that Anisha now was close enough to walk to our house.

She spent the night with us sometimes apparently without even telling her aunt. One time when Karen was taking her to school, she had to go by her aunt's apartment to pick up something and the electricity had been turned off. After that Karen told me that she was seriously concerned for Anisha's safety. She said, "If she keeps living like this, she could come up missing and no one would know. We need to do something about this little girl." I agreed.

Little Rock Central High School

Anisha had just started living with us and Karen had gotten her enrolled at Central High School, but because our house was not her legal address, they wouldn't let her ride the school bus that stopped nearby. I had my secretary call her principal and schedule an appointment for me. I wanted to make sure she knew that I was somebody high up before I asked for her help. I told her, "Anisha started coming by our house in the mornings because she lived where there was no electricity and would get locked out sometimes. Also, Anisha did not want to be adopted or formally separated from her mother, so we are making an informal arrangement with the folks at the Department of Human Services that simply allowed Anisha to stay with us. And since we live in the Central High zone, we would like you to register her at this address." She said, "Okay, I'll do it."

When the DHS supervisor came to visit us, Karen and I told the woman that we would support Anisha and not look to DHS for any money. We also said that Anisha did not want to cause any problems for her mother. And we were concerned that if DHS got a report that Anisha was not staying with her mother, there would be problems. The supervisor said, "I don't know anything about any of this. If something changes, you call me." That woman could have lost her job. She understood that we really were trying to help this child. And I never heard from her or saw her again until much later at a social gathering. We just smiled at each other and kept walking. I wouldn't know her now if I saw her. That was a long time ago.

Karen and Anisha Butted Heads

Taking a teenager into your home is a big commitment, and Anisha was a troublesome child. She and Karen definitely had trouble getting along. Karen struggled with accepting that even though Anisha was so young, she had been making her own decisions and coming and going as she pleased most of her life. Karen put normal expectations on Anisha, like helping around the house for her pocket-money allowance, as if she were a normal teenager, and they were in a constant power struggle. Karen got after Anisha as a mother would and Anisha pushed back as much as possible without going too far. No matter how mad she was at Karen, I'm sure Anisha really did want to be with us. She knew we both cared about her, and we gave her the stable home she needed.

Anisha and I got along much better, partly because I had been a troublesome kid too. Basically, I had done all the stuff Anisha could think of myself, so I could be a little bit more understanding and flexible. Also, I was less assertive in my parenting style, probably because of the way my Daddy dealt with me when I was going off track. Whenever she would do something stupid, I tried to stay calm like Daddy and not be reactive.

At one point, Karen's problems with Anisha got to the level where Karen was saying, "She has got to go." And I said, "Wait a minute, Karen, let me try one more time." I had decided to use what I called the "Drop Dead Hand" on Anisha, and I said to her, "I told you that I was going to work with you because I thought you were bright and you ought to have a shot at doing something with your life. But you have to understand that I am not going to let you destroy my marriage. I intend to stay married to Karen because I like her. I can't make you get along with her, so you have to do whatever you can yourself. And if that isn't enough, I will have to put you out." I think that Anisha understood I was not trying to be mean. After that she got along with Karen a little bit better. It wasn't perfect. Not like now. Hell, they are like the Momma and the favored daughter now.

A Very Good College for Anisha

School was easy for Anisha. She got good grades and graduated from Little Rock Central in 2003. When Anisha was in high school, Karen learned about a Little Rock program for black students who had potential that was not being fully realized. The program was run by an older white guy, Dr. Thomas Eppley, who encouraged black students to get out into the white world, and he helped them get scholarships to top-level colleges. Anisha wanted to go to Spelman or Howard, but Dr. Eppley gave her other choices. She was accepted by Barnard, Smith, and Wellesley, and she chose Barnard. It had a great reputation, so we were satisfied with her choice. I think Karen and Karen's friend Rose flew up to New York with her the first time. Karen and Rose also were there when Anisha joined a sorority. We brought her back home to Little Rock at the end of each school year, and we paid for her phone so we could stay in contact. Karen and I went to her graduation.

Part of Our Family

In 2018 Anisha talked about what it is like being part of our family as an adult:

> I know that even if we butt heads and even if sometimes we don't like each other's actions and even if I may perceive something negative going on, Karen and Olly care about me. It was their consistency that helped me learn to trust them. Their consistency proved to me that their hearts were and are in the right place, and they love me. But Olly is never very open with affection. Want to trip him up? Tell him you love him. It's not something he's says often, and he often stammers when he responds, but he always tells me he loves me when I tell him I love him.
>
> I have been calling Olly "Daddy" for a long time, but I still call Karen "Karen." Sometimes, though, I'd go back and forth. It was easy and still is easy for me to call Olly Daddy because I never had a father before. He just stepped into a place that no one had ever filled. But I already had a mother who was a good mother when she was not high. Even though my mother knows that I call Karen Mom sometimes, I have generally gone out of my way not to say it in front of her because I don't want to hurt her feelings. But nowadays, I don't focus on it as much. Now,

whatever name comes up is what I'm going with. And if my mother has a problem with it, that's on her.

Marriage

After Barnard, Anisha graduated from the University of Arkansas Law School in Fayetteville. She told me that she was interested in becoming a child advocate. She was especially interested in helping children, but she ended up getting married, having her children, and working as a law clerk. Anisha and her husband made a very attractive couple. They had two fine little children, a boy and a girl, and she brings them over to visit me almost every week. I look forward to seeing them. If her husband had been a little more loyal, Anisha could have stayed with him. She did her best to make the marriage work, but they ended up divorcing. Since she has been away from her husband, Anisha looks different. She is brighter. Karen knows more about this than I do.

Anisha seemed to have a pretty good understanding of what happened to her marriage when she talked about it recently. And I was happy to learn that I helped her along the way.

I married my husband in 2010, a couple months after I graduated from law school, and we have two children. But after eight years I decided it was time to divorce. I needed this marriage when I still suffered from childhood issues of abandonment and rejection. But I have learned you can be rejected and abandoned in a marriage too. I'm confident that I will be more than okay without him. And without bitterness or resentment, I wish him well.

Olly was the best throughout the whole marriage. I could call him at any time with anything. He would listen. He would give advice. He was simply there. When I made the decision to end my marriage, it meant the world to me when he said, "Nobody can say you haven't done everything to save that marriage." My decision was mine, but he knew everything, and the fact that he recognized all the work I had done mattered. Just like any other daughter needs approval from her father, his approval is important to me.

Career and Other Goals

Anisha took a position with the Federal Public Defender's Office in 2019. They serve indigent people in need of representation in the Eastern District of Arkansas. She is in the Capital Habeas Unit, where she works with her colleagues to research and present arguments seeking post-conviction relief for their death row clients. It seems to be a valuable use of her talent and intelligence.

She explains her career decisions and the progress she is making in her life much better than I can:

> After law school, it took me a little over two years to get a job in the legal profession. In 2012, I finally found a position at the Arkansas Court of Appeals. This was some years after Olly retired. For many reasons, it was a very good job for me. I liked the flexibility, and I was able to sharpen my research and writing skills. Also, children don't care why you are not there. It doesn't matter if you are absent because you are a drug addict or a judge or anything else. So while my children are young, I need a job that challenges me, pays well, but does not take me away too much.
>
> Olly and Karen have always encouraged me to do more. After my divorce and becoming a first-time home-owner, I felt ready for a new professional challenge. I've always wanted to work for children. Children don't pay taxes, so consequently, their lobby is not strong and legislative acts to help children fall short. I also have an interest in the death penalty and its uneven—to put it lightly—administration, specifically depending on class, race, and locality. So when I learned of a position in the federal Capital Habeas Unit, I jumped at the opportunity to apply and was hired as a research attorney. This is an important professional step for me as it gives me the opportunity to do meaningful work and make a difference.

Making Progress

Anisha goes on to explain her Christianity and spiritual life, as related to her past and future:

> I am a Christian. I am very spiritual and a member of New Life Church. The summer before my road to divorce started, I had prayed for a stronger relationship with God. That October was when I finally figured out for myself that God really loved me and I was on his radar. I had always known that he was with me. I can't look back at my life and say that God was not there and not doing things directly and indirectly through others like Olly and Karen. I just thought that he was an "in the nick of time" kind of God. But now that I have been working through the process of becoming a stronger person in Christ, it has spilled over making me a stronger person in other areas too.

I want to continue to grow personally in terms of self-esteem and con-fidence and professionally in terms of skill and influence. I want to do something important with my life in addition to being a good mother. I am making progress bit by bit. This is going to sound weird, but my ultimate goal is to have lived my life and to have done something that has made Karen and Olly proud. They dealt with so much in deciding to take me in. I want them to feel like it was worth it. That is not to say that they don't feel that way already. I think they do. I know that I have come a long way from where I started. But I want to do more. And I want them to see it.

Chapter 21
Nyerere Billups

Nyerere was born in Chicago on February 12, 1977, a month after his mother turned seventeen. His little brother was born in December of the same year. They stayed for a while with their mother in a shelter, but as with many children of single, teenage mothers, they were raised up almost entirely by grandparents. Nyerere was seven years old and in the second grade when he and his mother's parents moved back home to Lee County.

Nyerere's family did not have high expectations for him, and it seems that in his own way Nyerere rebelled intensely against the low expectations put on him.

This is how he describes it:

> In my family, all you were expected to do was get a job and survive. And I grew up knowing I didn't want to go through a bunch of the stuff I saw around me. I didn't want this path. As far back as I can remember, I would tell people that I wanted to be a doctor. I was really smart in school and there was never any question in anybody's mind that I was capable of being a doctor. Everybody just accepted that I was doing what I could to get where I wanted to go. My grandparents didn't ask questions and didn't worry about me getting in trouble.
>
> Everybody knew I was different, but at the same time I always was a part of my family. I was around for all the family drama, for all the scary times. And when I was only nine or ten years old, I started making adult-level decisions around the house. My grandfather couldn't read, and my grandmother's reading level was low, so when an official document came in, I would read it to them, and the interpretation I made was what they accepted.

Bright and Determined

My son Nic and Nyerere were friends, and I think that I heard about Nyerere's interest in medicine when he was twelve or thirteen. They started Lee High School at the same time, and Nic knew that I was trustee over the Addie Lee Wilson scholarship fund. Mrs. Wilson was a wealthy lady who lived near Marianna, and I did legal work for her. When Mrs. Wilson died, she left a big sum of money to help poor black kids get to college and into a medical profession. Nic told me about Nyerere, and I went to talk to him to see if he had made plans for a medical career.

Nyerere's grandfather was a decent guy, but he was an alcoholic. To me, Nyerere's grandmother was the most impressive person in his family. I don't know if she had enough global knowledge to be pointing him in any direction, but she was strong and she provided real cover for him. When I went to tell her I might be able to help Nyerere, she was enthusiastic and said, "Don't worry. His Momma will sign any paper you need." Anyway, his grandmother sure as hell didn't put out any slowdown in front of him.

When Nyerere and I talked, I hadn't put together a system about what I wanted to try to present to him. Not too long before this, I had been working with a couple of kids until they got hot and told me that they did not want another father. They turned off on me and anything I said. So, I was influenced by that experience, and with Nyerere I was being real careful. I told him, "I ain't trying to be your damn Daddy and I will not be your running buddy. But I am somebody you can count on. I am somebody who can help you get past your difficulties, so you can do what you want to do."

Nyerere was a sensible young man all the damn time. And at first, I couldn't figure out how he was so different from the others in his family. It was not that they weren't bright. His aunt, who had quite a reputation…, is a good example. She was an aide for the Lee County School District when Karen was superintendent there, and Karen told me that at work Nyerere's aunt could figure out things as fast or faster than anyone in the office. So it seemed that the people in Nyerere's family just came up in a situation that was not conducive to going anywhere. But I found Nyerere to be determined to bust out of how he came up. He had his own vision and he was going to stick to it.

Mentoring Nyerere

I helped Nyerere get his first Addie Lee Wilson scholarship when he was fourteen. It gave him money to go to summer camps and to statewide student organizations that he joined. One of them was the governor's youth commission, where kids worked to educate their peers and prevent them from misusing various substances.

Nyerere was involved with organizing regional and statewide conferences. And he was really good at being a behind-the-scenes grassroots-type coordinator. I believe he still uses this talent in his professional career. I drove him to those meetings in Little Rock because his family was not in a position to do that. If the meeting was on a Thursday and Friday, I'd pick him up in Marianna so he could be at the meeting. Then he would stay with me and Karen, and I would take him back home to Marianna on Sunday.

I helped Nyerere get to functions in places other than Little Rock too. He would come to me and I'd tell him how I could help either through a scholarship or driving him and other things too. I helped him get a job at the Clinic, and he worked there all of the four years he was in high school.

We got to know each other over a period of time on the drives between Marianna and Little Rock or wherever. We would talk the entire time. I would talk and he would talk. Nyerere was never shy. But he never talked about his family and he never came to me with any family problems. I was mostly an objective mentor, but I was so involved in his life that some people might have mistaken me for his father.

Knox College

When Nyerere graduated from Lee High School, he made the decision of where to go to college entirely by himself. He was accepted by quite a few schools and chose Knox College, a small school in Galesburg, Illinois. Nyerere told me that since he had grown up poor in a black community, he needed to learn how the rich kids lived and how the white kids lived. He chose a small, private, predominantly white college because growing up in Marianna, where he knew everybody, had not prepared him for life at a big university. He also said another important thing. He wanted to be part of a minority. He had read books about it and wanted that experience. All of this never occurred to me, but Nyerere knew himself and he made his own decisions.

I never felt comfortable up there at that white college, and I've never been big on emotional goodbyes. When it was time for him to go, we loaded his stuff in my truck, drove to Galesburg, and unloaded his stuff. I don't believe I even stayed the night. Before I left, I must have told him something like, "You know why you are here and I know why you are here. I hope you remember that and work hard." He arranged for the school to send his grades to me.

During the semesters when Nyerere was at Knox, we didn't have much contact, but when he needed an internship, he came to me, or if he didn't have a place to go during a break from school, he stayed with me and Karen. I helped him get two summer internships at the University of Arkansas for Medical Sciences in Little Rock. One was with Dr. Groesbeck Parham and the other one was with Dr. Phillip Rayford. The Addie Lee Wilson Scholarship provided money for some of his train transportation to and from school, and I would pick him up when he got to Little Rock. I might have paid for some of those trips out of my own pocket too, but I don't remember for sure. When Nyerere graduated from Knox, Karen and I were proud to be at his graduation.

Nyerere and the MCAT

When it was time for Nyerere to go take the MCAT (Medical College Admission Test), I think that he was prepared academically, but something happened to him physically. Knots or lumps would come up on his face. I don't know what it was, but there was something going on inside of him that was making it happen. I still can't explain it medically or psychologically, but I never believed his problems with the MCAT had anything to do with him not having the capability or the capacity to be a good physician. I do have to admit that I didn't do a very job of helping him with this problem. I sent him to a clinical psychologist who was a woman and a friend who gave me a discount. His problem with taking that big test didn't improve. He might have done better with a male psychologist, and I probably should have found another therapist. But we didn't have the necessary resources, and I just did the best I could at the time.

As Nyerere looked back on not fulfilling his long-held dream of becoming a doctor, he told me this:

> One of the things I don't talk about very much was that I was not well prepared to go to a good college like Knox. I spent my first two years there trying to catch up and did not get the best grades. In my second two years, I was finally up to speed and my grades improved. But it was an uphill climb to raise my GPA enough to be competitive for medical school. Getting into medical school is super competitive. You have to have an outstanding GPA and MCAT. I didn't have either when I applied to medical schools. But because my essays were strong, I still got interviews. I made the wait list at the University of Arkansas for Medical Sciences (UAMS), but I didn't get in because everybody showed up.

No Backup Plan

When Nyerere didn't get into medical school, he didn't have a backup plan, so I told him to come and stay with me and Karen. Nyerere was with us for two years and worked hard. He prepared and retook the MCAT again and again, and those physical symptoms appeared each time. He just could not do well on that test. He also searched for a graduate program that suited him. Neither medical school nor graduate school worked out, so he applied and was awarded a NASA fellowship to do research in a UAMS research lab. That grant connected him with some people at the Centers for Disease Control and Prevention (CDC), and he moved to Atlanta. Initially, he worked in medical research and then he moved into the private sector and worked his way up to becoming director of development for a company that develops cancer drugs.

While Nyerere was staying with us, Karen and I laid down some basic rules. He was free to stay with us, and we were happy to have him, but he had to fend for himself. We were not his chauffeurs. He could not drive our cars. And he couldn't have overnight guests. It became clear to us that Nyerere didn't have any intention of just laying around. He found some kind of a job and saved his money to buy a car and paid for his own car insurance.

All along, I was telling Nyerere, "I am not trying to be your father, but if I have something to say that I think will benefit you, I am just going to say it whether you like it or not. If you want to hear the truth, if you want to hear a balanced perspective, or you just want to hear my thoughts, I'm here for that." And sometimes I asked Nyerere to come with me when I went to speak at a school. As I talked to those kids, I would use Nyerere as an example of overcoming disadvantages, and I would brag about his accomplishments. Nyerere listened and this is what he took from those experiences and our relationship:

When Olly spoke at those schools, I heard what he really thought of me. And I also noticed how many people knew him, how many people waited to shake his hand, and how many people had a story of when he helped them or made a connection for them. It was over and over and over again. Even the janitor was, "Hey man, thanks for such and such."

Over time, I also saw Olly use himself as an example. He didn't shy away from talking about his failures. He didn't shy away from how messed up he thought he was and how he bounced back from disappointments. He was saying, "If I can survive all this and I can figure out how to do it, then you can too. You just have to want it. And when you get an opportunity, take advantage of it."

Olly's story is for me and you too. His life was guided by "How do I help others?" His example teaches that whatever you do, make sure you leave the door open for somebody coming up behind you, who looks like you or who is in a worse situation than you are. I learned from him that there is no such thing as the bare minimum. When you are committed to community service, you give your all. And if you are not going to be all in, you at least have to make sure you are not an obstacle.

When I think of Olly, I think of him being the father I never had. I also think of a man who worked in a post office, who had a successful stint in the military, who was an intelligent black scientist, who founded a community health clinic, who has been on this board and that board, who went toe to toe on civil rights issues, who was the first black prosecuting attorney, who became a circuit court and appellate judge. The guy is unique. He isn't 200 years old. How has he had time to do all those things?

Chapter 22
Karama Neal

My daughter Karama was born March 25, 1972. Her mother, Janet Cobb, had decided that she wanted me to be the father of her child with no more obligations on my part. I was Karama's father, and I was never very good to her. Today I wonder if I have done her harm. I can't go back and change anything. I just worry.

Karama's Visits

Janet and Karama lived in Little Rock, and I do think it was safer for her to grow up there. After 1979 I thought that I had a pretty good chance of surviving. But before that, I really did think I was going to be killed, and I did not want a little girl to be part of my crazy life. It was high stakes, and I didn't want anybody saying, "There she is. That's Olly Neal's daughter." During those years every time Karama came over, so I could at least see her, I was uncomfortable about the possibility of putting her in danger.

Karama has talked about those early visits, and it's pretty clear that she was not aware of any danger. She tells stories like this:

> I remember going to visit my dad when I was six or seven and my mother saying, "Karama, I think he would really like it if you called him Daddy." I was calling him Olly because my mother called him Olly and all my cousins called him Uncle Olly. I very much wanted more of him in my life and was eager to do whatever would be helpful. I called him Daddy from there on.
>
> After my mother passed, I found her 1981 daybook where she wrote down everything that happened that year. It showed me going to Marianna about every other weekend or every three weeks, something like that, at least for that year. It was actually quite adventurous. When I was seven, eight, nine, I would go by myself on the Greyhound bus. I would have my little pack of graham crackers and grapes. Those were different days.

Karama learned to read when she was very young, and I would brag to my friends about her. I'd tell them, "She reads the newspaper every day to keep up with the news." They didn't believe me because she was only four or five years old, so one day I told her, "Karama, go ahead and pick up the newspaper and read something to my friends." And she did. She picked up the newspaper, unfolded it, chose a story, and read it to us. Of course, she didn't read the newspaper every day, but she could do it, and I think that she liked making her Daddy proud.

Later when she was around ten years old and I had my law practice, Karama would help out at the office. She would run papers to the courthouse or to the bank, that kind of thing. We would go to Willie Mae McKnight's joint down the street from the old Clinic building. I'd buy her a hamburger and give her some quarters for the jukebox. Her favorite song was "Down Home Blues." There were periods when Karama's visits were more frequent and when they got to be much less frequent.

After I started my law practice, my office manager Pat Lamar helped me with Karama.

Pat remembered this in 2017:

> Olly's daughter Karama was really young when I first met her. I always thought she was his pride and joy, but he didn't always have much time for her. He worked hard. We did have to make a living and times were tough. When Karama would come to Marianna, I'd say to him, "What are you and Karama going to do? Don't be taking that baby to the juke joint." But he would. He seems to think this is why she came out well-rounded. Her Momma sheltered her and he let her see the world.
>
> When Karama was twelve or thirteen, I guess she had asked her Momma about wearing a bra and Janet had told her to see what her Daddy said, probably because Janet wanted Olly to remember he was a father to this girl. So, Karama wrote and asked Olly if she had his permission to start wearing a bra. And when he read that letter, he called at me, "Pat! Karama wants to wear a bra and she ain't got nothin'." I spoke back, "It's not about having nothing or having something. It's about being accepted. She's got to go to P.E. And every other girl has on a little training bra. Just let her go buy herself a bra. She'll be alright." So, I convinced him to let Karama wear a bra.

Not a Good Father

When Janet lost her job right before Karama went to college, I know that they experienced some hardship. Karama had scholarship money, but she wanted to go to Swarthmore and the scholarship package they offered was not enough. The school said since I was an attorney, I ought to have enough money to put toward my daughter's education. And Janet had to show them that I had never been financially supportive and there was no reason to expect this would change. Swarthmore revised Karama's financial help and it all worked out. I didn't know anything about this at the time.

When Karama was young, her Momma was good to her and to me by not sharing with Karama any of the negative thoughts she might have had about me. Karama still remembers this too. She says:

> I don't claim to know everything, but I do know that I was not an angry child. My mom didn't say bad things about my dad, but I would feel frustrated when I couldn't see him, and she would be frustrated because I was frustrated. And it made her sad when I was sad. That's all.
>
> I remember a bad period during the summer of 1989 or 1990, when I worked at the med school. This was before cell phones. I would call Daddy from a pay phone at least once a week just before I went into the lab and I could never get him. No one would answer and I'd leave a message, or Pat would answer and say that he was not available. Maybe he was and maybe he wasn't. I don't know. One time he did pick up the phone, and I could tell he was not happy that he had answered. I was like, "You know, Daddy, we haven't talked in a long time." And he said that he had a lot going on and was busy or whatever. And I told him, "Daddy, I think you would really like me if you got to know me." Soon after that he hung up.

As a father, I know that I was not consistent or dependable. But I have no memory of rejecting Karama's calls. I've learned in recent years that there were times when Karama was upset with me, especially when she was in college and we didn't talk much. Perhaps I didn't talk to her because I was not particularly happy with her mother. Janet had a way of quietly saying something that would stay with me and bang around in my head. Like when I ended a good year with $100,000 in my bank account and spent $35,000 of it on a new F250 diesel pickup. I really wanted that truck. And she asked me, "Now just why do you need to buy that truck?" She never yelled like my Momma, but her subtle criticism didn't sit well with me. So I could just have been putting some of that on Karama.

Forgiveness

Karama and Nic didn't grow up together, but they knew each other a little—and I never did do much for their relationship either. Somehow Karama found a way to forgive me for all my transgressions. I don't know how she did, but I am grateful.

Karama says this about it:

Not very often but sometimes I would hear from my brother Nic and we would talk. He is my half-brother and younger. There is no animosity or bad feelings between us. I care for him and I care for his children, but it would be dishonest to say that we have a traditional brother/sister relationship. I don't know all the particulars to his bond with our dad, but I know Nic lived with him during high school. And according to Nic, sometimes that worked well and sometimes it didn't.

After I was in graduate school, it became very clear to me that I did not want to have any guilt about my dad. This meant that if I called him and he hung up on me, I was going to be okay with it. I would call again later because I didn't want something to happen to him or to me and be left thinking, "If I had only called..." Then I reached a point when I decided that my Daddy really did love me, and I realized that people who love people do their best. That is part of the definition of love. As a child, what had been hard for me was that my mother loved me, and I saw what her best was. My grandmother loved me, and I saw what her best was. In comparison, my Daddy's best was not very good. But after I understood that Daddy loved me and was doing his best, how could I be mad at him? This is how I made peace with him in my own mind.

Our Happiest Times Are Now

When Karama was in college, in graduate school, and working in Atlanta, she was away from Arkansas for eighteen years. She had a serious boyfriend, Kwadjo Boaitey, and I met his family when they all came to visit in Little Rock. His mother, Akosua Mercy Obiri, was gregarious. She has strong principles and was a positive influence on her sons. In the early spring of 2005, Karama and Kwadjo came to visit again and were at the house when Kwadjo asked to talk to me. He said that he wanted to marry Karama, and I told him that I thought he and Karama would do well together. They were married September 3, 2005, at Karama's church, St. Andrews AME in Little Rock. I performed the ceremony. Kwadjo is a really decent guy. After they moved to Little Rock in December 2008, he got certified to teach and is now a middle school teacher.

Karama is her mother's only child. When Janet was sixty-eight, she was diagnosed with dementia. Before she started going downhill, Janet was walking for her exercise. Then, when she began to have difficulty, she would be out walking and sometimes couldn't figure out how to get home.

I remember finding her and taking her home a couple of times. One time she was so upset she was crying. This was all very unusual because Janet was a strong and independent woman.

As soon as Janet was diagnosed, Karama and Kwadjo wanted to move to Little Rock so Karama could be near her mom. In 2008, I had retired and was dragging around, and not doing very much. I still had my cows and I'd go to Marianna a couple times a week. So I was available to help too. Before they arrived back home, Karama was looking for an apartment in Little Rock. I didn't know too much about the neighborhoods, but I helped her find an apartment in an area that seemed okay. As soon as they came back, Karama submerged herself with caring for her mother. I helped with some legal stuff like Janet's power of attorney. And as much as I could, I tried to be emotionally supportive. Janet passed in April of 2010. She was sixty-nine.

Today, Karen and I live only a mile away from Karama, Kwadjo, and their daughter Ayoka. When Ayoka was little, I would walk over to see her every morning before school. We would chit chat while she ate her Cheerios and then I would walk her to school. It was wonderful. For quite a few years now, Karama and I have communicated frequently. We text. We talk. We email. We walk and talk on the track on Wednesday and Saturday mornings. And we have some very stimulating conversations. Karama is a thinker. Our discussions are always interesting and often intellectually challenging.

Karama can depend on me now and so can Ayoka. I am always pleased to be Ayoka's grandfather. Karama agrees, saying, "I can depend on my dad now and Ayoka has complete trust, complete love, complete adoration for her Granddaddy. When he can't come to see her performance at church or a school event, she doesn't worry that he might be mad at her or doesn't love her like I used to do. I believe that he is doing with her all the things he didn't do with me. Sometimes we visit him on Sunday afternoon and Ayoka needs her hair redone. He sits there in his chair and takes her braids or twists out—very gentle and loving. He shows her the affection that, as a child, I never felt from him."

I don't think that Karama will brag about me because she has heard so much different stuff about me from so many other people. And she says this:

I try not to name drop. When I was living with my mom in Little Rock and Daddy was in Marianna, if someone found out that my dad was an attorney, they used to assume that I was rich because attorney means rich, right? But he wasn't rich and even if he had been we weren't seeing any of it. They didn't know what they were talking about and this got to be annoying, so I didn't even bring it up.

Now that I am an adult and living in Little Rock again, I meet people who know my dad and don't know that we are related. For example, when I was at an event for the Arkansas Peace Week, I met a black woman who is the director of the Coalition to Abolish the Death Penalty. I see her every now and then at church too. But I hadn't seen her in a while, so I was hugging her and told her about her name coming up that morning when my dad and I were walking. I said, "I don't know if you know that Olly Neal is my dad." Another woman was standing with us and said, "Olly Neal is your father?!" And she started bowing. That kind of thing actually happens, and not infrequently. It's a little uncomfortable.

I realize that Karama understands and accepts me, though, when she says these things about me:

> Because he was a judge, my mother-in-law assumed my dad to be all puffed up, highfalutin, and stuffy. But as soon as she met him, she found out he is not at all like that. Daddy is a complex person. He is thoughtful about the law and is a great attorney, but he also talks loud, cusses all the time, and tells hilarious stories.
>
> I am proud that my dad cares about and has a real commitment to the people of east Arkansas. It is just in him. And he has become a real father to me and a wonderful grandfather to Ayoka. When my mom was alive she was pretty much everything to me. After she died and I was getting close to my dad, I remember thinking, "God, thank you so much because I'm not ready to have no parents. I can do sequential." That's what it is. I have had two amazing, sequential parents. And this is a blessing.

Education and Community Service

Even though I was not engaged in Karama's life much of the time, the underlying message about one thing from both me and Janet was consistent: We both prized and promoted education. I didn't say, "You must get a PhD." What Karama saw was that I valued formal learning and that even when I came under some hardship, I kept focused on my own education.

And she saw how the education I struggled to achieve allowed me to get into the career that suited me and served my commitment to civil rights.

As a child, Karama was reserved. Unlike me, she was shy, and very serious. I tried to help her break out a little bit. Every year I gave her a $100 bill for her birthday. I'd tell her, "Go spend the money. Act crazy. Live life. Have fun." And every year, I would get annoyed because she never spent it. She put it all in the damn bank. But blowing money at the mall or wherever just wasn't Karama's style. And it still isn't. She is serious and careful with money just like her mother.

I have always been involved in some kind of community service, and Karama takes after me in this regard. She is drawn to helping other people. And she is passing this on to her daughter. For example, Arkansas has a hunger relief alliance with a state food pantry network. Karama and her daughter participate in their gleaning project where volunteers go out into the fields and pick up fresh fruits and produce to put in the food pantries. They help glean watermelons and sweet potatoes, which is hard work. Karama didn't grow up in rural Arkansas. She didn't grow up working in the fields chopping cotton or anything like that. But on a Saturday morning when it is damn hot outside, they go out there to help the food pantry. It's a good example for Ayoka.

A Higher Power

Karama wanted to say one more thing:

> One time, Daddy, Uncle Willie, and I were going to visit my Uncle Donald in Colorado because Uncle Donald's daughter was getting married. This was before I could drive. Daddy and Uncle Willie drove from Little Rock to Colorado. I remember that the ride was a little scary and the same blues tape played over and over. In the flat of Kansas or wherever, Uncle Willie drove right in the middle of the highway at night!
>
> At Uncle Donald's house after we got everything out of the car, my dad sat down and said, "Thank you, Master!" Daddy grew up in a Baptist church. I am AME, and, based on what I know about Baptists, I don't think that he is a traditional Baptist. But when I reflect on this incident and other conversations we have had, there is very much an acknowledgement of a higher power.

Chapter 23
Karen Buchanan

I met Karen in 1986 at one of my friend Carol Willis's Super Bowl parties. And it wasn't long before we were in a steady, long-distance relationship. When we got together, I was living in Marianna and I had a stable general law practice. Karen lived near her family in Little Rock, where she was the principal of a respected elementary school. Living in Lee County was important to me, and Karen was happy in Little Rock. We saw each other nearly every weekend and we were not married.

Initially, Karen did not want to marry me, because she had a problem with our age difference. She is more than eleven years younger. After a while she changed her mind and thought that we should get married. The trouble was that I had been married three times before. I had not done well in any of my marriages and was reluctant to try again. Karen wanted to keep both of us satisfied with our relationship, and she told me something like this. "You might consider one of these options. We could get married and you can stay in Marianna, or you can move to Little Rock and we can live together and not get married."

I Chose Marriage

Karen knows me, and she is smart. When she put it that way, I chose marriage over leaving Marianna. And after agreeing to marriage, I still managed to put it off for quite a while. Karen worked on the school year calendar, so she wanted a June wedding, and I said, "Alright." But when it got to be April or May and time to do the preparations, I told her, "I can't do it. I can't get away in June. I've got this trial coming up and I'm afraid this thing is going to whip my ass." She just said, "Okay. Maybe we can do it in December." And again, I said, "Alright." But in September or October when she came to me about a December wedding, I looked at my calendar and I had this big case coming up, and it was a tough son of a bitch. I put her off again, and she didn't give me any trouble.

In December 1991 Karen didn't talk to me about marriage at all. She called Pat and asked if I had my 1992 calendar yet. Pat said, "Yes, it just came in." Karen asked Pat to mark "with Karen" for the week before June 20 and "with Karen" for the week after June 20. And Pat said, "Okay." She wouldn't have done that for anybody else, but Pat really liked Karen because Karen was always courteous to her on the phone. She didn't see anything wrong with me taking some time off to be with Karen because she knew that I liked her. Pat was being helpful.

So, being with Karen was marked on my calendar, and in April when she called to set things up again my answer was, "Ahh, I'm not sure." And Karen said, "Just look at your calendar. Look at your calendar." I looked and thought, "Oh no," but I couldn't say anything. If I hadn't been caught off guard, I would have had some story, but Karen had me, so I said, "Okay." And we started planning for a June wedding.

June 20, 1992, was on a Saturday and Karen made all the plans, but she forgot to tell me about the rehearsal dinner. I should have known about it. I should have asked, but I didn't. So, they had the rehearsal dinner on Friday night without me. And as I understand it, the preacher was there saying, "Where is the groom?" Karen had the presence of mind to be confident and say, "He'll be here. He'll be here tomorrow." It worked out. Nic and I drove over to Little Rock on Saturday morning and we got there in time for us to get married.

I don't know how she does it. If you say or do something that Karen doesn't like and she doesn't suspect you of doing it maliciously, she doesn't hang on to it. If you do something that I don't like, it might stay in my mind for a long time, but it looks to me like Karen can put it out of her mind. She knew that I should have asked, and I should have known about the rehearsal. But she has never expressed any concern about it to me. We have talked about it since then and she just sort of smiles. She knew I was coming.

What the hell... I moved.

After we got married, Karen and I continued living apart. We saw each other on weekends and were doing fine. But then Karen thought that we needed a base in Little Rock. I can't say that I was too excited about the idea but when we talked about us buying a house over there, I said, "What the hell. Go ahead and look for a house." Before I knew what was happening, Karen found this big old house close to her family. So now, I'll let her tell the rest:

> The house I found was on the same block with my mother, my brother, my grandmother, and my great-aunt. I had heard that the lady who lived in the corner house was planning to sell it in a year. Olly and I looked at it and the very next weekend I heard that the house was already up for sale! So, Olly had his back up against the wall, but being a

man of his word, he agreed to buy it. That was 1993.

Since Olly really didn't want to buy a house at all, he was passive and wouldn't get his paperwork together on time. And the kicker was the closing. That day he was in court in east Arkansas and he still hadn't gotten the money out of his bank in Marianna. By the time he was out of court, the bank had closed. When Olly called to tell me, I was damn mad! But the bank president opened his bank after hours and let Olly withdraw his money. Then, he had to drive all the way to Little Rock, and we didn't do the closing until almost midnight.

Olly was grouchy all through the move too. He fussed about everything. My friend Doris and her husband John came over and helped. When we bought our house, the area around it was really run down. Some of my friends were saying, "Why are you moving over there in the hood?" Well, the main reason was since Olly had already been married three times, if we ended up in a divorce, I didn't want to have a lifestyle that I couldn't maintain on my own. Plus, I didn't want Olly all stressed out having to pay big bills. I knew that if he was stressed out, he would be stressing me out all the time too.

Karen and I enjoy living in our house. This place has not put a strain on us. It is our home. I let Karen do whatever she wants to the house within reason, and we have made some improvements. After over twenty-five years, it is easy to see that our house was a very good investment. We paid $95,000 and now it's worth close to $300,000.

Upset with Karen

I only remember getting really upset with Karen one time. It was when I thought that she had stayed out too late. She tells the story this way:

My girlfriend Rose Barnes and I had gone to a party. I called Olly from the party and told him that we were going down to the River Market to listen to Kirk Whalum, who was in concert. I asked Olly if he wanted to come too. He wanted to know if we had tickets and we didn't. We were going to sit on the deck of a restaurant where we could hear the music for free. He said, "Uh huh, I'm not doing that."

When the music was over, it was sometime after eleven o'clock. Rose drove me home, and our neighbor Kim was out watering her yard, so I stopped to talk to her for a few minutes. Then, I went in the house and got in bed. I noticed that Olly had his back turned to me and wouldn't talk, so I went to sleep. He wouldn't talk to me or tell me what he was mad about for two or three weeks. And of course I was damned upset too.

My version is a little different. I always believed that Karen was out with her girlfriend, but for her to be out at three o'clock in the morning didn't make no damn sense and it didn't sit right with me. During those weeks when we weren't talking I was asking myself, "Why the hell are you here? What is the value of this whole relationship?" That's what I was doing. Was I uncomfortable during those weeks? Absolutely. Very uncomfortable.

I finally called Karen and asked her to go to lunch with me. We drove to the restaurant tense and not talking. When we got seated, Karen asked, "Does having lunch together mean we are talking again?" I told her, "I just don't think that my wife should stay out until three o'clock in the damn morning." And Karen responded by saying, "I don't either." So I asked her why she did it, and she told me that she hadn't been out that late at all.

Before that lunch, I had decided that however I was feeling, what Karen had done was not a deal breaker. Therefore, I had to figure out a way to get past it. I needed a justification for myself to get back together. She thought that I had looked at our clock without my glasses and mistaken the time. She might have been out-thinking me and making me doubt the time, but that didn't matter at all to me. The key was that I was trying to get past what had happened. I wanted to accept what she said. I let her convince me that I had screwed up reading the clock. So, both of us let the whole thing go. And I have to say that I am still all right with it. Karen is important to me.

Gifts

I absolutely don't do Christmas presents. Period. I don't like Christmas presents, but I do try to do those gifts that I know are important to Karen and have a little romantic tinge. For example, our wedding anniversary is June 20. Karen's engagement ring started off as a small marquise diamond. Ten years down the road, I gave her a full-carat marquise. For our twenty-fifth anniversary, I bought another small marquise diamond and put all three on the same ring with the big diamond in the middle and the small ones on either side. The next year I bought a special gold piece that holds the ring upright and in place. It looks like it is part of the ring and makes the whole thing look better.

Anyway, I like those marquise diamonds. I'm a marquise kind of guy. But I have to admit that in some ways I am still not altogether sure what

Karen sees in me. This is what she has to say: "Early in our marriage, it bothered me that Olly was not very emotional or affectionate. He doesn't do Christmas presents. He doesn't do a lot of hugging and touching. But then I realized that these things were not so important. How he lives his life is solid, and this is what really counts. It took me awhile to grow into understanding him. Now what I have to say is that Olly is the most supportive man I know."

Part Five: Legacy

I hope that giving and accepting a helping hand and finding forgiveness will be part of my legacy. There are other legacies that continue to inspire me, and I want to recognize them here. These are people who are continuing work I may have started or are going far beyond my wildest dreams.

Lazaro English, chairman of LCCC board; Dr. Kellee Farris, LCCC CEO; and me at the October 2019 picnic celebrating the Clinic's fiftieth anniversary.

Chapter 24
Lee County Sheriff Ocie Banks

Lee County was founded in 1873, after the Civil War during the time of Reconstruction. When I was in law school going over to Little Rock every week, I looked all this up in old handwritten records kept in the Secretary of State's Office. An African American state legislator, William Hines (W. H.) Furbush, who represented Phillips County, is responsible for both the founding and the naming of Lee County. Mr. Furbush also became the first black sheriff of the new county. We didn't get our second black sheriff until 2016 when Deputy Sheriff Ocie Banks was elected.

In the 1870s, the different political factions were like this. Lots of Democrats had the old Southern way of thinking that blacks were inferior and had to be kept in their place. The Republican Party was divided into two factions. One was the new post-Reconstruction group of both white and black Republicans who were interested in being fair to black folks. The other faction was the older white people who believed in Republican economic principles, but just like the Democrats, thought that blacks were inferior and to be controlled. Furbush was in the newer group of the Republican Party, but he was a "get along" kind of guy and could get along with all of them.

In the 1870s, transportation was by wagon, and the general rule was that a county was supposed to be small enough so everyone who lived there could drive to the county seat and back home in one day. That meant leaving home in the morning at five or six o'clock and getting back home before midnight.

Where Furbush and his constituents lived, they were too far away from Helena, the Phillips County seat, to get there and back home in a day. So, I believe it was 1871 when Furbush first brought up the idea to create a new county. I've forgotten what he wanted to name the county then but whatever it was, the legislature didn't vote for it. Two years later, he came back and brought it up again with a change. He told the legislature he wanted to call the new county Lee after General Robert E. Lee. This time the legislature agreed, and that is how Lee County was created.

How Furbush and Banks Became Sheriff

Part of the Furbush deal was that he would be the new county's first sheriff, and he served as the sheriff of Lee County for two terms: 1873–1875 and 1875–1877. We had to wait over 140 years to see another black Lee County sheriff, and Ocie Banks was elected in 2016 without any fanfare.

This is Banks's description of how he became sheriff:

> In 2003, Sheriff Jack Oxner asked me to quit the post office and come work for him as a full-time deputy. I was making more money at the post office in Memphis, but I told him, "Okay, Sheriff. I'll come work for you." I went to the academy that year and I was fifty-five. Most all the other guys were in their twenties and thirties.
>
> It was 2016 when Sheriff Oxner got ill. I'd been working for him over twelve years and was a major lieutenant deputy. About an hour before closing time for the election filing deadline, the sheriff called Deputy Captain Guynes and myself in to tell us that he wasn't going to run. And I said, "Sheriff, I told you that I would never run against you because I was loyal to you. But if you ain't going to run, I'll run." I shook Guynes's hand and I signed up. He just stood there. Nobody else signed up, so I won.

In my opinion, we can't get what we want only by complaining. In my career I've tried to make sure we created circumstances where black folks who want to be involved can be elected to public office, and rise into leadership roles. That doesn't mean that everybody I support has to be my clone. I am confrontational and Ocie is not. We all have our own style, and everyone has the right to serve in his or her own way. I know Ocie. He is a nice guy. And it seems like he is a little more like our first black sheriff, Furbush, a get-along kind of guy who knows how to get things done.

Sheriff Banks was sworn in on January 1, 2017. Ocie is a distant cousin of mine, and he asked me to be present. I was there and spoke a few words about him. Then I drove up to Forrest City to be present and speak about Dion Wilson when he was sworn in as circuit judge in the First Judicial Circuit where I served. It was a big swearing-in day for me. I don't claim much credit for either of these men. They both could have gone forward without me, but I was full of pride for their success and the leaders they have become.

Talking to the Kids

Ocie Banks was a military man. He went into the Army right after high school and stayed in the military for twenty-one years. In 1985 when he got out and came home, Ocie went to work at the post office in Memphis and stayed there for over sixteen years. He had to drive from Marianna to Memphis and back five days a week. In 1986 or 1987, Lee County sheriff Jack Oxner hired Ocie as a part-time auxiliary. He worked early at the post office and got back into Marianna in the afternoon.

Ocie started out talking to the kids. He walked the school campus, went to their ball games in uniform, and was a security officer. He would talk to the kids like this, "Olly Neal used to be just like you and look at him now. He is a big lawyer over on Chestnut Street. God-dog-it, boy, one day you could be a big man like Mr. Neal."

Ocie told me, "I could see that these kids are kinda like you, Olly, when you were their age. You never hurt anybody but you were always outspoken and getting into something. These kids are not real bad boys either. They are just mischievous."

Men of Action

When I was a deputy prosecutor and over the juvenile court, requiring a GED as part of some probations was not something I made up myself. Deputy Sheriff Ocie Banks came to me with the idea. He had been in Memphis seeing what they were doing over there to stop repeat offenders. And because we were distant cousins, I guess he didn't mind talking to me about this kind of stuff.

Deputy Banks also formed a new organization called the Lee County Men of Action. It was all about bringing men together to do things for the kids in the county. He asked me to let the Men of Action work with the kids who got in trouble. We created a special probation officer program. I asked another judge who had plenty of experience with juveniles to come and give them some lessons. And all the Men of Action were sworn in as official volunteer probation officers. Every time a boy got picked up, I called Ocie. After only three months, he and his men actually reduced the number of juvenile court sessions we had from twice a week to twice a month. I'm not making this up. He just stopped those kids from acting the fool. Ocie could get along with their Mommas, and he would go to their houses and talk to those boys.

It got so the parents would call Ocie whenever their boy took off out the window and was out late too many nights. Ocie still had to be at the post office in Memphis at 4:00 a.m. and after a while he got tired. He burned out and had to quit the Men of Action for a couple of years. Then, in about 2008, he started it back up again with ten or twelve older guys, and they went to work. Ocie would always let me know what they were doing. Men of Action did things like take young boys and girls to the zoo in Memphis and in Little Rock. They went to the Civil Rights Museum and to an air show in Memphis. Representative Murdock invited them to visit the State Capitol in Little Rock and see where the legislature meets. The school district would give Men of Action use of a school bus and pay for transportation to wherever they were going. Men of Action paid for the kids' lunches from a little money donated by people in the community. Banks says, "I have had several occasions later when one of those kids will come up to me and say, 'Mr. Banks, you remember me? We used to do this… We used to do that…' I ask them, 'How you doing? Where you living now?'"

Building a Better Community

Since Banks became Lee County sheriff, Men of Action is not as strong as it once was, but I still am a member and I've kept their cap because I am impressed with what they have done for the community. Now Ocie puts his time and energy into being a good sheriff. His notion of being a sheriff goes way beyond enforcing the law and keeping order. He says that he must make his community a better place to live. He works hard and has become an exemplary sheriff. Sheriff Banks was reelected in 2018 for a four-year term. James Guynes ran against him, but Banks was confident and won by a comfortable margin. Sheriff Banks is very popular and everyone can see that he is strong and healthy. He says that he will be ready to run again next time too.

Banks is a sheriff who goes out and communicates all over the county. As he says, "I just want to keep building the connection I had prior to becoming sheriff. If I see a group of guys out in a field standing around by their tractors, I go up to them and say, 'Hey, you guys. Y'all ready to go to jail?' And they all say, 'Yep, we ready.' I may have enemies in the community, but I think everybody respects me, and I respect everybody until they do something to cause me to change."

Sheriff Banks has done a number of things to make the county safer, like speaking to the Housing Authority about putting up security lights and to the school board about new issues in school security. The sheriff's office supported a defensive driving class at the high school and an "active shooter" training for the whole community at the Marianna Civic Center. He promotes trash clean-up for community pride, holiday lights for added neighborhood security, and farm equipment awareness during summer months for road safety. He also is responsible for some extras, such as when his office sponsored an inspirational speaker to talk to parents on the importance of supporting their children's education.

Sheriff Banks likes to be out in the community meeting folks. He attends school board and Chamber of Commerce meetings. He is a member of the local Arkansas Community Foundation, the Single Parent Scholarship Foundation, and the Marianna Housing Authority Board. He has established a good relationship with Marianna's white community through participation in organizations that used to be all white, such as the Rotary Club and the American Legion. He even served as the American Legion Commander for one year.

Sheriff Banks says this about white/black relations in the county:

> I never run into black/white problems. Everyone wants to see you do something positive, and that is what I am trying to do. I learn from white folks too. I know some black people who say that whites got everything, and it is all easy for them. But the young white guys who are trying to run a business are creative minded, and they get out there and work hard. They are just like me. If you get out and work hard, you will be successful. That is true for both black and white. You could say that I care about everybody. I go check on some of the older white folks too. When I was campaigning to be sheriff, I stopped to ask this white woman to vote for me. She said, "I like what you are doing and I would vote for you, but I have never voted in my life." After the election, I went out there to help her get registered. I sure did.

Looking toward Lee County's Present and Future

Regarding what is going on today in Lee County and what is on the horizon, Sheriff Banks says this:

> There are some opiate drugs in the county, but that problem is not too bad here. We have maybe two or three cases a year, but they have to do with somebody trying to sneak drugs into the state prison. Personally, I think the biggest problem we have in the county today is parents not giving enough support to their kids and our public schools. I want to support good parenting. I want to recognize the parents when their kids do well. I want to encourage more parents to see the value of an education and get behind their kids. I wish we had more activities for the kids. We need to work together. If we worked together, I know we could have

a park where parents played ball with the kids. To make a park we need something like the Marianna City Council to say that we will do it for our young people. I don't think we can do it without them.

I don't like it when I see the young guys coming into court, and their appearance is not so good—face not washed and wearing messy clothes. I tell them don't be coming to court looking like trash. I advise them to clean up to be treated right. I do see some improvement though among the young people. More are seeking jobs. Now, it is like when I came out of the military. There aren't jobs here at home. They have to go off to find a job like I did when I went to Memphis. I also encourage them to try the military if they don't have anything going for them. And some come back to me to ask how to go about applying. They have to go over to the office in West Memphis.

I try to speak to the young guys and the older guys too and encourage them to run for public office in Lee County. I tell them to go to different meetings and do things that will prepare them for the job they want to do. I talk about being a community person and about running to help the people not just to be in the office. I think one of my black deputies might step up, rise to the occasion and get himself prepared.

My Influence on the Sheriff

Banks got to know me when he was a deputy sheriff because of my farm. I had a big longhorn bull out there that never stayed home. Whenever he and my cows got out and I wasn't around, Sheriff Oxner sent Deputy Banks to put them back in. He called my longhorns "big, old ugly things." I don't know—maybe he had never seen longhorns before.

When I was in my Marianna office not too far from the sheriff's office, I remember one day Deputy Banks came over there to tell me, "Olly, there's this guy in the jail cell saying he wants to talk to you." And I asked, "Has he got any money? No? You tell him when he gets some money to call me." You see, back then, Ocie didn't know that lawyers worked for money. I guess he thought I was some kind of a volunteer.

Ocie talked about me setting an example and giving support:

> Olly has led by his example. That is what I want to say. After I retired from the Army and come back and started working in the community, Olly influenced me because he was a person of ideals and he was a person who was not afraid to speak out. Some is afraid to speak because they are scared of what their buddies are going to say. Olly was never that way. And he would listen to whatever I wanted to talk about, and

he was supportive of whatever I was trying to do or start up. When he supported the Men of Action, he would tell us, "You all are doing a good job, keep it up."

I always looked to him for support. I do that right now too. The first thing I did when I found out that I was going to be the sheriff was call Olly Neal to tell him. There is just something about him that I believe in. He always tries to help and give support. He calls me once in a while to ask me, "How you doing?"

"Doing fine."

"Good. You need anything, call me."

"Yes, sir."

I say, "yes, sir" to him.

Chapter 25
Karama Neal and the Arkansas Heirs Property Law

As a resident, civil rights activist, and lawyer in the Arkansas Delta, I became aware of the problems the old Arkansas heirs property law created for many poor and middle-class black families. This is how it worked. The estate of many black families is limited to modest property, and often there is no will (called intestate). When the older generation dies out, under Arkansas state law, the real estate passes to all the heirs as "tenants-in-common," a vulnerable form of ownership. "Tenants-in-common" are vulnerable because one of them can force partition of the property. Under the old law what happened was that a real estate speculator would buy out one of the "tenants in common" and file a petition in court for a "partition action." This meant the whole property had to be sold. The court set the sale date. A legal description of the property and notice of the auction date appeared in the newspaper, and the property was auctioned off. Usually, none of the family knew what was going on, and the property sold at a very low price. In this way, the whole property could be acquired by a speculator for an amount well below market value. And, the heirs would lose their inherited wealth! I saw this over and over again in the Delta.

Calvin King and I had been unsuccessful in getting the law changed in the 1990s, and more recently in 2008. In our latest attempt, we had gotten help from the Uniform Laws group, but we never even considered going to the Arkansas Bar Association for their support. We thought that between the two of us, we could work with enough legislators to get a better law passed. What we didn't understand was that most of them were just not interested in doing anything to help low-income families. I also planned on going to Governor Mike Beebe for his help, but we never got that far—and I'm not sure he would have helped us anyway. I didn't know him very well, and I suspect that he saw me as someone who was too loud and not deferential enough.

My daughter Karama's interest in Arkansas's heirs property law is personal. She inherited property from her mother, Janet, whose great-grandfather Griffin Henry Belk was a slave until he was seventeen years old. As a free man, he eventually bought 160 acres in Ozan just outside of Hope in southwest Arkansas, and he fathered five children. Apparently, someone told Belk that if he didn't have a will, his property could never be sold out of the family. So he chose not to write a will, and he died believing that his descendants would always have a place they could call home. Nice thought, but he was misinformed.

Belk's land is a fairly remote, second-growth pine forest. Each of his five children had a five-acre homestead there and in the 1980s, Karama's great-uncle ran cattle on the property. Now all the family homes are long gone, and only the family cemetery remains. In the past the family had a regular process for taking care of the taxes. Karama's grandmother collected the money from her siblings and first cousins and made sure the taxes were paid each year. Today, there are about 200 heirs. Some probably don't even know about the property, and none of them are as tied to the land as were the previous generations who were born there and lived there. Since the time her great-great-grandfather bought the property, Karama is the first one in her line of descendants not born on the land.

Typical of Karama, she wanted to do right by her family and she had a plan. This is how she tells it:

> Fortunately, the taxes aren't high, and I am sure we can continue to pay them in the future. Now that my mother and grandmother and so many of their generations are gone, different ones of us step up. Although we have kept the taxes current, the process and contributions have become kind of random. When the land became partly mine, I started thinking about what I could do to make it a financial asset as well as a place to bring all of the Belk descendants together. To alter or invest time and money in a property so that it can become productive, the title must be clear. So I talked to my dad about finding the relatives. I planned to write down the Belk family tree and reach out to everyone, so we could clear the title and try to make the property more productive.

When Karama came to me about contacting all the Belk heirs and clearing the title, I had to tell her, "Karama, you really ought to step back from that a minute because you may find some relatives who hear about the land and simply want their money out of it. According to Arkansas law, all the descendants own that land as tenants-in-common and someone could force a sale of the *entire* property. Then, you all would lose the whole thing." Karama certainly didn't want that to happen, so she stopped hunting for all the heirs.

The Uniform Laws Commission is based in Chicago and has been around since 1892. It has commissioners from every state, and they develop model legislation that they believe should be the same in all states. This is the summary of the Uniform Partition of Heirs Property Act (UPHPA) on the commission's website:

The Uniform Partition of Heirs Property Act (UPHPA) helps preserve family wealth passed to the next generation in the form of real property. Affluent families can engage in sophisticated estate planning to ensure generational wealth, but those with smaller estates are more likely to use a simple will or to die intestate. For many lower- and middle-income families, the majority of the estate consists of real property. If the landowner dies intestate, the real estate passes to the landowner's heirs as tenants-in-common under state law. Tenants-in-common are vulnerable because any individual tenant can force a partition. Too often, real estate speculators acquire a small share of heirs' property in order to file a partition action and force a sale. Using this tactic, an investor can acquire the entire parcel for a price well below its fair market value and deplete a family's inherited wealth in the process. **UPHPA provides a series of simple due process protections: notice, appraisal, right of first refusal, and if the other co-tenants choose not to exercise their right and a sale is required, a commercially reasonable sale supervised by the court to ensure all parties receive their fair share of the proceeds.**

Karama says:

> After my dad and I talked, I felt kind of stuck, so I went online and googled, "heirs property?" When I read about the UPHPA, I saw that this law would not solve all of our problems, but it would address some of them, and it could help many other families like mine. So in 2013, I started working on changing Arkansas's heirs property law. And this is how we got the new law passed. In retrospect, it is a story of what Margaret Mead meant when she said, "Never doubt that a small group of thoughtful, committed citizens can change the world. Indeed, it is the only thing that ever has."

Karama became passionate about changing the heirs property law in Arkansas because she wanted to help Arkansas families who were in a situation like her own. She started a newsletter. She put up a website. She promoted the UPHPA on the radio. And she went to various family reunions to tell them about the new law and how it could help them. When she contacted Arkansas's Uniform Law Commissioners Elisa White and Lynn Foster, they became active, and what they did was key. They asked the Arkansas Bar Association to add the UPHPA to the Bar Association's legislative package, and the Bar Association decided to include UPHPA as one of the laws they wanted passed during the 2015 legislative session. Once it was on their list, the Bar Association paid for the lobbying. This meant that their lobbyist Jack McNulty would push for the UPHPA.

Karama was excited with this big step for her project. She says this:

> Jack McNulty was wonderful. I told him, "I just want to see this passed. If you want me to shout, I'll shout. If you want me to be quiet, I'll be quiet. Just tell me what to do." When I talked to him, he easily could have looked at me and thought, "You are not an attorney. I don't know who you are, lady. Just stay out of this." But instead, he took the time to thoroughly explain the strategy. He said, "This is not a situation where the story of a family struggling to keep and then losing their heirs' property will help." That made sense to me, so I stopped talking and I didn't publish anything after that. He told me, "Since the new law is coming from the Arkansas Bar Association, most legislators will simply think that if the Bar Association wants this passed, we should pass it." And that is exactly what happened. It passed on February 24, 2015, and went into effect January 1, 2016.

Other states (including Alabama, Georgia, Iowa, Missouri, South Carolina, and Texas) have passed the UPHPA. The 2018 federal farm bill now offers owners of heir property in states that have passed he UPHPA priority consideration for farm loans, federal programs, and assistance in clearing the title for their property. In Missouri and Iowa the UPHPA is called the Save the Family Farm Act because the law is so effective. And there are many more states moving to enact the UPHPA legislation.

Since the UPHPA passed in Arkansas, families with heir property have the due process protections of property appraisal, sale notice, right of first refusal, and, if necessary, a commercially reasonable price with the sale supervised by the court. In conjunction with the University of Arkansas at Pine Bluff (UAPB) and Calvin King's Arkansas Land and Community Development Corporation (ALCDC), the University of Arkansas at Little Rock Bowen School of Law (my alma mater) has presented a new kind of clinic to help families clear the title on their property. This type of clinic was not possible before the UPHPA because the old law made it too risky for families to reach out to long-lost relatives so they could clear the title.

The ALCDC and others are making an effort to help heir property families find productive uses for their land. Going forward, we still need to protect the UPHPA from speculators and land grabbers who used to make money under the old law and now want to weaken the new one. Karama and others who are interested in heir property continue to monitor legislative activity on this issue during each session.

Chapter 26
Future of the Lee County Cooperative Clinic

S tarting and directing the Lee County Cooperative Clinic was the most important job I had in my life. Not the biggest but the most important. It definitely was my greatest challenge, and it gave me the confidence and contacts needed for my law career.

In October 2019, the LCCC commemorated its fiftieth anniversary with a week of celebrations, including a full-house formal gala on a Thursday night. I was impressed. The gala was a "Sunday best" celebration. Afterwards, even those who couldn't afford to be there were bubbly and proud of it. It seems to me that this gala was a demonstration of the new generation moving everything forward in their own way. And the music was part of the generation change. In the past the music would be a Lee County chorus or local students' singing group. This time it was a hot singer from Little Rock who performs at the River Market and for big fundraisers. Many, including my daughter Karama, were there dancing to the very end.

When I think of the LCCC celebrating this anniversary, I feel gratified— gratified that I came up at the right time and had the ability to get it going. I should also say that I am especially gratified that I had sense enough to recognize and associate with people who could make the Clinic go forward. In a way, I just gave them room to do their work. Two key people come to mind. The first was our top-level accountant Clarence Coleman, who kept our books so accurately that whenever Senator John McClellan sent special auditors from Washington, we could show them that our finances were on the up and up, and that we were doing nothing wrong.

I'm also thinking of Dr. Irwin Redlener, who came to the Clinic through our doctor recruitment efforts and stayed with us for two years. Dr. Redlener was the one who designed the Clinic facility that has lasted for over forty-five years. He also pressed me hard so that I had to get involved in promoting rural sanitation with the NDWP even though I really didn't feel like I had the time.

Dr. Redlener confirms how he got to Marianna and pushed me into the water and sewer program, saying this:

> I was in the final months of my pediatric residency at Denver Children's Hospital and about to begin a pediatric cardiology fellowship. Everything was set to go, until I saw a poster in the doctor's dining room.

It had been written by Olly Neal and Dr. Robbie Wolf. And I was transfixed by the message. "VISTA DOCTORS NEEDED IN LEE COUNTY. JOIN NOW! IF YOU'RE NOT PART OF THE SOLUTION, YOU'RE PART OF THE PROBLEM." The message was accompanied by a black-and-white photograph of Dan Blumenthal with his little black doctor's bag walking down one of Lee County's barren roads.

That was it. The following weekend, I flew to Memphis to check this place out. Olly picked me up at the airport and drove me into Marianna. During the ride, Olly talked and talked about how the Lee County Co-operative Clinic was developed, about what was needed, and about the opposition he faced. I've never told him this, but by the time we got to the outskirts of Marianna I was convinced. I knew that I needed to be working at this clinic. Days after returning to Denver, I resigned from my fellowship and made plans to move to Lee County, and I've never looked back.

But what really was it that made me turn my life around and make such a dramatic change in my career? I certainly wanted to work with the wonderful folks I met in Marianna and I wanted to be part of the Clinic's important mission. But truth be told, my decision came about because of the charismatic force of nature known as Olly Neal. He was a powerful and irresistible community organizer. He was comfortable speaking with any audience, from impoverished farm families to governors or U.S. senators. And working with Olly became a life-changing lesson for me on how to make a difference under the most challenging conditions, including profound poverty, racism, and isolation.

Clean water and sanitation were the most basic needs to prevent many of the conditions I saw in my young patients at the Clinic. I was the one who told Olly that he had to make it happen, and I appreciate him crediting me with urging him to deal with this critically important issue. But at the end of the day, it was Olly who led the National Demonstration Water Project to fund water and sewer systems in Lee County, all over rural Arkansas, and in many other states with impoverished rural counties. In a very short time (and while attending law school), he transformed himself from a brilliant community organizer to one of the most effective public health champions anywhere in the country.

Clinic and Quality of Life

Following the Clinic's fiftieth anniversary, I am excited that the Clinic may be able to do more in the future to improve the quality of life for its patients. The people of the Arkansas Delta may no longer suffer from lack of clean water and sanitation, but they still face serious lifestyle challenges to their health. I am especially happy to see the Clinic's CEO Dr. Kellee Farris committed to including preventive health care alongside excellent basic health care. I'm not sure exactly what the Clinic will accomplish, but there are all kinds of possibilities, like regular exercise classes for the elderly and arthritic patients, education about eating healthy foods like fresh garden vegetables, and education supporting mental health.

Dr. Farris is the daughter of a longtime Marianna resident and LCCC dentist. She returned to Marianna after earning her PhD in public health, and her training and experience have prepared her for the task at hand. She has a clear vision of what she wants the Clinic to be in the future, saying this:

> The Clinic can be a dynamic centerpiece for our area, and we have work to do. My vision is for us to go back to being a community-driven organization. We have managed to stay connected to the larger community by being available whenever another organization needs something. But I want to bring organizations and special programs into the Clinic, so everybody can get more services right here in this one place. I want my community to thrive. I want to encourage business leaders to become more community oriented. I want to ensure that there are opportunities for stability and access to health care. We can do this by taking opportunities to the citizens and not waiting for them to come to us.
>
> I am pleased with our strong telemedicine component, our mental health screening for all patients, and Alzheimer's training for staff members. I am proud of the Clinic's support staff, as they make our patients feel welcome. And I am exceptionally proud of our medical staff, who are highly skilled and especially dedicated to caring for their patients. I want our Clinic to have the latest medical technology and the best diagnostic equipment, and I want our building to become a community center with meeting space for local health-related organizations and classes. Good health is more than taking your medications. Environmental and social issues affect our well-being too. We need to promote a lifestyle that prevents getting sick. I'm talking about a healthy diet, which also will treat some of our most common problems: diabetes, high blood pressure, and high cholesterol. I'm also talking about regular exercise. There is no workout facility in Marianna and figuring out how to fund exercise equipment and trainers here is a challenge.

Many of our patients need help getting to the Clinic to see their medical provider. Thus, we have a transportation department with vans that carry patients to and from their appointments. However, since patients with different appointment times must come in together, this contributes to another problem that is difficult to solve: patient wait time. And we are working hard to get the average patient wait time to under an hour. There are additional factors affecting wait time as well. In general, we have found that when we keep focused on reducing patient wait time, it decreases to a more acceptable level.

Preventive Medicine

From my own experience, I know that exercise and good diet can work to combat a chronic disease, like my rheumatoid arthritis and my tendency to depression. I don't know where I'd be if I just sat in my chair and didn't have my wife pushing me to get out there and do the right thing. Having enthusiastic and consistent support and making it fun is definitely the way to go. I don't really think of exercise as fun until I realize how much I enjoy walking the track and talking with my daughter and granddaughter.

There are other activities for good health besides exercise too. If you have a group who wants to sing, you've got a singing group. You just need a place for that singing group to meet. If they want to sing and they get to sing, singing together will help lower their blood pressure. When I was the Clinic's CEO, we used to have a community choir. I wasn't the one who organized it, and I wasn't the choir leader. But folks knew they had my support because I was there singing with them. They kept that choir going for quite a while too. All the people who led it are old now, and I think that the last time they put it together was to sing at the Reverend Spencer Brown's funeral. But my point here is you can't do it all by yourself. When there is an interest in doing something good and someone is willing to take the lead, all you have to do is to say yes, and if possible, give it your support in a visible way.

Strong Leadership and a Bright Future

Lazaro English, chairman of the LCCC board at the time of its fiftieth anniversary, expressed his views:

> The Clinic board's greatest attribute is that we know the Lee County Cooperative Clinic is important to the health of people in our communities and will do all we can to keep it moving forward. We have improved our services. We brought the pharmacy back and have a full-time pharmacist. We have health days in different communities on

various topics. With the cooperation of the extension service, we offer nutrition education about the importance of diet for diabetics. We have formed a partnership in Forrest City to open a clinic at the high school. We will be starting a demonstration greenhouse to promote eating fresh vegetables.

I have a lot of confidence in our CEO Dr. Farris. She wants the Clinic to provide the best services, and I think she can lead the way. As chairman of the board, I am committed to the Clinic's future. We have an excellent medical staff, and our clientele is increasing. In ten years I want to be celebrating a new building and want the Clinic to be as high tech as anybody out there.

The Clinic's board chairman is a strong person. There still may be hard times ahead, but I am optimistic and have confidence in the people behind the Clinic. Doing what is new can be challenging. But anything is possible when leadership understands disease prevention and high-quality care, and can do a good job selling what is being done and communicating what more is needed. I expect the Clinic to continue attracting skilled staff and wise board members with a deep understanding of the Arkansas Delta and its people. With the dedication of a great board and staff, the Clinic has a bright future.

Closing Thoughts

I lived my life and did what I had to do.

I didn't always find satisfaction in what I was doing, but I have been given profound help and support along the way. There is no way to say how important many people have been to me. I am far from perfect, but the people who reached out to help me saw something in me and gave me what I needed far beyond expectation. A helping hand might have been a small thing for them, but it was big for me. Help came in all different forms too. Sometimes they didn't even know that they were helping me at all. I just took encouragement from the good I saw.

Kindness

Everybody considered Mrs. Grady to be a good teacher. I always sort of liked her, but I never thought about her very much until at least twelve years after I was out of high school. That's when she told me she knew I was stealing the library books and she kept replacing them. Mrs. Grady just wanted me to keep reading. After that she and I became friends, and I have never forgotten her kindness.

Straight Talk

In basic training, I got in some trouble and was on my way to much worse until my platoon sergeant Alfonso Chavira sat me down. He said, "If you soldier for me, I'll cover for you. But if you don't I will have to break you because I have to do what is best for the rest of the troops." He probably didn't think very much about what he said to me. But his straight talk saved me when I was young and didn't have any sense. I learned from him that if it's not possible to change something, you have to just make the best of it, and bide your time.

Sustained

At the Clinic, 1970, 1971, and 1972 were awful hard years. But every now and then something would come along that was sustaining. Governor Bumpers was very helpful. In 1971 when he appointed me as one of only two blacks on the Arkansas Health Planning Council, it was a huge boost. That appointment told me, "What the Clinic is doing makes sense and all these white folks are not going to keep rejecting everything I do."

Inspired

In 1972 and 1973, Martha Flowers, Gloria Fender, and I organized two big conferences for black medical students with Arkansas roots. They came from all across the country to see the exciting new health work being done in their home state. The second conference was in Marianna. We had just opened our new Clinic building and could show them that it was possible to practice in a rural community and not be isolated. This was a high point for me. It was inspiring to see their interest in what we were doing.

New Life

In 1973 after we had been working the National Demonstration Water Project (NDWP) for about a year, I went over to the legislature to request some money for what we were doing. Afterwards, I was sure that I had failed to get anybody's attention, but then John Miller, who was on the house appropriation committee and chairman of the legislative council, contacted me. He told me liked what I had said and he wanted to help me get the money we needed. Before that I didn't even know John Miller. He breathed new life into our project.

Permanence

I never said this out loud, but back in 1970 I did not expect the Clinic to make it. I knew it was a place to wage a damn good fight, but I didn't see how we could survive. My thought didn't change until 1973 when we finally got the $1.2 million grant to build our new building. That brick building said "Permanent." They couldn't get rid of us now.

Satisfaction

I felt real satisfaction when J. B. Smith told me this story. J. B was working to get support for the NDWP when he overheard Mississippi County judge Shug Banks say this about me, "I don't give a damn what you all think about this boy. He helped some of my communities get their sewer and water systems and I am with him." Shug Banks was a racist white man, but when he said this, it showed he was doing the right thing in spite of his prejudice.

A Sign of Success

The U.S. Post Office mailman delivered an envelope addressed to "Olly Neal, Nigger." No town. No return address. No signature. The postmark was Harrison, Arkansas. The paper inside said something like, "You better get out of town or we got something for you." I guess I was supposed to be afraid. It was a threat letter, but I felt no threat. Looking back I can see it was much more. It signified that I was the voice of my people and I had been loud enough. I had been heard.

Support

In 1974 when I went to see LeMoyne College President Horton about finishing my undergraduate degree, he said they would work with me. My coursework was ten years old and might have been dismissed, but he gave me credit for all the courses I took in 1958, 1959, and 1960. I had to get the approval of Dr. Beuler, who had been my chemistry professor before, and I didn't expect him to want me back. He must have known that Charles Nichols and I used to steal ethanol from the lab and get drunk. But Dr. Beuler allowed me to take the three courses I needed in one semester. I had thought that I was a *persona non grata*, but they helped me beyond my understanding. It was huge and completely unexpected. What they did meant that I could graduate in time to go to law school in the fall. Their support shaped the rest of my life.

Hope

I didn't know it at the time, but when I applied to law school, the University of Arkansas in Fayetteville was attempting to increase the number of black students at the law school there. I got a call from Steve Nichols saying I was accepted up there, but then I had to tell him that where I really wanted to go was the night school in Little Rock. He thought this was impossible but sent my application on to them anyway. After only four or five days I got another call saying that I was admitted to Little Rock. I don't know how it happened, but that acceptance was my big chance and it gave me hope.

Help

When Daddy died during my last semester of law school, I was depressed and decided to quit. As far as I know, Henry Jones had no reason to come talk to me. He never knew my Daddy, and I didn't know him very well either. But his visit and talking to him about Daddy was what I needed. He got me over the worst of what I was feeling. I went back to law school, and I will never forget his help when I needed it most.

Compliment

When I was on the circuit court bench in Helena, I ruled against Herman Young in a timber poaching case and he had to pay a big chunk of money. On the way out of court, I overheard him say to his attorney, "That nigger is the best damn judge we got over here!" Herman Young was a white man who cared about nobody but himself and usually thought that no "nigger" ought to be doing anything but working for him. I could have gotten hot because he referred to me like that, but somehow, I had made a crack in his thinking and it felt more compliment than insult.

Forgiveness

I'm not telling you I have it all right, but I don't hate certain white folks anymore. I am especially thinking of Leroy Webb, the white boy in Marianna who punched my brother Prentiss during one of our demonstrations. At the time I couldn't let personal revenge damage our movement, but I hated that son of a bitch and planned to get even someday. Then about fifteen or twenty years ago, I got to thinking, "Hell, Leroy was just doing what he thought he needed to do." I've forgiven people I used to hate. For me, this is a beautiful thing.

Acknowledgments

We are grateful to the **Arkansas Humanities Council** (AHC) for a mini-grant that supported research completed in 2017. And we wish to thank the **Improvement Association of East Arkansas** for sponsoring this grant.

We extend a wholehearted thank you to all our interviewees, some whose stories are included in this book and others who helped with background information and fact-checking: Earl Anthes, Sheriff Ocie Banks, Judge Kathleen Bell, Nyerere Billups, Dr. Carolyn Frazier Blakely, Ayoka Boaitey, Ollie Brantley, Joe Bruch, Karen Buchanan, Mack Cleveland, Clifton Collier, Ernest Cunningham, Jesse Daggett, Helen Dickey, Bob Donovan, Harry Durham, Dr. Kellee Mitchell Farris, Jesse Gist, Dr. Mildred Barnes Griggs, Justice Josephine Hart, Antony Hobbs, Evanstene Peters Holmes, Andrea Hope Howard, Keith Ingram, Calvin King, Dr. Sterling King, Pat Lamar, Sheriff Bobby May, Grace Meacham, Robert Morehead, Dr. Karama Neal, Nic Neal, Rowan Neal, Shirley Brady Owens, Patricia Palmer, April Peer, Wilbur Peer, Anisha Phillips, Robert Scott, J. B. Smith, Ora Barnes Stevens, Grif Stockley, Governor Jim Guy Tucker, T. F. Vaughn, Betty Neal Walker, Dr. Ethelyn Williams-Neal, and Judge Dion Wilson.

We appreciate and recognize the valuable advice, information, and resources given by: Ernie Dumas, Cherie Anthes, Dr. Dan Blumenthal, Corinne Cass, Susan Daggett, Bill Husted, Gloria Neal Howard, Dr. John A. Kirk, Dr. Irwin Redlener, Karen Redlener, Eugene Richards, Dr. Colleen Walter, Gary Wingert, and Dr. Robbie Wolf.

We are indebted to our friend Gene Richards for the cover photograph and to our readers who contributed their honest opinions and thoughtful comments: Carol Hoffman, Jerry McFarlen, Donna Peacock, Peggy Sankey, and Suzi Limoni Woerfel.

To the people of Butler Center Books at the Central Arkansas Library System: Rod Lorenzen, Ali Welky, and Michael Keckhaver, who pushed, improved, and reassured this book to publication, we value and credit all your work to help us produce *OUTSPOKEN*.

Thank you again and again to those who were always there to encourage us and ensure that we had the time and space to work on this book: Karen Buchanan, Sarah Czar, Dr. Karama Neal, Jerry McFarlen, Joel McFarlen.

If your name should be on any of these lists, we thank you too and apologize for our shameful oversight.

Index

About the Authors

Olly Neal Jr., a courageous activist for social and political change, led the Lee County Cooperative Clinic through its contentious founding years in the 1970s, directed the National Demonstration Water Project, and championed public health in the Delta. He participated in major voting rights litigation, became the first black district prosecuting attorney in Arkansas, and served as a notable circuit and appellate court judge. He lives in Little Rock with his wife, Karen Buchanan.

Jan Wrede, a high school science teacher, was one of the VISTA health advocates who devised the plan for an outpatient clinic in Lee County, Arkansas, in the 1970s. Later, she became an environmental educator and writer with two books published by the Texas A&M University Press. She lives in Boerne, Texas, with her husband, Jerry McFarlen.

CPSIA information can be obtained
at www.ICGtesting.com
Printed in the USA
FSHW010730060720
71762FS